ROBERT LOUIS STEVENSON
AND THE FICTION OF ADVENTURE

Robert Louis Stevenson

AND THE FICTION OF ADVENTURE

ROBERT KIELY

CAMBRIDGE, MASSACHUSETTS
HARVARD UNIVERSITY PRESS
1964

* * * * * * *

Distributed in Great Britain by Oxford University Press, London

Publication of this work has been aided by a grant from
The Hyder Edward Rollins Fund

Library of Congress Catalog Card Number 64-21788

Printed in the United States of America

* * * * * * *

FOR JANA

PREFACE

It was admiration for Joseph Conrad that led me into this study of Robert Louis Stevenson. I was interested in Conrad's peculiar ability to employ some of the most commonplace conventions of the adventure yarn to suggest moral and psychological conflicts with power, subtlety, and variety. In fact, my reason for rereading Stevenson was to satisfy a foregone conclusion that his action tales were stylish and entertaining, but inconsequential, that in his hands the familiar conventions remained relatively inert. Professor Albert J. Guerard suggested that I combine three essays on the uses of adventure in the fiction of Stevenson, Conrad, and Graham Greene. But as it turned out, I never got past Stevenson.

I discovered, on rereading old favorites and looking at much else of his for the first time, an interest I had not anticipated. For one thing, I found that Stevenson foreshadowed Conrad in all kinds of curious ways. But it was not that which finally concerned me. There was a striking originality in this "sedulous ape," an unexpected pessimism in this happy moralist, and a maturity in this writer of boys' books which had been skimmed over or ignored even by the critics who admired him most. My intent, therefore, was to investigate the nature and development of these qualities as reflected in Stevenson's best writing—his adventure fiction.

I would like to thank Professor Douglas Bush and Dr. Monroe Engel for their good and spirited counsel during the preparation of this essay and for the high example they set as humane doctors. I am also deeply indebted to Professors Jerome Hamilton Buckley and Walter Jackson

Bate for reading the completed manuscript in its original version and offering valuable advice and generous encouragement when they were most needed. I wish also to express my thanks to the Henry P. Kendall Foundation for its generous contribution toward the preparation of this manuscript.

For those friends—Barbara Charlesworth, Albert Gelpi, Joel Porte, and Stephen Rogers—together with whom the love of literature became a way of life, gratitude seems such an inadequate word as to be almost embarrassing.

R. K.

Cambridge, Massachusetts
January 1964

CONTENTS

* * * * * * *

. . . Shortly after the publication of *The Mayor of Casterbridge* [May, 1886] . . . he wrote to ask if I would permit him to dramatise it, as he had read the story, and thought Henchard 'a great fellow,' adding that he himself was keeping unusually well. I wrote back my ready permission; and there the matter ended. I heard no more about the play; and I think I may say that to my vision he dropped into utter darkness from that date: I recall no further sight of or communication from him, though I used to hear of him in a roundabout way from friends of his and mine.

—Thomas Hardy, *I Can Remember Robert Louis Stevenson*

* * * * * * *

INTRODUCTION

A LITERARY REPUTATION

* * * * * * *

The posthumous reputation of a novelist who has been very popular in his own lifetime is invariably distorted, and often seriously damaged, by that popularity. And if his fame rested largely on romance and high adventure, he risks, like Scott, Dickens, Melville, Twain, and Conrad, being placed in children's libraries. There is nothing unjust in that fact by itself. Each of these authors wrote books which are appealing—and, up to a point, comprehensible—to the young. The mistake, which in these five cases has been rectified in the last few decades, is to assume that a novelist who can entertain an adolescent cannot possibly have much of value to say to an adult.

That is essentially the modern attitude toward Robert Louis Stevenson. He is not held in disrepute. Most readers look back on their first encounter with *Treasure Island, Kidnapped,* and *A Child's Garden of Verses* with pleasure and nostalgia. The other works, as Hardy once said of the man, have all but "dropped into utter darkness." But Stevenson was not always thought of as one who wrote exclusively for the young. He was the author of a great many books, and the two or three we remember from childhood represent relatively early efforts in a career which extended over nearly a quarter of a century. Even when his juvenilia were at the height of their popularity, he was regarded by his contemporaries as a gifted and serious artist, and thought by many to be the greatest living master of English prose. George Saintsbury in his *History of Nineteenth Century Literature,* published two years after Stevenson's death, called him "the most brilliant and interesting by far . . . of those English writers whose life was comprised in the last half century . . . . His method and results were extremely typical of the literary movement and character of our time."[1]

Far from being patronized as a charming scribbler of children's books, he was the respected friend and colleague of some of the most distinguished writers of the day, including Sidney Colvin, George Meredith, Edmund Gosse, Henry James, William Ernest Henley, Leslie Stephen, Andrew Lang, and John Addington Symonds. He corresponded with Mark Twain and James M. Barrie and is known, on at least one or two occasions, to have written letters of encouragement, as from the old master, to the young Rudyard Kipling and William Butler Yeats. The point of repeating these names is not to build an associative halo of fame around Stevenson, but simply to suggest the position (partly social, but primarily literary) he held among his contemporaries.

Even those who sometimes questioned the seriousness of Stevenson's subject matter credited him with being peculiarly gifted as a stylist. He regarded the technique of his craft with the devotion of a poet—one is reminded particularly of the attitude of the young Alexander Pope and John Keats—and apprenticed himself to those whom he considered masters of language. Though the admission has occasionally been cited to "prove" his lack of originality, Stevenson was not in the least apologetic in acknowledging his youthful role as "the sedulous ape to Hazlitt, to Lamb, to Wordsworth, to Sir Thomas Browne, to Defoe, to Hawthorne, to Montaigne, to Baudelaire and to Obermann . . . That, like it or not, is the way to learn to write; whether I have profited or not, that is the way. It was so Keats learned, and there was never a finer temperament for literature than Keats" (XIII, 258-264).*

In a letter written to Robert Bridges in October of 1886 Gerard Manley Hopkins, himself an uncommon stylist, compares Stevenson's artistry to that of his contemporaries:

> In my judgment the amount of gift and genius which goes into novels in the English literature of this generation is perhaps not much inferior to what made the Elizabethan drama, and unhappily it is in great part wasted. How admirable are Blackmore and Hardy! Their merits are much eclipsed by the overdone reputation of the Evans—Eliot—Lewis—Cross woman (poor creature! one ought not to speak slightingly, I know), half real power, half imposition . . . But these writers only rise to their great strokes; they do not write continuously well: now Stevenson is master of a consummate style and each phrase is finished as in poetry.[2]

When Arthur Quiller-Couch received word from Samoa that Stevenson had died, he wrote a memorial essay for *The Speaker* which contained an outburst that appears to the contemporary reader sentimental in the extreme: "Put away books and paper and pen. Stevenson is dead. Stevenson is dead, and now there is nobody left to write for." Quiller-Couch anticipated the difficulty future generations might have in understanding the unique regard in which Stevenson was held. "Surely another age will wonder over this curiosity of letters—that for five years the needle of literary endeavour in Great Britain has

---

* The "Thistle Edition" of Stevenson's works, published by Charles Scribner's Sons (26 vols., New York, 1902) has been used throughout, unless otherwise indicated. Quotations from this edition are referred to in the text by volume and page number. *The Letters of Robert Louis Stevenson,* edited in four volumes in 1911 by Sidney Colvin, is referred to as *Letters.*

quivered towards a little island in the South Pacific, as to its magnetic pole."[3] So soon after the death of Ernest Hemingway, another "blighted youth" who had lived for a time in self-imposed exile, it is not so difficult to see why Stevenson appealed to the imaginations of his late-Victorian contemporaries.

Then, as now, art seemed peculiarly in danger of drifting away from what was alive and human. The prospect of an author living like one of the characters in his own books presented the possibility of a pose, a great lie, or the hope that among all the seeming contrivance, the man was foolhardy and courageous enough to try to write and be without distinction. The reason that the death of such an artist inevitably provokes a shock of admiration even from those who questioned his sincerity while he lived is that it is the one event in a man's life which is too serious and too final to be regarded as an act. What Henry James wrote to Fanny Van de Grift Stevenson in his letter of condolence has been repeated about Hemingway, in the years since his death, countless times: "There have been—I think—for men of letters few deaths more romantically right."[4]

There is little question that Stevenson's whole existence—including the circumstances of his death in Vailima at the age of forty-four—was "romantically right." Critical commentary—even more than is usual in the late nineteenth century—makes little effort to separate this colorful man from his work. W. E. Henley's verse portrait set the personal tone while Stevenson lived:

> Valiant in velvet, light in ragged luck,
> Most vain, most generous, sternly critical,
> Buffoon and poet, lover and sensualist:

A deal of Ariel, just a streak of Puck,
Much of Antony, of Hamlet most of all,
And something of the Shorter-Catechist.[5]

After Stevenson's death, there was more heard of Ariel and less of Puck. "The most striking individuality in English letters of to-day has gone from us," wrote Joseph Jacobs in the *Athenaeum*. "He was the laureate of the joy of life, of the life here and now . . . The world was getting tired of analysis and introspection . . . He took us out into the open air and made us care for the common life and adventures of men."[6]

The cult of personality reached extremes so quickly in Stevenson's case that to read through essays and articles written in the 1890's, just preceding and following his death, is to witness something like critical hysteria. In 1890 Arthur Conan Doyle stated in the *National Review* that Stevenson was in the trinity of great short-story writers with Hawthorne and Poe.[7] Lionel Johnson, in a review of Stevenson's *The Wrecker* for *The Academy,* found only one living author who seemed to share Stevenson's artistic virtues: "Of modern writers only Mr. Pater shares with Mr. Stevenson this fine anxiety not to play life false by using inaccurate expressions . . . The one is more meditative, more learned, more gentle than the other, but both are men who feel the pathos, the heroism, the living significance of things."[8]

In 1894, hoping to establish some balance amid what seemed to him an excess of praise, Arthur Symons cautioned that Stevenson's literary merit was probably comparable to that of Thoreau, that is, "with the men of secondary order in literature."[9] But in 1895 Walter Raleigh suggested that the lack of clear-cut morality in much of Stevenson's fiction was a sign that he possessed powers of imagination and sympathetic identification reminiscent of Shakespeare.[10]

As the superlatives increased and the comparisons reached rarefied heights, the talk was less frequently about Stevenson's books and increasingly about his qualities as a man. He was revered as a rebel against social convention, an adventurer, but above all an invalid who smiled and tried not to notice he was dying. The final apotheosis is reflected in the concluding lines of a short study of Stevenson by Alice Brown, published privately in Boston in 1895:

> One man has looked hell in the face and stayed undaunted. One man has peered over the gulf where suns are swinging and unmade stars light up the dusk, and yet retained the happy sanity of our common life. He returned from his Tartarean journey lifting to the unseen heaven the great, glad cry of ultimate obedience. Therefore will we not despair, nor wish one thorn the less had sprung before his feet. We are the stronger for his pain; his long conflict helps to make ours calm. For very shame, we dare not skulk or loiter now; and whither Stevenson has gone, there do we in our poor, halting fashion seek the way.[11]

Miss Brown made of Stevenson a redeemer, who in his lifetime descended into hell, rose again, and ascended into heaven. And although her manner of expression is rhetorical even for 1895, she provides us with one of the most important clues to Stevenson's enormous popularity. She makes of him the suffering lamb, a divine symbol of a sick and dying generation, scourged by Darwin and Lyell, broken by industrialization, and mocked by Zola and the realists. Living out his last years in a small feudal kingdom of his own making, Stevenson became the modern personification of the wounded lord in a medieval romance. The days of youthful heroism were gone; the knight had passed his prime, but he was dying nobly and, best of all, with color and a certain style. What Tennyson had described in *Morte d'Arthur* and Arnold in *Tristram and Iseult,* Stevenson seemed to embody.

Even for those Victorians who regarded themselves as modern and forward-looking, there was a deep reserve of nostalgia for an earlier time when moral and social distinctions seemed clearer, when God was still supreme in heaven, the king on his throne, and the lord on his manor. Granting the naiveté of using sentimental reminiscence as a meaningful representation of the English past, to do so does reflect the frame of mind to which Stevenson made his most immediate and direct appeal. His life and much of his fiction were regarded as a product and a symbol of a prevailing mood. To recognize that mood helps to explain the extent of his reputation in 1895 and its decline almost immediately after the First World War. Elevated initially on relatively emotional and personal grounds, he seemed to an age hardened by a catastrophic disillusionment to be a little egotist on gilded stilts.

It is true that Stevenson was an egotist who sometimes wrote too willingly to please the crowd. It is also true that throughout his life he earned his living by the pen and was well aware that being a public idol was, among other things, good business. He allowed his generation to romanticize him for a variety of reasons, but it is unfair to imply that money or fame was the prime motivation of his art. The delayed reaction against him as an excessively commercial writer is partially the fault of those who tried to deify him after his death. It seemed abhorrent and shocking to discover that a saint had been troubled with financial concerns or had let his head be turned by public flattery.

Immediately after Stevenson's death, his closest friends, especially Edmund Gosse and Sidney Colvin,* and his relatives (under the firm hand of Fanny Stevenson) did everything in their power to enlarge the image of R.L.S. as an innocent and childlike man, responding with bravery and good cheer to a life of torment. They called him "the perennial boy," "thou restless angel," "friendship incarnate," and sometimes depicted him as a kind of secular holy man without blame or blemish. "He became the most exquisite English writer of his generation," wrote Gosse, "yet those who lived close to him are apt to think less of this than of the fact that he was the most unselfish and most lovable of human beings."[12]

If the partial truth of this angelic portrait helped Stevenson's reputation to soar in the decade following his death, it has contributed correspondingly to its decline since the 1920's. The inevitable books appeared—some with undisguised scorn, some with the honest scholarly intent of getting at the truth—uncovering evidence of sexual promiscuity, revealing a bourgeois concern for the financial welfare of his family, exposing ill-temper, melancholy, and moments of despair, even hinting at drug-addiction, alcoholism, and homosexuality.

One of the most common ways to undermine popular veneration for a writer of "wholesome" books is to prove

* Colvin's editing of the letters was notoriously unscholarly and, in some instances, creatively protective of their author's "respectability." Fortunately, most of Stevenson's purely literary remarks were not tampered with, and recent biographers have corrected the major misconceptions about his life to which Colvin's additions and omissions once contributed. Nonetheless, one looks forward eagerly to the publication of the new scholarly edition of Stevenson's letters being prepared by Professor Bradford Booth of the University of California at Los Angeles.

that the author's life is not anything like that of his own fictional characterizations. If his heroes are manly, chaste, and true, the writer must be proved decadent and dishonest. In the case of Stevenson it is a critical game of Jekyll-and-Hyde which has been played with nearly as much gusto and inaccuracy as the early attempts at canonization. When the game does not work, when the author's personality does seem to be reflected with some clarity in his fiction, there is always the comfort of regarding it as bad art. What Andrew Lang wrote of Stevenson in 1905, as an expression of approval, could hardly be uttered half a century later without ironic overtones: "He was the most autobiographical of authors, with an egoism nearly as complete, and to us as delightful, as the egoism of Montaigne."[13]

The reaction against Stevenson was not altogether delayed until the 1920's. Arthur Symons warned in 1894 that reckless hyperbole would eventually do more damage than good to the novelist's future reputation. In an article in *Pall Mall Gazette,* in 1901, W. E. Henley, the old friend with whom Stevenson had had a falling out, called for critical restraint. But it is not until thirty years after his death, in the biography published by John A. Steuart in 1924, that we observe the pedestal upon which Stevenson's contemporaries had set him being used as the ram to batter him with:

> Stevenson cultivated the art [of egotism] with a sleepless assiduity throughout his entire career. And he had his reward in the doting fondness of a host of readers who innocently fancied he was laying his heart bare for their delight and edification. There, they said in tones of rapture, was the most beautiful, the most adorable personality in contemporary, or, as some courageous souls averred, in all, literature . . . While [his] personality is

> an abiding charm in his miscellaneous writings, it is, so far as it obtrudes itself in his fiction, a blemish, in reality a cloak used, perhaps unconsciously, to cover meagreness of creative power, a limitation sharply emphasised by the frequency with which . . . he throws himself on the screen.[14]

Even in America, where Stevenson's popularity had once exceeded that in Great Britain, there was a feeling that the man whose character and talent had been puffed up almost beyond recognition needed to be reduced to size. In *The Mauve Decade,* published in 1926, Thomas Beer includes a hasty, unsympathetic, and not very well-informed verdict on the Stevenson vogue:

> His intellect was not legitimately rebellious at all, and the wistful apology of "The House of Eld" is the whole statement of his case . . . His levity impressed timid, bookish folk as red rashness, and for fourteen years a moving syrup of appreciation supported the gay invalid on its sweetness. His subjects were inoffensive—murder and more murder, fratricidal hate and madness, blood lust and piracy in seven forms. His prose chimes gently on, delicately echoing a hundred classic musics, gently dwindles from the recollection as do all imitations, and is now impressive only to people who think that a good prose is written to be read aloud.[15]

The need for a reassessment of Stevenson, now that there is something of a lull in the storm, has been reflected in the last fourteen years in balanced and sound biographies by Malcolm Elwin (1950), J. C. Furnas (1951) and Richard Aldington (1957); two short but excellent critical studies by David Daiches in 1947 and 1951; selections from the correspondence with Henry James edited by Janet Adam Smith in 1948; a collection of Stevenson's letters to Charles Baxter, edited in 1956 by DeLancey Ferguson and Marshall Waingrow; and an account of Stevenson's years in the Pacific by Elsie Noble Caldwell, published in 1960.

There is little doubt that as a phenomenon in literary history Stevenson deserves to be taken seriously. What remains an open question is whether as a writer—particularly as a writer of fiction—he has a value for the mature reader which transcends the entertaining accidents of his life and the virtuosity of his prose style. My object in the following pages is to investigate that question and to suggest some of the reasons why I would answer it affirmatively. Although the emphasis is textual and thematic, I do not think it would be feasible or desirable in a critical study of Stevenson to avoid references to the man's life altogether. What I do hope is that biographical information can occasionally shed light on the work rather than burning through and obliterating it as it has done so often in the past.

In the time I have spent with Stevenson I have become aware of the temptation of falling under the spell of his life. After all, his personality had sufficient effect on such dissimilar writers as George Meredith, Henry James, and John Steinbeck to inspire each to model a character after him.[16] In addition to his controversial marriage to a strong-minded American divorcée eleven years his senior, his life is filled with curious and occasionally incongruous personal relationships. James M. Barrie commented in 1890 on the "marvel" of the professional admiration and close friendship between James and Stevenson: "One conceives Mr. James a boy in velveteen looking fearfully at Stevenson playing at pirates."[17]

But if there was a man alive in the nineteenth century who can be less readily envisioned in conversation with

Stevenson than James, it was Henry Adams. In October of 1890, while Adams was touring the Pacific with John LaFarge, a visit was paid to Stevenson which, if it were not so well documented, might be regarded as the satirical invention of a George Bernard Shaw. Adams was appalled by the "squalor" of the Stevensons' island home, which he compared to a "two-story Irish shanty." He thought Fanny looked like a "half-breed Mexican," and Louis, though intelligent and entertaining, like "an insane stork." But Adams's rudest shock came when he discovered that Stevenson knew of LaFarge by reputation, but had never heard of Henry Adams:

> His early associates were all second-rate; he never seems by any chance to have come in contact with first-rate people, either men, women, or artists. He does not know the difference between people, and mixes them up in a fashion as grotesque as if they were characters in his New Arabian Nights. Of course he must have found me out at once, for my Bostonianism, and finikin clinging to what I think the best, must rub him raw all over, all the more because I try not to express it; but I suspect he does not know quite enough even to hate me for it.[18]

In a life filled with comic and sometimes tragic inconsistency—the move to Samoa, the sudden and unpredictable popularity, the seemingly endless list of unlikely admirers—all begins falling into a curious pattern. We read, almost without surprise, that less than a year before Stevenson's death, the young John Galsworthy and his friend E. L. Sanderson, having been called back from a voyage during which they had intended to visit Stevenson in Samoa, sailed home on the *S. S. Torrens,* and struck up a lasting acquaintance with her chief mate, Joseph Conrad.[19] It is the kind of information which has so much romantic appeal by itself that we are apt to overlook the fact that it tells us almost nothing about Robert Louis Stevenson. The details of Stevenson's life and times—whether peripheral or central to the private man—have, to a degree almost unique in nineteenth-century letters, obscured the writer. They are like exotic creatures with an independent existence: difficult to tame and all but impossible to ignore.

The one personality, aside from Stevenson's own, which has come between the critic and Stevenson's novels is Sir Walter Scott. Of the hundreds of comparisons drawn between these two authors, that of Gerard Manley Hopkins is most certain to please Stevensonians: "I think Robert Lewis Stevenson shows more genius in a page than Scott in a volume."[20] Alas, all commentators have not shown Hopkins' clarity of vision and, therefore, have not permitted the case to rest with his sensible statement. For almost a decade after Stevenson's death, it is difficult to find an article or book which does not eventually come around to evaluating Stevenson's work in relation to that of his prolific predecessor. The reasons for this are fairly obvious, and many of them are valid. But the name of Scott began to assume in Stevenson criticism a shorthand hieroglyphic significance which no one bothered to decipher. Stevenson was called a minor Scott or a delicate Scott; a sentimental Scott and a superior Scott; a modern Scott and a mature Scott, a decadent, feeble, brave, timid, humane or depraved Scott. Whether he was more or less than Scott finally seemed to make little difference so long as the critic recognized the indefinable pivot around which all Stevenson criticism must turn. It is primarily as an antidote to this that I have mentioned Scott so rarely. If Stevenson's works deserve to stand, they should be able to do it without continual anecdotal support from the author's life. And if they deserve to fall, they should be

* * * * * * *

What, then, is the object, what the method, of an art, and what the source of its power? The whole secret is that no art does "compete with life." Man's one method, whether he reasons or creates, is to half-shut his eyes against the dazzle and confusion of reality.

—A Humble Remonstrance

* * * * * * *

I

THE AESTHETICS OF ADVENTURE

❁ ❁ ❁ ❁ ❁ ❁ ❁

For many years Robert Louis Stevenson was a man to be dealt with, both while he lived and after he died. "It has been his fortune," wrote Henry James in 1900, ". . . to have had to consent to become, by a process not purely mystic and not wholly untraceable—what shall we call it? —a Figure."[1] Whether you liked him or not, whether you read him or not, his personality and his books somehow demanded attention and definition. He seemed bound to remain a kind of literary enigma, changing his style, his face, his habitation, his genre, taunting his readers and daring his critics to give him a name that would cover all situations. Of course the critics took him up on it. They called Robert Louis Stevenson a child.

As might be expected, Stevenson's close friend and correspondent, Henry James, gave the consensus its most graceful and intelligent expression. In an article which Stevenson read in proof in 1887 and approved, James wrote:

> The part of life that he cares for most is youth . . . Mingled with his almost equal love of a literary surface it represents a real originality . . . The feeling of one's teens, and even of an earlier period . . . and the feeling for happy turns—these, in the last analysis . . . are the corresponding halves of his character . . . In a word, he is an artist accomplished even to sophistication, whose constant theme is the unsophisticated.[2]

Apt as James' statement is—and his two essays on Stevenson remain the finest criticism written about that author—there is the tendency already in 1887, when Stevenson had seven of his most productive years still ahead of him, to come to "the last analysis," to put his literary character "in a word," to label and have done. Perhaps now, seventy years after his death, it would be worthwhile to investigate again the nature of his "real originality," to pursue the man who, Chesterton said, had "barricaded himself in the nursery . . . [because there] dwelt definite pleasures which the Puritan could not forbid nor the pessimist deny."[3]

2

The most consistent characteristics of Stevenson's elusive and quixotic disposition are, as James suggests, his devotion to the art of letters and to the less sophisticated, though not necessarily childish, life of adventure. The two do not seem to go together, but if we are to take him as he was and if we are to avoid the invariably awkward acrobatics of juggling form in one hand and matter in the other, we shall have as often as possible to talk about both simultaneously. Stevenson, it is true, was capable of taking the adventure story in its conventional, almost sub-literary, sense as a mode in which change for its own sake was uppermost; motion counted more than direction, physical action overshadowed interior motivation—a concatenation of faraway places, bizarre characters, sea voyages, mysterious benefactors, abductions, duels, endless flights from hostile pursuers, and seemingly endless quests for unattainable goals.

But to stop here is to stop short of Stevenson's full understanding of adventure. He spent much of his life thinking about outlandish enterprises, writing about them, and occasionally succeeding in embarking upon them. In a very real sense, adventure was the material of his mind, and it is unlikely that over a period of forty-four years it would not have taken on some of the peculiar shape and coloring of that mind. Of course, this might be said of the material of even the most indifferent writer if he spent long enough at his business, but Stevenson's concept of adventure was also part of a highly serious and carefully developed theory of fiction.

In the early 1880's, when Stevenson rose to the defense of the romantic novel in three of his most famous critical essays, Scott, Marryat, and Kingsley were dead, and Charles Reade was an old man. The novel of romance had all but gone out of vogue, and what George Saintsbury called the "domestic and usual novel" had taken its place. "It is certain that for about a quarter of a century, from 1845 to 1870, not merely the historical novel, but romance generally, did lose general practice and general attention . . . Those who are old enough . . . will remember that for many years the advent of a historical novel was greeted in reviews with a note not exactly of contempt, but of the sort of surprise with which men greet something out of the way and old fashioned."[4] It was the period when Anthony Trollope and George Eliot were at their height in England and Émile Zola was clamoring that naturalism was "the intellectual movement of the century."[5]

But in the decade of the 1880's there were signs of a small but vigorous countermovement in Great Britain. *Treasure Island* (1883) and H. Rider Haggard's *King Solomon's Mines* (1885) were received with a popular acclaim and serious critical attention which neither their authors nor publishers could have predicted. William Ernest Henley, who was instrumental in getting both books published, served the "revival" as poet, critic, and, on occasion, as agent. Another even more versatile defender of romance was Andrew Lang, the Scottish classicist, poet, folklorist, literary critic, and journalist. His graceful praises of Scott, Dumas, Mrs. Radcliffe, and later of Stevenson and Haggard, gave wit and authority to the small current which was running steadily against the tide of literary realism. In an essay entitled "The Supernatural in Fiction," he wrote:

> As the visible world is measured, mapped, tested, weighed, we seem to hope more and more that a world of invisible romance may not be far from us . . . I can believe that an impossible romance, if the right man wrote it in the right mood, might still win us from the newspapers, and the stories of shabby love, and cheap remorses, and commonplace failures.[6]

It is thoroughly characteristic of Stevenson that, in the midst of a general enthusiasm for literary domestication and realism, he should join the dissenters and raise his voice in behalf of romance. In 1882 he wrote a sentence in "A Gossip on Romance" which has been quoted so often that its meaning has worn thin: "Drama is the poetry of conduct, romance the poetry of circumstance" (XIII, 329). Stevenson always associated drama with drawing-room realism, partly because of the kind of play being written in the seventies and eighties, but also because properties, costumes, and stage sets could duplicate the concrete paraphernalia of everyday life in a way that the novel obviously could not. But Stevenson also meant to emphasize something much more serious and general than this obvious distinction between dramatic and narrative literature.

He was using aesthetic armament to fight a philosophical and moral battle against an epoch which seemed to him to be making an idol out of the scientific method. Émile Zola was the most persuasive and vociferous evangelist of the new gospel as it applied to literature. For him, conduct and circumstance needed no longer to be regarded as separate because, through experimentation, man would eventually learn how to control circumstance and make of it a predictable consequence of conduct.

> This, then, is the end, this is the purpose in physiology and in experimental medicine: to make one's self master of life in order to be able to direct it . . . Their object is ours; we also desire to master certain phenomena of an intellectual and personal order, to be able to direct them. We are, in a word, experimental moralists, showing by experiment in what way a passion acts in a certain social condition. The day in which we gain control of the mechanism of this passion we can treat it and reduce it, or at least make it as inoffensive as possible. And in this consists the practical utility and high morality of our naturalistic works, which experiment on man, and which dissect piece by piece this human machinery in order to set it going through the influence of the environment.[7]

It is in juxtaposition to a statement like this that Stevenson's attitude toward all art, particularly the art of writing, becomes clear. He neither believed nor hoped that man would discover the mystery of his existence by regarding himself as a machine to be dismantled and analyzed. Zola had said, "The metaphysical man is dead; our whole territory is transformed by the advent of the physiological man." And again later: "I insist upon [the] fall of the imagination."[8]

But Stevenson, too, was capable of stinging and memorable phrases: "I would not give a chapter of old Dumas . . . for the whole boiling of the Zolas" (*Letters,* II, 85). And in 1883 he wrote to Will H. Low: "Continue to testify boldly against realism. Down with Dagon, the fish god! All art swings down toward imitation, in these days, fatally. But the man who loves art with wisdom sees the joke . . . The honest and romantic lover of the Muse can see a joke and sit down to laugh with Apollo" (*Letters,* II, 171).

Although Stevenson's concept of the imagination was more limited than that of the earlier English Romantics, he spent his life trying to prove to himself and a skeptical age that every man possessed a creative power of mind which science could not (and should not) reach. (It was not until later in his career that he began seriously to probe the possibility that the source of nonrational mental activity might produce destructive as well as creative effects.) It was this instinctive and unself-conscious element in man which Stevenson saw as participating in and responding to the rhythm of natural circumstances without being able to "regulate" or "direct" them like a machine. The language he uses, in contrast to that of Zola, is deliberately nonscientific. He repeatedly emphasizes the pleasure and value of mood, emotion, atmosphere, intuition, coincidence.

Stevenson passionately believed that the greater part of life was chance. And although his own published statements on the subject usually came as unsystematic responses to the pronouncements of his contemporaries, they arose from a consistent, even tenacious, conception of art. Stevenson has been accused of frivolity in his criticism and fiction—and, in a sense, justifiably so. He often resorted to frivolity—an impulse he regarded as more purely artistic than that of "practical utility"—in order to liberate fiction from the impingement of sociology, genetics, and political science. In doing this, Stevenson may not at first have been able to avoid the hazards of aesthetic indulgence, but that should not obscure his salutary efforts to distinguish art from propaganda.

The concept of chance seemed to provide some of the mystery and imaginative range found by artists of other periods in revelation or inspiration. Chance, as Joseph Conrad's Marlow was to argue, might be the one remaining escape hatch in a modern and closed universe. It was also a byword for a young Edinburgh writer who was convinced that so long as art was treated primarily as an instrument of reform, it was incapable of fulfilling its highest function. Chance and frivolity were Stevenson's ammunition against the stultifying threat which determinism and utility posed to literature. Those artists who shared his fears—however different they were from Stevenson in other respects—responded to his essays with surprising fervor.

Gerard Manley Hopkins found an almost Shakespearian freedom from prevailing biases in Stevenson's definition of romance, and rallied to its defense as to an ally newly discovered:

> [Stevenson's] doctrine, if I apprehend him, is something like this. The essence of Romance is incident and that only . . . no moral, no character-drawing . . . As history consists essentially of events likely or unlikely, consequences of causes chronicled before or what may be called chance, just retributions or nothing of the sort, so Romance, which is fictitious history, consists of event, of incident. His own stories are written on this principle: they are very good and he has all the gifts a writer of fiction should have, including those he holds unessential.[9]

In the great century of biography and character portrayal, Stevenson stressed the importance of event. And at the dawn of science's confident claim that it could predict and perhaps form behavior, he emphasized the random nature of the human adventure. Neither Hopkins nor Stevenson thought of man as a puppet totally manipulated by unknown forces, but they also did not like to think of him as the plaything of his own scientific and political "schools." The unpredictability of incident, if nothing else, could save him from that, and it became paradoxically a kind of protective talisman. Stevenson uses the words "active" and "passive" in "A Gossip on Romance" not to indicate the degree of physical and mental participation in an event, but the degree to which the individual willingly brings about or controls the circumstances in which he finds himself. In this sense, much of Jim Hawkins' experience in *Treasure Island* is "passive" since things keep happening to him which he cannot foresee or prevent; whereas a character like Madam Merle, who exerts little physical energy, plays a relatively "active" role in the events of James's *Portrait of a Lady*. Since Stevenson believed that much of life is ungovernable circumstance, he would argue that Hawkins is the more representative of the two characters.

In 1883 Stevenson continued his defense and definition of romance in "A Note on Realism." He rejects the claim that the French naturalists have found a way of representing a larger truth than that possible in a stylized romance. He argues that all art which is "conceived with honesty and executed with communicative ardour" has a claim to veracity. The disagreement is rather one of method. "The question of realism, let it be clearly understood, regards not in the least degree the fundamental truth, but only the technical method, of a work of art."[10] The realist has made the mistake of confusing detail with truth, while the romantic novelist persistently keeps his eye on the whole and admits detail into his narrative only as it contributes to a total vision.

Over thirty years later, Joseph Conrad wrote to Stevenson's friend Sidney Colvin that although he (Conrad) had been called a "writer of the sea, of the tropics, a descriptive writer, a romantic writer," his real concern had always been "with the 'ideal' value of things, events, and people."[11] In 1883, Stevenson anticipated Conrad's claim by making a similar one for himself and for all serious writers of romance:

> The idealist, his eye singly fixed upon the greater outlines, loves . . . to fill up the interval with detail of the conventional order, briefly touched, soberly suppressed in tone, courting neglect. But the realist, with a fine intemperance, will not suffer the presence of anything so dead as convention; he shall have all fiery, all hot-pressed from nature, all charactered and notable, seizing the eye . . . The immediate danger of the realist is to sacrifice the beauty and significance of the whole to local dexterity, or . . . to immolate his readers under facts . . . The danger of the idealist is, of course, to become merely null and lose all grip of fact, particularity, or passion . . . But though on neither side is dogmatism fitting . . . yet one thing may be generally said, that we of the last quarter of the nineteenth century, breathing as we do the intellectual atmosphere of our age, are most apt to err upon the side of realism than to sin in quest of the ideal.[12]

3

Significantly enough, Stevenson's most important single piece of criticism is an essay in response to James's "The Art of Fiction," in which truth to life was emphasized as the essential criterion for judging a novel's value. James's emphasis is clearly very different from that of Zola, yet he too upholds a method which Stevenson rejects:

> As people feel life, so they will feel the art that is most closely related to it. This closeness of relation is what

> we should never forget in talking of the effort of the novel. Many people speak of it as a factitious, artificial form, a product of ingenuity, the business of which is to alter and arrange the things which surround us, to translate them into conventional, traditional moulds . . . Catching the very note and trick, the strange irregular rhythm of life, that is the attempt whose strenuous force keeps Fiction upon her feet. In proportion as in what she offers us we see life *without* rearrangement do we feel that we are touching the truth; in proportion as we see it *with* rearrangement do we feel that we are being put off with a substitute, a compromise and convention.[13]

In his reply, "A Humble Remonstrance," published in *Longman's Magazine* in 1884, Stevenson praises much that James has to say, but disagrees with his basic premise that the function of art is to come as close as possible to resembling life. Stevenson takes a directly opposite position:

> No art—to use the daring phrase of Mr. James—can successfully "compete with life"; . . . To "compete with life," whose sun we cannot look upon, whose passions and diseases waste and slay us—to compete with the flavour of wine, the beauty of the dawn, the scorching of fire, the bitterness of death and separation—here is, indeed, a projected escalade of heaven . . . Life is monstrous, infinite, illogical, abrupt, and poignant; a work of art, in comparison, is neat, finite, self-contained, rational, flowing and emasculate. (XIII, 347-350)

Stevenson argues that art should not try too hard to be like life because the copy is bound to appear pale and spurious beside the real thing. At first glance, he would seem to be working from Coleridge's famous distinction between "imitation" and "copy." Imitation, according to Coleridge, is always the more beautiful and successful in its own terms because, unlike the detailed waxwork copy, it begins by acknowledging the essential difference between it and the object being imitated.

> In all imitations two elements must coexist, and not only coexist, but must be perceived as coexisting. These two constituent elements are likeness and unlikeness . . . If there be likeness to nature without any check or difference, the result is disgusting.[14]

Stevenson, early a reader of Romantic prose, particularly Coleridge, Hazlitt, and Wordsworth, evidently has the general argument, if not this precise statement of it, in mind. But he carries the point to a rather un-Romantic conclusion by stressing that aspect of art which is most unlike nature, rather than seeking, as Coleridge did, a balance between sameness and difference. If art cannot hope to compete with life, then, suggests Stevenson, let it cease the effort, and accentuate instead those characteristics in which it is most obviously and peculiarly itself. In content as well as form, let it be openly and unashamedly "neat, finite, self-contained, rational, flowing, and emasculate."

The ultimate implications of this aesthetic for fiction are extreme; yet on and off, until the later years of his life, he reiterated his position and attempted in his creative work to put the theory into practice. As a doctrine it is worth exploring, partly because it is in itself a unique and refreshing combination of familiar critical assumptions; moreover, it provides an insight into aspects of Stevenson's intelligence which we are not normally aware of in his fiction and poetry. Eventually, in his increasing inability or unwillingness to follow his own literary rules, we discover a mind in rebellion against itself—a philosophy, a morality, and a way of writing undergoing change in spite of early and earnest attempts to establish a permanent orthodoxy.

The tenets of that orthodoxy as set forth in "A Humble Remonstrance" must be understood before we can discover, through analyzing the fiction, how and why he gradually came to modify his own "dogmas," and to disregard some of them altogether. First, the novel or story is to be "neat" and "finite," that is to say, without loose ends—no unexplained mysteries or ambiguous characters left for the reader to wonder about after the last chapter. Life puzzles and mystifies enough; that is not the task of art. Nothing in the shape or the matter of the work should be extraneous; he agrees with Poe that every word and phrase must contribute to a common effect or purpose; otherwise, the story would do better without it. Conclusions must be appropriate and consistent with the whole. If they can be inevitable in the Aristotelian sense, well and good, but they must never be shocking or morbid if the plot presents any alternative:

> It is the blot on *Richard Feverel,* for instance, that it begins to end well; and then tricks you and ends ill . . . the ill ending does not inherently issue from the plot . . . It *might* have so happened; it needed not; and unless needs must, we have no right to pain our readers. (*Letters,* IV, 144)

A work of art is neat and finite because it is fully comprehensible in its sum. The novelist may deal, if he likes, with unclear subtleties of psychology, with the vagaries of philosophy, and the complexities of human conflict, but if he is wise he will sharpen his focus somewhere before the end. He will clarify distinctions, and give his creation a simplicity life does not have. The novel, Stevenson asserts, "is not a transcript of life, to be judged by its exactitude; but a simplification of some side or point of life, to stand or fall by its significant simplicity" (XIII, 357).

Thirdly, art should be "self-contained." In Stevenson's opinion, narrative fiction has an advantage over drama because in drama "the action is developed in great measure by means of things that remain outside of the art," that is, by real people as actors, properties, costumes, heard voices, and actual movements and gestures. If the best art is that which depends as little as possible upon the world outside itself, then the novelist can make up his own rules of logic and morality, or, if he likes, dispense with them altogether. Stevenson is fairly adept, especially in his early fiction, at sidestepping moral questions. As for logic, he had a properly Romantic contempt for it in a formal sense. "The heart," he wrote, "is trustier than any syllogism"; and he praised the novel of adventure for making its appeal "to certain almost sensual and quite illogical tendencies in man."

When he goes on to call art "rational," then, he does not mean it in a strictly philosophical sense. Nor does he so much refer to reason as it operates in daily life—sorting out existing possibilities and selecting real alternatives—but rather as it might operate in a fanciful world beginning with unlikely, even preposterous, assumptions, and moving from them to other more or less unlikely positions in an orderly and systematic way. In saying that art is rational, Stevenson is also reminding us that its realm is the mind. It is not only conceived and created in the mind of the artist, but its appeal, however simple or sensational, is through the senses to the intelligence:

> We admire splendid views and great pictures; and yet what is truly admirable is the mind within us, that

> gathers together these scattered details for its delight, and makes . . . that intelligible whole. (XIII, 88)

The next adjective Stevenson uses to define art is "flowing," a word with which Hazlitt liked to describe the "warm, moving mass" of a painting or the vitality of a poem. In a way, Stevenson means much the same thing. What is wanted in fiction is coherence and movement, not only a reasonable connection between episodes and an observable relationship among characters, but motion, which for a writer of romance invariably means physical action on the part of the characters and its imaginative counterpart in the reaction of the reader:

> In anything fit to be called by the name of reading, the process itself should be absorbing and voluptuous; we should gloat over a book, be rapt clean out of ourselves . . . This, then, is the plastic part of literature: to embody character, thought, or emotion in some act or attitude that shall be remarkably striking to the mind's eye. (XIII, 327-333)

For Stevenson, then, although he recognizes that he lives in an age in which "it is thought clever to write a novel with no story at all," one of the cardinal sins the novelist can commit is to arrest the flow of action, to allow his story to fall into a "kind of monotonous fitness," —in other words, from his point of view, to be static and dull. This interpretation of "flow" veers from Hazlitt in much the same way Stevenson's aesthetic differs from that of Coleridge and James—that is, with regard to art as an imitation of life. When Hazlitt says that poetry "describes the flowing, not the fixed," he introduces that statement by asserting art's essential commitment to vitality. "Poetry," he says, "puts a spirit of life and motion into the universe."[15] Stevenson accepts the principle and necessity of motion in art, but to an extreme which seems deliberately to avoid the "spirit of life."

It is true that life is in a state of continuous flux, but the modes of change are various, uneven, and at times almost imperceptible. What is physiologically necessary in human nature is dramatically essential in narrative art: that periods of near-stasis precede and follow moments of extreme agitation. As an invalid Stevenson knew the corporeal validity of this better than most men, and perhaps it is as an invalid that he rejected it as a principle of fiction. "Seriously, do you like repose?" he asked Cosmo Monkhouse in a letter written in 1884. "Ye Gods, I hate it. I never rest with any acceptation . . . Shall we never shed blood? This prospect is too grey" (*Letters,* II, 204-205). If life must now and then slow down almost to a stop, give in to inertia and to the tedium of rest and impotent anticipation, art need not succumb to the same limitation. The novel, particularly the romance, can spin out an endless series of hectic and exhausting episodes with rarely a pause between. When Stevenson wrote this kind of book, he achieved more or less what he wanted. The result is not very much like life; it is an invention of perpetual motion which, because of its relentlessly consistent rate, resembles the mechanical much more than it does the organic.

It is partly the realization of this lack of what Hazlitt calls "the living principle" in art which brings Stevenson to his final and most telling adjective, "emasculate." True, art has neither organic life nor gender; it cannot generate itself and it cannot die. But considering the chasteness of Stevenson's early experiments in adventure fiction, the choice of this strong metaphor evokes, deliberately or not, literal substantive connotations as well as figurative and formal ones. It has often been noted that, except in a few isolated instances, mostly found in the work of his later years, he avoided sex in his fiction. He did not simply avoid realistic treatment of physical sexuality (which is true of most Victorian novelists), but he shunned dealing with any but the most superficial relationships between the sexes, and often excluded women from his fictional world altogether. "This is a poison bad world for the romancer, this Anglo-Saxon world; I usually get out of it by not having any women in it at all" (*Letters,* IV, 12).

He sounds here as though he is lamenting the prudish morality of the age which prevented artists from dealing honestly with sex, and since this letter was written in 1892 (by which time he had begun bringing women more often into his fiction), the complaint is probably in earnest. But long before this, Stevenson, without the trace of a complaint, regularly avoided romantic love, even of that delicate, sentimental, and social variety permitted, indeed encouraged, by his age. As his definition suggests, sexlessness, in theory if not always in practice, is essential to his early concept of fiction.

It can be argued that Stevenson's prejudice is not strictly directed against women, but that he discriminates against matured masculinity as well. Not only are many of his heroes young boys and adolescents, but even his grown men lack potency and aggressiveness in their relations with other characters in the story and in the impression they leave upon the reader. His adult heroes, including Harry Hartley, Robert Herrick, Loudon Dodd, Henry Durie, and St. Ives, think of themselves as children not quite at home in the adult world. Neither their personality nor their gender has been fully developed. And this is precisely as Stevenson would have it. He wants no hero of his to be so carefully and elaborately described that his personality or his sex comes between the reader and narrative incident. "When the reader consciously plays at being the hero, the scene is a good scene" (XII, 339). Therefore, the disposition of every protagonist must be generalized and vaguely enough realized so that, at the appropriate moment of crisis, the reader can ignore him and "enter" the plot himself.

Hopkins, once again, provides a sympathetic and cogent interpretation of Stevenson's intention: "The persons illustrate the incident or strain of incidents, the plot, *the story,* not the story and incidents the persons."[16] Until later in his life Stevenson was so committed to this idea of characterization that he wrote a letter to Henry James in 1884 making a request which strikes the modern reader —and must have struck James—as curious indeed: "Could you not, in one novel, to oblige a sincere admirer . . . cast your characters in a mould a little more abstract and academic . . . and pitch the incidents, I do not say in any stronger, but in a slightly more emphatic key—as it were an episode from one of the old (so-called) novels of adventure? I fear you will not" (*Letters,* II, 256).

We hear again and again in Stevenson's remarks on the form and function of art, echoes of earlier critics and anticipatory murmurings of those who followed him. There is nothing noteworthy about that; it happens in criticism all the time. It is the peculiar, almost cavalier, combination of familiar critical concepts which constantly surprises us, and makes us pause before attaching a simple label to Stevenson.[17] He will chastise Fielding for writing novels in the spirit of the playwright, for being ignorant of the "capabilities which the novel possesses over the drama," and at the same time plead for necessary causation of incident, the ascendancy of action over character, and the inevitability of conclusion, all of which bear striking resemblance to Aristotle's first principles of drama.

He can agree with Coleridge on the futility and artlessness of attempting to reproduce life by means of an "exact" copy, and even borrow his words in praising Hugo for achieving "unity out of multitude" in his romances. But if we expect him to agree with Coleridge on the organic principle of art, the *forma informans,* we are disappointed. While Coleridge speaks of works of art in terms of natural metaphor, as "the loveliest plants," "of living power as contrasted with lifeless mechanism,"[18] Stevenson makes a comparison which abruptly and unexpectedly abbreviates the association with Romanticism, and casts out new lines of speculation toward the early twentieth-century formalism of T. E. Hulme: "A proposition of geometry does not compete with life," asserts Stevenson; "and a proposition of geometry is a fair and luminous parallel for a work of art" (XIII, 350).

In an essay entitled "Victor Hugo's Romances" he writes that one of the greatest advantages narrative fiction has over drama is the tremendous expanse it provides for the writer to cram with details of local color and historical background. "Continuous narration is the flat board on to which the novelist throws everything . . . He can now subordinate one thing to another in importance, and introduce all manner of very subtle detail, to a degree that was before impossible" (XIV, 21). He goes on in the same vein to comment on what to him is the inexplicable absence of historical particulars in the novels of Fielding: ". . . It is curious . . . to think that *Tom Jones* is laid in the year forty-five, and that the only use he makes of the rebellion is to throw a troop of soldiers into his hero's way" (XIV, 22). In this mood of attachment to historical incident and picturesque detail Stevenson sounds like the kind of Romantic that has prompted the familiar comparisons with Scott. Yet only eight years later, in "A Humble Remonstrance," he strikes a remarkably neoclassical, in fact Johnsonian, note while arguing in favor of generalized treatment of subject matter: "Our art is occupied, and bound to be occupied, not so much in making stories true as in making them typical; not so much in capturing the lineaments of each fact, as in marshalling all of them towards a common end" (XIII, 349).

It would seem, on the basis of these scattered quotations, that Stevenson could not make up his mind about art, that he was slowly undergoing a change, or that some of these apparently inconsistent critical opinions are not in fact as contradictory as they at first appear. Each explanation has some truth in it. Stevenson, for example, did try his hand at the more expansive novel. Most notably in *Kidnapped* and *The Wrecker* there is a proliferation of detail, a reliance on digression, a looseness of structure, which, like the romantic works of Dumas and Scott, make some concessions to the untidiness of life. But his dominant tendency—from *Treasure Island* to *The Ebb Tide* and *Weir of Hermiston*—was to subordinate incidental detail to more general considerations of thematic pattern and narrative economy.

Stevenson had his own troubles with structural integrity, but his better judgment usually told him that he was not the kind of writer who could cope successfully with massive quantities of fact. Though he may have looked with admiration—and occasional envy—upon the sprawling works of some of his Romantic predecessors, his restless temperament usually had little patience with art when it became too heavily encumbered with the minuteness of life. Stevenson was in accord with Lang's approval of

Hawthorne for not choosing to "compete with life," that is, for not making "the effort—the proverbially tedious effort—to say everything."[19]

It should be remembered that Stevenson's ventures into aesthetic theory, looked at in the context of his whole career, were exploratory rather than definitive. Even when he sounds most doctrinaire, one discovers a tendency, not uncommon among artist-critics, to state with special emphasis ideas still very much in the formative stage. Perhaps what is most remarkable is that in spite of the occasional and diffuse quality of his critical statements between 1874 and 1887, there emerges a surprisingly coherent rationale for his profession in the art of adventure.

4

In Stevenson's eyes a physically active and exciting existence bears to everyday life, especially the everyday life of a semi-invalid, something of the same relationship art bears to nature. Participation in a hazardous enterprise—climbing a mountain, fighting a duel, exploring an island—is a way of simplifying reality and therefore a way of pretending. Intense physical activity can induce an uncomplicated state of mind or an absence of mind; it is capable temporarily of abstracting a man from his ego. Stevenson employs curiously ornate and static diction throughout *An Inland Voyage* to describe a moderately rugged canoe trip he took down the Oise River in France during a period of good health. He reserves the vocabulary of adventure, not for rapids or storms or mysterious innkeepers, but for the serene mental state induced by the bodily fatigue which is the result of coping with these "hazards." "This frame of mind was the great exploit of our voyage . . . the farthest piece of travel" (XII, 114).

But though it may provide unexpected moments of harmony, adventure, like art, is doomed to fail in its attempt to achieve a permanent ideal goal. Insofar as adventure is the active search for a state of perfect happiness, supposedly achieved through the attainment of limitless treasure, the discovery of utopian kingdoms, or union with a flawless woman, it is fated, as is art in its reaching out after ideal beauty, to fall short of its ultimate aim. The pleasure and value of both may more often than not be found in the process rather than in a clear perception of the end. In "Providence and the Guitar," first published in 1878, the strolling player's wife says of her husband and his friend the painter: "They are people with a mission—which they cannot carry out" (I, 384). And in "Precy and the Marionettes," from *An Inland Voyage,* Stevenson says that even the poorest actor has the stature and the dignity of an artist because "he has gone upon a pilgrimage that will last him his life long, because there is no end to it short of perfection." And a few sentences later: "Although the moon should have nothing to say to Endymion . . . do you not think he would move with a better grace and cherish higher thoughts to the end?" (XII, 127)

It is the venture itself—the "mission," the "pilgrimage," the graceful movement—which is stressed in these statements and throughout so much of Stevenson's work, with little thought and less hope of achieving the distant ideal that draws the artist and adventurer on. One inevitable result of this attitude is that process becomes its own goal. Particular moral aims, political causes, and social crusades are swept under by the timeless and overwhelming wave of human energy. Because it cuts across the limitations of historical period and regional custom, gathering strength and momentum by virtue of the sheer sameness of its manifestations, bold physical exertion addresses man with a simple immensity which can make it appear glorious for its own sake. Like those of his contemporaries who found art to be its own justification, Stevenson defends the appeal of adventure as immutable and universal, transcending the historical accidents which make the manners and morals of one century or of one country different from those of another. "Thus novels begin to touch not the fine dilettanti but the gross mass of mankind, when they leave off to speak of parlours . . . and begin to deal with fighting, sailoring, adventure, death or child-birth . . . These aged things have on them the dew of man's morning; they lie near, not so much to us, the semi-artificial flowerets, as to the trunk and aboriginal taproot of the race" (XIII, 238). Adventure, for Stevenson, like art for the aesthetes, has a kind of sacred purity about it which ought not to be tainted with moral or psychological convention: ". . . To start the hare of moral or intellectual interest while we are running the fox of material interest, is not to enrich but to stultify your tale. The stupid reader will only be offended, and the clever reader lose the scent" (XIII, 352).

We would seem to be leading to the inevitable conclusion that Stevenson, like most "action" novelists, regards fiction, and therefore adventure, which is the material of his fiction, as an escape—an escape from the self and from time, a rejection of the present, of mortality, and of the responsibility of making moral judgments. There is an undeniable truth in this, and no one could assert it more clearly than Stevenson himself in a letter written to John Meiklejohn in February of 1880:

> When I suffer in mind, stories are my refuge; I take them like opium; and I consider one who writes them as a sort of doctor of the mind. And frankly, Meiklejohn,

> it is not Shakespeare we take to, when we are in a hot corner; nor, certainly, George Eliot—no, nor even Balzac. It is Charles Reade, or old Dumas, or the Arabian Nights, or the best of Walter Scott; it is stories we want, not the high poetic function which represents the world . . . We want incident, interest, action: to the devil with your philosophy. When we are well again, and have an easy mind, we shall peruse your important work; but what we want now is a drug. (*Letters,* I, 322)

There is a tone in this statement that brings one of the various moods of Keats to mind, and perhaps it is a good thing that it does. Because, although we have already learned that we cannot always depend upon Stevenson to fulfill his Romantic promises, there should be a warning to us in the parallel, not to make the mistake so many critics once made with Keats—to take a few references to hemlock, Asian poppy, and poetry as a "friend to man," and with them to conclude that Keats is a poet of escape, and that is all that needs to be said about him.

If, in periods of mental suffering, Stevenson escapes by reading tales of adventure, it is safe to assume that much of his writing is done either in that state of mind or in anticipation of its advent in himself or in his readers. But the word "escape" is not finally very helpful in the description of a literary form. All art, inasmuch as it is selective and exclusive, is an escape from something whether it means to be or not. It is only fair, before we label a writer an "escape artist," as though that were a kind of charlatanism not worthy of serious literature, to determine first what he selects and what he excludes, what he is escaping from and what he is escaping to. Otherwise we risk falling into Zola's misconception that the novelistic school of realism, as opposed to the school of romance, necessarily comes closer to the whole truth and complexity of life. In some ways it obviously does, but it is salutary to remind ourselves that both are bound to the limits of *fiction*.

Much more typical than his references to art as doctor, drug, or medicine, are Stevenson's descriptions of it in terms of physical exercise and endless exploration, a bracing and healthful activity, stimulating to the body and purifying for the mind:

> O the height and depth of novelty and worth in any art! and O that I am privileged to swim and shoulder through such oceans! Could one get out of sight of land —all in the blue! Alas not, being anchored here in flesh, and the bonds of logic being still about us. But what a great space and a great air there is in these small shallows where alone we venture! (II, 146)

This too may be regarded as a kind of escapist view of art, especially for a semi-invalid, but it is not an absolute avoidance of life so much as it is a simplification, a trimming down to what is clean, fresh, and controllable. There is much of the latter-day classicist about Stevenson, particularly in his reverence for the general, the categorical, and the formal. His first impulse may be Romantic, but his second thought is almost always classical. We find him again and again in his criticism beginning with Coleridge, concluding with Aristotle; promising Hazlitt, delivering Johnson. The same tendency is visible in much of his fiction as well. How often his novels and short stories open in Romantic suggestiveness with inviting scenes of rustic nature or in dark corners of Gothic kirk-yards, with hints of vague mysteries or unspeakable passions, only to develop the clear outlines, in his early career, of a child's game and later on, of moral fable.

5

Where Stevenson differs most notably from the Romantics, especially Keats, is in his almost total inability to exist in uncertainty. This may seem a peculiar conclusion to draw about a man who spent most of his professional life experimenting in literary form and substance, theologically a skeptic, a supporter of liberal and often upopular political and social causes. And yet limitation, boundary, explanation, is what he repeatedly seeks in his early and middle fiction as well as in his moral and aesthetic theory. His letters have been compared with Keats's and it is true that in his correspondence he may begin like Keats, probing the possibilities of the creative imagination, but he does not end like him, in uncertainty.

The metaphorical terms Stevenson uses to convey his idea of the poetic provide an interesting contrast with earlier Romantic images and reveal his tendency to circumscribe. In "A Chapter on Dreams," published in January 1888, he describes the unconscious activity of the imagination during sleep as accomplished by "Little People": ". . . what shall I say they are but just my Brownies, God bless them! who do one-half my work for me while I am fast asleep" (XV, 262).

In "The Lantern-Bearers," February 1888, he compares the inner poetic faculty of every man to a child's oil lantern hidden under a cloak: " . . . and all the while, deep down in the privacy of your fool's heart, to know you had a bull's-eye [lantern] at your belt, and to exult and sing over the knowledge" (XV, 241).

In the same essay Stevenson introduces the familiar symbol of a singing bird as a sign of the poetic essence of romance:

> There is one fable . . . of the monk who passed into the woods, heard a bird break into song, hearkened for a

> trill or two, and found himself on his return a stranger at his convent gates; for he had been absent fifty years . . . It is not only in the woods that this enchanter carols . . . He sings in the most doleful places. The miser hears him and chuckles, and the days are moments. With no more apparatus than an ill-smelling lantern I have evoked him on the naked links . . . A remembrance of those fortunate hours in which the bird has sung to us . . . fills us with . . . wonder when we turn the pages of the realist. There, to be sure, we find a picture of life in so far as it consists of mud and of old iron, cheap desires and cheap fears . . . but of the note of that time-devouring nightingale we hear no news. (XV, 243-244)

Dream, flame, and a singing bird, have been used not only by the Romantics (though they were particularly common among them) but by writers of all periods as means to suggest the poetic, either at its creative source or in its ideal state of perfection. But Stevenson's treatment of these familiar images is unique. There is the obvious diminution of dream into the work of "Little People" and of the poetic flame into a flicker inside a boy's tin lantern, but there are other modifications and peculiarities as well.

The attempt, for example, to determine who the "Little People" are and how they go about their work is half-playful, but Stevenson is serious enough about establishing the relationship between dream and conscious artistry to conclude the essay with a fairly precise account of contributions from his world of sleep to his world of written fiction: "I can but give you an instance or so of what part is done sleeping and what part awake"; and then he goes on to explain how he dreamt part of *Dr. Jekyll and Mr. Hyde*. "All the rest was made awake, and consciously, although I think I can trace in much of it the manner of my Brownies. The meaning of the tale is therefore mine . . . indeed I do most of the morality. . . . Mine, too, is the setting, mine the characters. All that was given me was the matter of three scenes, and the central idea of a voluntary change becoming involuntary."

Stevenson is careful to show exactly how much dream has gone into his story, to describe its quality, and to distinguish between it and the moral and stylistic additions of his conscious mind. The tendency, however whimsical, is not like that of Coleridge in *Kubla Khan* or Keats in *Sleep and Poetry,* to enlarge the concept of the imagination by associating it with the dark realm of dream, but rather to clarify and confine it by dutifully acknowledging which elements in his stories come from the unconscious and which do not. Even in his most playful mood, he cannot ask with Keats, "Surely, I dreamt today, or did I see?" Stevenson insists upon noticing the difference between waking and dreaming. Even symbolically, Keats's question seems to have no relevance for him. Dream is not a challenge to his rational life or a symbol of the infinite possibilities of art; it is a contributor to his fiction—diminutive, quaint, and controllable, "some Brownie, some Familiar, some unseen collaborator, whom I keep locked in a back garret."

That Stevenson's image of the poetic flame should be confined within the narrow tin walls of a child's lantern is by itself characteristic. But he goes even further in his reaching out after certainty by assigning specific qualities and functions to his fire. He speaks of simple men without external signs of virtue or talent, "but heaven knows in what they pride themselves! heaven knows where they have set their treasure!" Interpreted cynically, this sounds like a justification for delusions of grandeur; taken sentimentally, we find in it some of the pathos of Gray's *Elegy*

Written in a Country Churchyard; but, reduced to essentials, it seems a fairly reasonable description of the psychology of self-respect.

The poetic flame becomes associated with each man's ability to retain the youthful conviction that his ego is the center of the universe. Since this comforting assumption is neatly caged, there is no chance that it might prove a serious threat to the rational mind by coming into disenchanting contact with the "outside" world and growing uncontrollably from the pleasant into the painful. At the first signs that it might, Stevenson clangs shut the lantern gate or the garret door, and arrests his imagination with an excess of rhetoric and rationalization.

Perhaps the most interesting of the three images which Stevenson associates with the poetic is the bird. Here the metaphor itself does not undergo the external changes of the tampering toymaker, but remains a respectable Keatsian nightingale singing in the trees. It is the nature of the song and its effect on the listener that has changed. Stevenson recalls "those fortunate hours in which the bird has sung to us," tells how the "miser hears him and chuckles," and names him the "delight of each" who has fallen under his spell. The sense of coming momentarily in contact with death and eternity, which is so strongly sensed throughout Keats's ode, has vanished. The bird is no longer an obscured symbol, now seductive, now threatening, a perfect sign of immortal life or a cold reminder of death. Stevenson wants to say exactly what his nightingale is. It is an entertainer. It cheers and amuses. It does not draw us out of life, but takes us more quickly through it than a clock or a calendar.

Insofar as Stevenson's symbol, like Keats's, promises a release from the tedium and oppressiveness of daily life, it, too, is an emblem of escape. But whereas Keats pursues his restless search for ideal beauty to the edge of death and immortality, Stevenson pursues instead the more immediate pleasure of "love, and the fields, and the bright face of danger." While Keats's "escapism" sometimes seems the longing for eternity of a poet already "half in love with easeful Death," Stevenson's "escapism" is more often the life-wish of a man who thought himself only half-acquainted with the world of the living.

Throughout much of his adulthood, Stevenson was sickly and melancholy and subject to long periods of morbid depression. In the correspondence of over twenty-five years he refers continually to death; sometimes with irritation, as after recovering from a serious fever and wishing "a thousandfold" that he had "died and been done with the whole damned show forever" (*Letters,* I, 231); sometimes with whimsical resignation, as when he compared his body to a badly made jar, "and to make every allowance for the potter (I beg pardon; Potter with a capital P.) on his ill-success, [I] rather wish he would reduce [me] as soon as possible to potsherds" (*Letters,* I, 242); but most often, Stevenson's attitude toward death is one of pathetic fatigue and boredom: "For fourteen years I have not had a day's real health," he wrote in 1893. "I have wakened sick and gone to bed weary . . . I was made for a contest, and the Powers have so willed that my battlefield should be this dingy, inglorious one of the bed and the physic bottle . . . I would have preferred a place of trumpetings and the open air over my head" (*Letters,* IV, 243).

In 1894, less than three months before he died, he wrote to Charles Baxter: "I have been so long waiting for death, I have unwrapped my thoughts from about life so long, that I have not a filament left to hold by" (*Letters,* IV, 351).

Stevenson frequently contemplated death fondly as a comfort and a release from suffering, but he hesitated to reject life without ever having been physically strong enough to live it like other human beings. A healthy body was in its own way as much of a lure for him as easeful death. And though he broods over mortality in his letters and essays, he does not let it enter his fiction in a serious way until quite late in his career. His art, as he willingly admits, is to be an antidote to his life, not an image of it. Still, as Stevenson himself gradually came to realize, the peculiar nature of a medicine has its own way of reflecting and defining the disease for which it is prescribed.

Nonetheless, with the exception of an occasional poem or tale, Stevenson's artistic treatment of death in his early years has very little in common with that of the Romantic poets. The idea of death attracted and repelled Keats as dangerous and cold, but perfect and unchanging, like an exquisite urn or an unseen bird. Contemplation of it led him out of himself; it was his lure, and to put it in terms of the romancer rather than the Romantic, it was his intrigue and his adventure. For Stevenson, in the great bulk of his early fiction, what was mysterious, unknown, enchanting, was the idea of life. And he did not at first intend it in a very complicated or elevated sense. Just walking about with a good appetite, normal digestion, a strong leg and a clear head—that was what was wanted. In the years of young manhood when his health was particularly poor, he wrote yearningly of the simple pleasures of physical well-being:

> O for the good fleshly stupidity of the woods, the body conscious of itself all over and the mind forgotten, the clean air nestling next your skin . . . the eye filled and content, the whole MAN HAPPY! Whereas here it takes

> a pull to hold yourself together; it needs both hands and a book of stoical maxims, and a sort of bitterness at the heart by way of armour. (*Letters,* I, 213)

To be able to stay out in the rain without catching a fever or to work hard enough at manual labor to get blisters—these things take on positively exotic overtones for Stevenson. And it is at this point that he takes leave of the Romantics and joins hands with Fielding and Defoe. Shamelessly he will steal from the Romantics their exuberance and exaltation (which do show signs of wear in Stevenson); he will snatch Shelley's flame and Keats's nightingale, but only on his own terms. At the first signs of morbidity, he is off to play with Robinson Crusoe and Joseph Andrews. As already mentioned, his early adventures contain the same curious combination of Romantic suggestiveness with neoclassical formalism that his critical essays do. The emotional quality of natural settings has importance even in Stevenson's earliest fiction; yet peopling his mysterious and incompletely perceived world are robust heroes with good and simple hearts, and dark-complexioned villains who have no particular motive for villainy other than that they happen to be "ornery."

6

As Stevenson's career progresses, we find works in which the walls of separation are weakened, and the weird and beautiful powers of nature encroach on the sturdy and mechanical characters, seeping into their blood, weakening their "type" and complicating their singularity. It would make life simpler for critics if novelists would change their creative habits more smoothly and consecutively than they do, but that is rare. In Stevenson's fiction, for example, we discover tentative signs of the integration of character, incident, and locale, as early as 1878, 1881, and

1882, which are the respective publication dates of "Will o' the Mill," "Thrawn Janet," and "The Merry Men." But it is not until 1888 and the publication of *The Master of Ballantrae* that Stevenson is able to sustain "unity out of multitude" at any length.

Without constructing a series of artificial stages through which he never passed in a systematic way, we might usefully select that year as the most significant turning point in his literary career. Aside from *The Master of Ballantrae,* it is the year of publication of several of his finest essays, including "Pulvis et Umbra," as well as the time when his health improved sufficiently for him to embark on the expedition to the South Seas from which he never returned. The justification of art and idea of adventure as described and interpreted thus far have come almost exclusively from letters, essays, and fiction written in the decade between 1878 and 1888. It is the period of *An Inland Voyage* and *Travels with a Donkey;* of *Virginibus Puerisque, Memories and Portraits,* and *Familiar Studies;* of *Treasure Island, New Arabian Nights, Prince Otto, The Merry Men, Dr. Jekyll and Mr. Hyde,* and *Kidnapped.* It is, in fact, the period of Stevenson's most popular juvenile works, and still the ones the modern reader is most likely to remember.

During this decade the elaborate style of the essays and the simplified accumulation of unlikely dangers in the fiction had become Stevenson's way of fending off the ordinary and the ugly. The language of the expository pieces is rich with metaphor, inversion, hyperbole, balanced phrases, and interior rhyme. Words become above all the media of a gorgeously decorative abstract art, like the figures in a Persian carpet, meaningful primarily as design, and appealing in their almost unearthly ability *not* to suggest nature. Simultaneously, the hazardous incidents of the early fiction are presented in terms so direct and simple as to suggest the comfortable monotony of ritual, the limited intensity of a child's game, and the lifeless validity of a mathematical proposition. The theory and the practice of this period are full of optimism and bravado, of carefree self-confidence, and perhaps a slightly excessive and artificial *élan,* which seems particularly strained when in reading the letters we realize it comes from a man with such slight reserves of physical and nervous energy.

The tone of Stevenson's work does gradually change and deepen, however, until in "Pulvis et Umbra," first published in April of 1888, it becomes evident upon close reading that he has admitted much to his judgments of life and art that we have not found earlier. The trouble is that he constructed the childish image of himself so well that people continue to read the Stevenson of 1888 as they read the Stevenson of 1881, in the same patronizing albeit affectionate way they would listen to a child of ten, extracting "cute" phrases and optimistic tidbits, and ignoring the rest. One can find reasons even in "Pulvis et Umbra" for Stevenson's admirers to regard him as an infant phenomenon rather than as a full-fledged adult professional. He does have a way of sounding like one schoolboy exclaiming to another, even when his subject is human misery:

> Ah! if I could show you this! if I could show you these men and women, all the world over, in every stage of history, under every abuse of error, under every circumstance of failure, without hope, without help, without thanks, still obscurely fighting the lost fight of virtue, still clinging, in the brothel or on the scaffold, to some rag of honour, the poor jewel of their souls! (XV, 295-296)

It is this almost frenzied expression of felicity in the

face of disaster that has endeared Stevenson, and especially "Pulvis et Umbra," to generations of schoolmarms and their victims. But if we read the essay without a mind for extracting moral slogans to live by, if we read it as a whole piece without predetermination, it becomes evident that it is anything but one salvo of addle-brained optimism after another. (I do not mean to imply that it is unintelligent to be optimistic, but rather that one's reasons for being optimistic and the expression of those reasons can very easily be foolish. These charming follies unfortunately have been what Stevensonians have too often singled out of Stevenson.)

But one becomes aware on a careful reading of "Pulvis et Umbra" that the good cheer comes precariously close to hysteria; that the gay celebration of life in the midst of catastrophe, which has become a Stevenson stereotype, is mingled with an unfamiliar admission of ugliness and disenchantment. His description of the origins of life on earth might have pleased even Zola:

> This stuff, when not purified by the lustration of fire, rots uncleanly into something we call life; seized through all its atoms with a pediculous malady; swelling in tumours that become independent, sometimes even (by an abhorrent prodigy) locomotory; one splitting into millions, millions cohering into one, as the malady proceeds through varying stages. The vital putrescence of the dust, used as we are to it, yet strikes us with occasional disgust, and the profusion of worms in a piece of ancient turf, or the air of a marsh darkened with insects, will sometimes check our breathing so that we aspire for cleaner places. But none is clean: the moving sand is infected with lice; the pure spring . . . is a mere issue of worms; even in the hard rock the crystal is forming. (XV, 291-292)

Certain parts of Stevenson's surprisingly repulsive description of organic life suggest that he, like the poet laureate, was forcing himself to come to terms with Darwin:

> All these prey upon each other, lives tearing other lives in pieces, cramming them inside themselves, and by that summary process, growing fat: the vegetarian, the whale, perhaps the tree, not less than the lion of the desert; for the vegetarian is only the eater of the dumb. Meanwhile our rotatory island loaded with predatory life, and more drenched with blood, both animal and vegetable, than ever mutinied ship, scuds through space with unimaginable speed. (XV, 292-293)

But Stevenson reserves his keenest disgust for man himself, and presses his point with a Swiftian energy unprecedented in his earlier works:

> What a monstrous spectre is this man, the disease of the agglutinated dust, lifting alternate feet or lying drugged with slumber; killing, feeding, growing, bringing forth small copies of himself; grown upon with hair like grass, fitted with eyes that move and glitter in his face; a thing to set children screaming;—and yet looked at nearlier, known as his fellows know him, how surprising are his attributes! (XV, 293)

Of course, the final sentence turns off Swift and brings back the undespairing and familiar Stevenson. But the words of revulsion have been uttered, and with a force which cannot adequately be halted by a dash, an optimistic cry, and an exclamation mark. Stevenson's distaste for physical life extends not only to what we ordinarily think of as the immediate causes of bodily suffering—sickness, hunger, decay—but to all the creative life processes, including reproduction, nourishment, and growth. In its combination of disgust and fascination, it is a response comparable to that of an adolescent to the first signs of his own puberty. Even the terminology of the essay suggests this in its references to simple organisms "swelling in tumours that become independent"; to reproduction "with its imperious desires and staggering consequences"; to man "grown upon with hair like grass"; and to the general notion that life in its most advanced stages is so filthy "that we aspire for cleaner places."

It is significant that Stevenson treats this "dying into life" much more clinically and grotesquely than his Romantic predecessors did. It suggests not simply a different and perhaps less powerful imagination, but, more importantly, it indicates a diminished faith in the power of the mature imagination to transcend the burden of natural life, a skepticism as well as a view of nature which Stevenson shared with his age. He is describing, and in a sense enacting in nineteenth century post-Romantic terms, the perennial fall from the childhood state of angelic innocence—golden, sexless, clean, and beautiful—to the mature state of manhood—unexpectedly brutish and knowing.

Stevenson explains in an early essay on "Child's Play" that what most distinguishes the child from the adult is his ability to exist in a tidy, make-believe world which has almost no reference to concrete reality:

> Children are content to forego what we call the realities, and prefer the shadow to the substance . . . Whatever we are to expect at the hands of children, it should not be any peddling exactitude about matters of fact. They walk in vain show, and among mists and rainbows; they are passionate after dreams and unconcerned about realities. (XIII, 144-147)

As many have been quick to point out, Stevenson's descriptions of children invariably serve equally well as descriptions of himself—at least of that part of him that was most in evidence before 1888. But what has not so often been noted is that the child's talent for disregarding or simplifying "matters of fact" had been, according to Stevenson's earliest aesthetic theory, an essential trait for all artists. Without Wordsworth's and Keats's faith in the powers of the mature imagination, Stevenson thought his choice was either to grow up (and therefore *out* of art) or to remain a child, deliberately, stubbornly, and as he half-suspected all along, unsuccessfully. One of the obvious difficulties is that the refusal to age, especially for a man past twenty-five, is a pure act of will which can be realized only in the imagination.

We are accustomed to a great many nineteenth-century authors—including Dickens, Mark Twain, Kipling, and J. M. Barrie—who, like Stevenson, created child-heroes with whom, in one way or another, they identified themselves. The enormous popularity of J. D. Salinger's *The Catcher in the Rye* and William Golding's *Lord of the Flies* suggests that modern sympathies may extend more readily to the older child undergoing disenchantment—that is, to the adolescent in crisis. Whereas Stevenson's Jim Hawkins can effectively don and shed exotic roles at will, Holden Caulfield's insecurities are only heightened by his comic-pathetic impersonations. The boys on Golding's island may be successful at assuming new roles by smearing their faces and rearranging their clothes, but then most of them are unable to change out of their disguises again. Going in search of buried treasure, Jim Hawkins becomes engaged in an invigorating and harmless adventure, but Salinger's adolescent hero finds the "great wide world," like his own efforts at changing personality, "phoney." And Golding's English schoolboys discover not pieces-of-eight but the devil on their island paradise. For the contemporary adolescent hero the treasure chest is either empty or harboring a serpent.

But Stevenson would have it otherwise. He fought like one struggling for life to keep evil, confusion, sorrow, and mutability out of his art. He built a literary theory like a fortress, constructed plots which he himself called "machines," and sharpened his style like a weapon on the masters of English prose. But by reading only his early works we have tended too readily to assume that his defenses were impregnable. On the contrary, there is a time when, even for Stevenson, the child has to let in the man. He writes of it sadly as late as the fall of 1894:

> As I go on in life, day by day, I become more of a bewildered child; I cannot get used to this world, to procreation, to heredity, to sight, to hearing; the commonest things are a burthen. (*Letters,* IV, 353)

The key word here is "bewildered," because, as Stevenson realized from the beginning, the moment the child is sufficiently intruded upon by the world to become bewildered by it, he has begun to yield up his innocence and his youth.

The history of Stevenson's gradual and painful maturing as an artist is a narrative of conflicting tendencies—practice rebelling against theory, the increasing encroachment of the "monstrous, infinite, illogical, abrupt, and poignant" upon the "neat, finite, self-contained, rational, flowing, and emasculate." It is not until the novel fragment, *Weir of Hermiston,* interrupted by his death in 1894, that we have a work which for complexity, integrity, and range, for narrative interest and sheer lyrical beauty, may be called a mature masterpiece. And still the old love of adventure remains—deepened and enlarged—but recognizable nonetheless. It is not, as some critics have implied, this imaginative devotion to the active life which is the source of his immaturity, but rather his prolonged failure to find an artistic harmony between the externals of action and the intangible truths of human morality and psychology. The early stories like *Markheim* and *Dr. Jekyll and Mr. Hyde* which do make moral and psychological claims are as schizophrenic as their protagonists. The "meaning" does not inhere to the action. It is introduced *ab extra* and, as a result, is not only detachable but disposable.

The child in Stevenson—that quality of mind which allowed him to close "the dazzle and confusion of reality" out of his art—was a long time dying. But it did die. And Stevenson was never so unaware of himself as to doubt seriously that it would:

> So in youth, like Moses from the mountain, we have sights of that House Beautiful of art which we shall never enter. They are dreams and insubstantial; visions of style that repose upon no base of human meaning; the last heart-throbs of that excited amateur who has to die in all of us before the artist can be born . . . But . . . though these dreams of youth fall by their own baselessness, others succeed, graver and more substantial; the symptoms change, the amiable malady endures. (XV, 184-185)

To understand the nature and increase of that "malady" we must begin where it does, in the "dreams of youth."

✲ ✲ ✲ ✲ ✲ ✲ ✲

Let us try to remember how fancy works in children; with what selective partiality it reads, leaving often the bulk of the book unrealized, but fixing on the rest and living it; and what a passionate impotence it shows—what powers of adoption, what weakness to create.

—Popular Authors

✲ ✲ ✲ ✲ ✲ ✲ ✲

I I

ADVENTURE AS BOY'S DAYDREAM

* * * * * * *

Robert Louis Stevenson had fewer delusions about childhood than most people suspect. He had a canny, or perhaps I should say uncanny, perception of the workings of the young mind far too detached and analytical to resemble the way children see themselves. Of course his perception was different, he would probably agree if he could read this, for, in his view, one of the things that makes children unique is that they *do not see* themselves at all.

And here is the crux of his whole treatment of youth, both fictional and expository. Again and again he repeats that the child's most distinctive characteristic, his greatest strength as well as his most vulnerable weakness, is the capacity for not seeing. "Sensation does not count for so much in our first years as afterwards; something of the swaddling numbness of infancy clings about us; we see and touch and hear through a sort of golden mist. Children, for instance, are able enough to see, but they have no great faculty for looking" (XIII, 137).

Aside from the mention of "golden mist" there is a hardheadedness in Stevenson's expression which makes us hesitate to link his view of childhood with the transcendental conception of some of the early English Romantics. Stevenson did not think symbolically enough to make a good Platonist. With metaphor, simile, even allegory, he was relatively comfortable, but perhaps his Scotch Presbyterian training made him too mistrustful of the possibility of representing ideal reality in concrete terms to find intimations of spirituality in infancy. Stevenson celebrates childhood—he has what James calls a "passion for youth"—but he does not sanctify children nor endow them, even figuratively, with a kind of transcendent wisdom. On the contrary, childhood and early youth are the only times in which a man has the right to make a fool of himself. And Stevenson does not use the word "fool" ironically to suggest ineptitude in the practical ways of the world and sagacity in some other transcendent sphere. The only ways there are for Stevenson are the ways of this world. The significant difference, therefore, between the mind of a child and the mind of a man is that the child perceives these ways less completely than the man. And if to mature is to see the world as ugly, oppressive, and petty, there is an advantage in being a child.

Stevenson, in spite of his refusal to join the public lament of the pessimistic realists of his day, and in spite of his famous though half-playful verdict that the "world is a brave gymnasium, full of sea-bathing," did not see the universe from an altogether happy and complacent point of view. It is a profound sense of the difficulty of human endeavor and the meanness of life in the nineteenth century that provokes him as early as 1878 to comment indulgently on the impetuosity of Shelley:

> Shelley was a young fool; so are these cock-sparrow revolutionaries. But it is better to be a fool than to be dead. It is better to emit a scream in the shape of a theory than to be entirely insensible to the jars and incongruities of life and take everything as it comes in a forlorn stupidity . . . For God's sake give me the young man who has enough sense to make a fool of himself. (XIII, 63-64)

Stevenson seems to be chiding Arnold in advance for his famous judgment of Shelley, published three years later, as a "beautiful and ineffectual angel, beating in the void his luminous wings in vain." Of course, an "angelic" poet is ineffectual in this world, Stevenson admits, for the same reason a child is. Neither sees the world for what it is and therefore neither is quite able to live in it except on his own terms, which is to say, ineffectively. But, adds Stevenson, again in almost prophetic repudiation of Arnold's critical fastidiousness, "to equip a dull, respectable person with wings would be to make a parody of an angel."

The young Stevenson and mature Arnold provide an interesting study-in-contrast of the Victorian mind. For Arnold, the critic, the great task was to see things as in themselves they really are, whereas Stevenson preferred to see *some* things as they really are and leave the rest alone. The young Stevenson, like Pater, Swinburne, and Wilde, chose for essentially aesthetic reasons to notice in his art only that part of life which pleased him. The association of names seems a peculiar one because Stevenson's artistic output, even in his early days, is on the surface so different from that of the aesthetes. Yet the formative process and initial attitude are essentially the same.

This highly controlled and selective view of life and art is obviously a rather extreme manifestation of dissatisfaction with "things as in themselves they really are." There is little doubt that Stevenson was not pleased with the half of the nineteenth century into which he had been born. Until the last years at Vailima, by which time some profound changes had taken place in his mind—perhaps partly because he had removed himself from the Victorian milieu—we find relatively little mention of contemporary history in his letters, essays, or fiction, and that usually when he has something to complain about. In one of his rare references to Gladstone, he criticizes him for being bourgeois, and in the same month writes to Colvin, "I fear England is dead of Burgessry, and only walks about galvanized. I do not love to think of my countrymen these days: nor to remember myself" (*Letters,* II, 266). The immediate cause of Stevenson's unhappiness was the abandonment of Gordon in the Sudan, but his disillusionment with public affairs is general and pervasive. He traveled extensively in France, yet we have only a passing reference to Napoleon III and the Franco-Prussian Wars. He was in his early teens during the American Civil War, yet for all his love of soldiery and trumpets in the abstract, there is no trace of that conflict in his writing. Until the essays of the late eighties he gives us reason to believe that if he has ever heard of Engels, Owen, Darwin, and Huxley, he prefers not to think about them.

His novels and stories, with relatively few exceptions, take place in time past—the Middle Ages, the Renaissance, most often the eighteenth century, and usually not later in the nineteenth century than 1820, a safe thirty years before he was born. With the lesson before him of Arnold, Carlyle, Mill, and Tennyson—Victorians who had suffered agonizing periods of dereliction, a premature sense of aging and impotence in a state "between two worlds, one dead, the other powerless to be born,"—Stevenson appears to squint at the nineteenth-century universe like a suspicious child, trying to avoid with his mind, as he rarely could with his body, as many deadening intrusions from the outside world as possible.

It would seem a perverse kind of scholarship to take every boy's Stevenson, the adventurous invalid, the happy moralist, and turn him into an aesthete and a pessimist.

It would be not only perverse, but inaccurate. Still, it is of importance in trying to understand his fiction and the part adventure plays in it to realize that his optimistic dream is based on a highly serious, even somber, view of himself and of life. In a letter to the French sculptor Auguste Rodin he describes his state of mind late in the year 1886: "Sans capacité mais sans regret; sans espérance, c'est vrai, mais aussi, Dieu merci, sans désespoir . . . je m'y résigne" (*Letters,* II, 355). Two of his favorite parables for the human condition involve a city on the slope of a volcanic mountain always threatening to erupt and the proverbial leaky ship slowly sinking as she goes.

His allegory often extends beyond the death of the individual to the generally discouraging trend of human progress. Stevenson is enough of a realist to recognize that nothing can be done to avoid his own personal demise and enough of a Victorian pessimist to believe the entire human race had passed its prime; still, he is a romancer, and prefers singing to wailing on the way down. "Old and young, we are all on our last cruise," he wrote in "Crabbed Age and Youth." "If there is a fill of tobacco among the crew, for God's sake pass it round, and let us have a pipe before we go!" The taste for this kind of balladry has given way in twentieth-century literature to understatement, silent endurance, or the loving dissection of human deterioration. Stevenson's artistic response may be his century's and his own, but he is like us in the realization that he had been born into a world in which irrational and destructive forces seemed frighteningly out of control.

Once we have looked, if only briefly, into his philosophical attitudes in the years preceding 1888, it does not come as a surprise that Stevenson's first full-length work of fiction is a "sea-song with the chorus 'Yo-ho-ho and a bottle of rum.'" The response which *Treasure Island* has provoked over the years would almost certainly have delighted Stevenson's whimsical nature. In its variety of sober, sentimental, irritable, embarrassed, adulatory, and apologetic moods, Stevenson criticism includes some of the most entertaining literary hobby-horses of the last half century.

He has been called a Christian theologian, an atheist, primarily a novelist, essentially an essayist, a poet above all, and a sickly adventurer with no particular literary merit; he has been accused of hating his father, wanting to marry his mother, of being impotent and a notorious Don Juan; he has been regarded as just another commercial hack, a children's writer, and seriously compared with Homer, Keats, Defoe, Hazlitt, Hawthorne, Twain, Poe, Scott, Sir Thomas Browne (whom he studied and admired), and Joseph Addison (whom he claimed never to have been able to read). That a critic would take the trouble as late as 1918 to say that "no reasonable Stevensonian claims for him a place beside Homer, or Dante, or Shakespeare,"[1] suggests that there must have been "unreasonable" Stevensonians even then who were doing precisely that.

G. K. Chesterton, in an otherwise highly suggestive and original study, concludes that Stevenson was a "Christian theologian without knowing it," and goes on to imply a mysterious connection between his writing of boys' stories like *Treasure Island* and an unconscious reversion to the doctrines of the early Church:

> He would have been the first to say that such dogmas were dead and that we cannot put back the clock to the fifth century. Yet he did not explain why he was so often trying to put back his own clock to his fifth year.[2]

Twenty-three years later, J. C. Furnas, in an extensive

and admirable biography, is at great pains to explain the Vailima Prayers not as a sign that Stevenson "was degenerating back into the chirping piety of his childhood," but rather as the most effective way to express "ethical values that he took seriously himself and considered Samoans to need—such as truthfulness, charity, industry."[3] Stevenson's friendly attitude toward Christian missionaries, Furnas reassures us, "is not religious at all," since his references to them contain "small word of souls, much of behavior."

In 1925 George Hellman published a volume called *The True Stevenson* with such lurid chapter headings as "The Crucial Mystery," "The Sex Question," "The Henley Mystery." Almost half of the book is devoted to "proving" by means of letters, unpublished fragments, and surviving "witnesses" that the Stevenson "who has for generations been held up for the emulation of youth" was in fact "an oversexed man"[4] who engaged in premarital relations with a blacksmith's daughter named Claire and with Fanny Osbourne, later to become Mrs. Stevenson.

In an introduction to a 1954 edition of *The Master of Ballantrae,* Leslie Fiedler published an essay (reprinted in the collection, *No! In Thunder*), in which the suggestion is made that the relationships between Jim Hawkins and Long John Silver (who significantly has but one leg) and David Balfour and Alan Breck are covertly homosexual: "In *Kidnapped* . . . the relation of the Boy and the Scoundrel, treated as a flirtation in the earlier book [*Treasure Island*], becomes almost a full-fledged love affair, a pre-sexual romance; the antagonists fall into lovers' quarrels and make up, swear to part forever, and remain together."[5] After some development and elaboration of this theme, Fiedler passes effortlessly, in the fine tradition of diagnosis-by-fiction, into Stevenson's private life: "I do not think it is an accident that R.L.S. had no children of his own."

Although Stevenson himself thought one hundred pounds "a sight more than *Treasure Island* is worth," his friend Andrew Lang praised it with hyperbole not common among Scotsmen: "Except *Tom Sawyer* and *The Odyssey,* I never liked any romance so much" (*Letters,* II, 16). But in a severe little critique published in 1937, Doris N. Dalglish, also a Scot, refers crossly to "that boring book *Treasure Island* and the repulsive *Jekyll and Hyde*."[6] Miss Dalglish regards Stevenson's early works of adventure fiction as responsible only for "efforts wasted and time lost on return journeys from fanciful destinations to the main road of progress."

The temptation is strong to continue through the catalogue of Stevenson criticism, but it is perhaps best to admit that now and then, even in the most eccentric commentary, one finds new and valuable insights and, at the very least, is reminded of the infinitely various ways of reading even the simplest books. And *Treasure Island* is a very simple book. It is not the *Odyssey* and it is not *Tom Sawyer.* There is not a trace of wit or irony in it—not as Mark Twain understood those words. But it is not a boring book, and it is by no means an irrelevant byway, a *faux pas,* on the "main road" of Stevenson's progress.

2

Treasure Island is one of the most satisfying adventure stories ever told primarily because it is the most unhampered. The great pleasure in reading the first few chapters depends not only on the gathering mystery, but on the exhilarating sense of *casting off* which Stevenson gives us. I mean casting off both in the nautical sense of leaving port and in the conventional sense of throwing off encumbrances. It is the perennial thrill of the schoolboy tossing away his books on the last day of the term or the youth flinging off his sticky clothes for the first swim of the season. What this amounts to is a temporary change of roles, a peeling down to what seems for the moment our least complicated and perhaps our most essential self.

Stevenson begins the process in *Treasure Island* with shameless dispatch by getting rid first of geographical place and time present and all the demands that go with them. We are relieved of place in the first sentence when Jim Hawkins explains that he will keep "nothing back but the bearings of the island, and that only because there is treasure not yet lifted." He then speaks of taking up his pen to write the story "in the year 17—," but, like other "historical romanticists," fails to fill in the last two numbers or to say how long before 17— the adventure actually occurred. He says at the beginning of the second paragraph, in introducing Billy Bones, "I remember him as if it were yesterday," and here we have another notch in our release from time. Not only are we well removed historically, but we are offered as our only authority the imperfect memory of a boy who assures us casually that he recalls past events as though they had all happened the previous day.

We become aware almost at once that Jim Hawkins' memory is anything but flawless. He recalls his first impression of Bones upon his arrival at the Admiral Benbow:

> . . . a tall, strong, heavy, nut-brown man; his tarry pigtail falling over the shoulders of his soiled blue coat; his hands ragged and scarred, with black, broken nails; and the saber cut across one cheek, a dirty, livid white. (II, 3)

And, of course, the stranger immediately breaks into a chorus of "Fifteen men on the dead man's chest." There seem to be a great number of details here, but they would hardly help distinguish Bones, tanned, scarred, and pig-tailed, from the general run of disreputable seamen, especially as conceived in the mind of a child who had never seen one. "Character to the boy is a sealed book," Stevenson wrote in "A Humble Remonstrance." "For him a pirate is a beard, a pair of wide trousers, and a liberal complement of pistols." Here then is the next item dismissed from the book. We are early relieved of personality except as a costume or disguise which may be put on and off at will.

Before the *Hispaniola* can sail in search of the treasure, the characters must all shed their old selves, determined up until then only by the faintly vocational fact that one is an innkeeper's boy, one a doctor, one a squire, and so forth, and assume the new roles required by the nature of the adventure. As in any game, the assumed roles should and do have some connection with the original talents or inclinations of the character. Just as a strong arm and a straight eye make the best "pitcher" and the smallest boy the best "cox," so the characters of *Treasure Island* are assigned roles which best fit their previously if sketchily established selves. Even the selecting is accomplished, as in a boy's game, by a self-appointed leader who achieves the desired transformation merely by stating it:

> "Livesey," said the squire [to the doctor], "you will give up this wretched practice at once . . . we'll have the best ship, sir, and the choicest crew in England. Hawkins shall come as cabin-boy. You'll make a famous cabin-boy, Hawkins. You, Livesey, are ship's doctor; I am admiral." (II, 48)

Only Long John Silver takes on a role not befitting his

pre-established character as buccaneer. When he becomes sea-cook aboard the *Hispaniola,* the first ominous rumblings begin which threaten to spoil the game, but really make it interesting.

Perhaps a corollary to the dismissal from the novel of historically measurable time and the complexity of human personality is Stevenson's cavalier casting off of the serious consequences of mortality. It is not that people do not die in *Treasure Island.* They drop on all sides throughout most of the book. There are, of course, the expected casualties among the pirates and the loyal but minor members of the crew, once the fighting gets under way on the island. But the fatalities before that are rather different and particularly indicative of the efficient purpose death serves in the story. The first demise, which takes place in Chapter III, is that of Jim's sick father, who we know is ailing somewhere in an upstairs bedroom, but whom we never meet face to face. Jim's account of the event is characteristically matter-of-fact and inaccurate. "But as things fell out, my poor father died quite suddenly that evening, which put all other matters on one side."

Actually, the death of Jim's father puts nothing aside at all. He is buried in the next paragraph and not mentioned again, while the incidents of the mystery continue to accumulate at the same headlong rate which had been established while he was still alive and ailing. The only thing the death of Jim's father puts aside is Jim's father. Critics are forever trying to read something of Stevenson's youthful difficulties with his own father into the recurring theme of filial isolation in his fiction.

It is true that Stevenson's early manhood was marked by several shattering disagreements with his father—especially on the subject of religion and the choice of a profession. Although the quarrels were usually smoothed over and Stevenson paid a moving tribute to his father's character in *Memories and Portraits,* the old contention undoubtedly left deep scars on the sensitive son of the "morbidly" orthodox, physically hardy, and professionally successful Thomas Stevenson. But we need not reach very far into an author's private relationships to recognize the universal truth that boyish adventures, especially games involving danger, are possible only when the limiting authority symbolized by the male parent is absent. It might be mentioned in passing that both Robinson Crusoe and Frank Osbaldistone in *Rob Roy* are estranged from their fathers before embarking upon their adventures. The father of Amyas Leigh, the young hero of Kingsley's *Westward Ho!,* dies before the boy sets out for foreign seas; and H. Rider Haggard devotes considerable space at the beginning of *She* describing the last wishes and demise of Leo Vincey's father. Also the young heroes of Twain and Melville are often, for all practical purposes, fatherless. A mother may be overridden, convinced, left temporarily behind. But the father must give way altogether so that his place may be taken by a kind of romantic opposite, dusky and disreputable, a Nigger Jim, a Queequeg, a Long John Silver.

The next two deaths, occurring in fairly rapid succession before Treasure Island is reached and the main part of the story begins, efficiently eliminate characters who had served as narrative and psychological preliminaries to Long John Silver. Billy Bones and Blind Pew are the first to intrude seriously on the life of the inn at Black Hill Cove as representatives and messengers from a vast and mysterious other world where terror prevails; they also introduce separately the two apparently contradictory aspects of personality combined in Long John Silver.

One role we first see played by Billy Bones, the browned and burly pirate, lusty, loud, and frightening to behold, but basically good-natured and kind. His strong exterior hides not only a kind heart, but a weak one, which is the eventual cause of his death by apoplexy when he receives the black spot. This is the bogieman who turns out to be less of a threat than he had seemed, both kinder *and weaker* than he looked. When Bones dies of a stroke he has served the narrative purpose of bearing the sea-chest containing the chart of Treasure Island into the story and the psychological purpose of presenting Jim and the reader with half of what we can expect from Long John Silver. Jim dispenses with Bones quickly, and interestingly enough associates his tearful reaction to his death with left-over emotion from the death of his father.

The other half of Long John Silver and the next character to threaten the order of the Admiral Benbow Inn from a faraway renegade world is Blind Pew. He is the nightmare of every child, and perhaps of every adult —the deformed stranger, apparently harmless, even feeble, offering friendship and requesting help, and suddenly demonstrating unexpected reserves of cruel strength. Jim describes Pew as "hunched as if with age or weakness," obviously blind, and seemingly innocuous. He asks Jim,

> "Will you give me your hand, my kind young friend, and lead me in?" I held out my hand, and the horrible, soft-spoken eyeless creature gripped it in a moment like a vice. (II, 24)

This is a simple but classic example of the sudden horror of the realization of misplaced trust, the confusion and paralysis of being caught in a human trap. When Blind Pew has delivered the black spot, a warning of doom, to Bones, he too has served his narrative purpose and may die. He is stamped to death by horses, but the scene is too swift to be gory: "The four hoofs trampled and spurned him and passed by. He fell on his side, then gently collapsed upon his face, and moved no more." Hawkins does not even spare him the abbreviated sympathy he had given Bones; he mentions him only once more, "Pew was dead, stone dead," and passes busily on to other matters: "As for my mother, etc . . ."

Death in *Treasure Island* is quick, clean, and above all, efficient for the rapid advancement of the plot. It never provokes a sense of real pathos even in the case of Jim's father, and it is not an impediment in the lives of the surviving characters. On the contrary, especially in the early part of the book, removal of characters by natural or "accidental" means is another step in the process of casting off the potential obstacles to free movement in the adventure to come. Bones and Pew could perhaps have wandered off, run away, disappeared from the plot without dying, when their respective missions were completed. But they would then have lurked in the background of the rest of the story, complicating its essential simplicity with minor but unanswered questions. It is appropriate anyway that these two advance guards from the pirate world, these two preludes to the character of Long John Silver, should die before that legendary and duplex buccaneer is born into the novel twenty pages later.

Long John Silver is the kind of character critics like to give hyphenated names to: villain-as-hero, devil-as-angel, and so forth. Certainly the duplicity of the man justifies these labels even if it does not seem adequately explained by the clichés they have become. Silver appears to be physically weak because of the loss of one of his legs, yet Jim repeatedly notes what a husky man he is and how well he maneuvers even aboard ship. He is capable of being generous, kind, and reasonable, as he demonstrates both on the voyage out and at the end of the story when his position on the island is weakened. But he is also capable of uncomplicated cruelty. In both moods he holds a kind of parental sway over Jim. In the early chapters Jim attaches himself to Silver and obeys him for much the same reasons he obeyed Billy Bones, partly out of curiosity, partly out of admiration, and partly out of pity for his physical disability. As for Long John, there is no doubt that he regards Jim Hawkins with paternal affection. "'Come away, Hawkins,' he would say; 'come and have a yarn with John. Nobody more welcome than yourself, my son.'" And much later, on the island, Silver offers Jim a kind of partnership in piracy in words not unlike those of a self-made man inviting his son to join the family business: "I've always liked you, I have, for a lad of spirit, and the picter of my own self when I was young and handsome. I always wanted you to jine and take your share" (II, 210).

But Jim has also seen Silver, like Pew, reveal startling physical power in spite of his debility, and brutality, in spite of his previous kindness. Jim is watching when Tom Morgan, a loyal member of the crew, refuses Silver's invitation to mutiny. The sailor stretches his hand out to Long John: "'Hands off,' cried Silver, leaping back a yard, as it seemed to me, with the speed and security of the trained gymnast." And when the sailor turns his back and begins to walk away,

> John seized the branch of a tree, whipped the crutch out of his armpit, and sent that uncouth missile hurtling through the air . . . Silver, agile as a monkey, even without leg or crutch, was on the top of him next moment, and had twice buried his knife up to the hilt in that defenceless body. (II, 107)

At moments like this it is obviously fear mixed with awe at the athleticism of this supposed cripple that compels Jim. Stevenson, in a letter to Henley (who had had a foot amputated in 1875), admits that this combination of infirmity and power appealed to him: "It was the sight of your maimed strength and masterfulness that begot John Silver in *Treasure Island* . . . the idea of the maimed man, ruling and dreaded by the sound, was entirely taken from you" (*Letters,* II, 138).

What, finally, are we to make of Long John Silver? Is he after all the heroic villain or the angelic devil? In a general way he is both. But this anxious reaching out for a permanent judgment overemphasizes the moral dimension of Silver's character and of the whole novel. David Daiches, in an excellent essay, "Stevenson and the Art of Fiction," suggests that "all of Stevenson's novels have a highly sensitive moral pattern . . . Consider even *Treasure Island,* that admirable adventure story . . . What we admire is not always what we approve of . . . That Stevenson was here consciously exploring the desperate ambiguity of man as a moral animal is perhaps too much to say."[7] I would agree that the structural design of Stevenson's later moral tales is visible in *Treasure Island,* but the "desperate ambiguity of man" seems to me to have been left deliberately—and successfully—unexplored. We should take Stevenson at his word when he explains to Henry James that the luxury in reading a good adventure novel, *Treasure Island* in particular, "is to lay by our judgment, to be submerged by the tale as by a billow."

Silver is a player with two faces, that of the blustering buccaneer with a good heart (like Bones) and that of the cripple with a vicious heart and almost superhuman strength (like Pew). For us to ask which is the "real"

Silver, to push aside the whiskers and try to see which of the two roles is better suited to the countenance behind is unfair, irrelevant to the spirit of the novel, and not worth the trouble because it is impossible to do. It is also unconvincing to attempt integrating Bones and Pew in order to show Silver's double nature as springing from a single psychological source. The contradictory tendencies are not presented as part of a complex personality fraught with tension and paradox. Such a union of traits is not impossible for a novelist to achieve in a sea dog. Melville and Conrad both accomplish it. But Stevenson does not do it in *Treasure Island.* And that is another reason for questioning the value of the hyphenated labels. Not only do they stress moral issues where they barely exist, but they imply an integration of Silver's dual roles whereas Stevenson seems to have taken some pains to keep them apart.

One of the pleasures in reading *Treasure Island* is in observing Long John Silver making his repeated "quick-changes," alternating rather than growing or developing, bounding back and forth between "Bones" and "Pew." Stevenson again and again allows him to assume his most Pew-like part, unctuous and perfidious, only to be defied and shattered by a verbal barrage from a loyal member of the crew which transforms him into "Bones," a roaring but impotent husk. One of the best examples of Silver's capacity for rapid change is when Captain Smollett replies to his treacherous offer of "protection" if the pirates are given the treasure chart:

> "You can't find the treasure," [said Smollett]. "You can't sail the ship—there's not a man among you fit to sail the ship. You can't fight us—Gray, there, got away from five of you. Your ship's in irons, Master Silver . . . and they're the last good words you'll get from me; for, in the name

> of heaven, I'll put a bullet in your back when next I meet you. Tramp, my lad. Bundle out of this, please, hand over hand, and double quick." (II, 151-152)

Smollett speaks to Silver as though he were a bad boy, not only naughty, but bungling in his attempts at villainy. And at once, the fearsome and oleaginous enemy becomes a comic, almost pathetic, buffoon, bellowing hollow threats. Retreating without dignity, he literally "crawled along the sand" to safety.

Jim, too, gets in his verbal "licks" against the pirate chief when he falls into the enemy's hands and things are looking blackest for him. He pelts the Pew-disguise with a furious tirade and concludes by shouting: "I no more fear you than I fear a fly."

What self-respecting pirate would take this kind of talk from a child? None at all, of course, but then as we have pointed out, Silver is given no self to respect. There is no basic personality from which he may derive strength when challenged or to which the reader may assign responsibility when Silver himself is doing the threatening. He is a weed that flourishes in ideal conditions but shrivels almost without resistance at the first sign of opposition. The point of the story as well as the pleasure in reading it is in the active conflict, not in its cause or even its final result. To try to speak seriously of good or evil in *Treasure Island* is almost as irrelevant as attempting to assign moral value in a baseball game, even though a presumable requisite to enjoying the contest involves a temporary if arbitrary preference for one side or the other.[8]

The fuss that some critics have made over Silver's escape with a small part of the treasure at the end of the book as a sign of Stevenson's moral softness or of his "liberation" from strict Calvinist dogma seems rather foolish. Silver has murdered, robbed, and lied, but he has also been a good cook, a remarkable physical specimen in spite of his lost leg, and a rather affectionate if irresponsible replacement for Jim's dead father. Above all, he has been entertaining, and in a timeless, placeless, nearly conscienceless world, Stevenson seems justified in paying him off and sending him packing. To have killed him would have implied a punishment, a moral judgment Stevenson apparently did not want to make in this book. By the same token, to have rewarded him too generously or to have brought about his conversion would also have introduced a moral element not anticipated by anything earlier in the novel and therefore hardly appropriate at the conclusion.

If evil can be said to exist at all in one of the characters of Stevenson's early period, it is an illusion which wilts when exposed to daylight. Deacon Brodie, the two-faced "villain" of a play written with Henley in 1880, sees his own wickedness as a "blindness," a "nightmare," which vanishes when he awakes and his "eyes are opened." This prototype of Dr. Jekyll comes to an unhappy end, but not before absolving himself by declaring: "I see now that the bandage has fallen from my eyes; I see myself."

Later on, most obviously in *Dr. Jekyll and Mr. Hyde* and in *The Master of Ballantrae,* Stevenson returns to the theme of the double personality and tries with varying success to raise in the midst of melodrama serious moral and psychological questions. But it is important to see that his first impulse is to play a game and to teach us nothing more or less than how to play it with him. *Treasure Island* belongs not in the ironic mold of *Huckleberry Finn,* in which the adult world is seen through the eyes of a boy for what it really is. Without the transcendental overtones, it follows more closely in the tradition of Blake's *Songs of Innocence* and Wordsworth's "We Are Seven." The child is isolated from the adult world, protected from it by his own lack of experience, and does not really see it at all except in imperfect and distorted glimpses. We learn precious little about the psychology of evil from Long John Silver and nothing of real consequence about nineteenth-century morality from reading *Treasure Island.*

William Golding's *Lord of the Flies,* as a serious variation on the theme of boys' adventure, may make twentieth-century readers suspicious of the ingenuousness of a *Treasure Island* or a *Swiss Family Robinson.* In fact, it must have been intended, in part, as an antiromantic antidote to that "escapist" genre. But it ought to be remembered that, unlike *Treasure Island* and despite its popularity among adolescents, *Lord of the Flies* depends almost entirely on adult assumptions for its effectiveness as a novel. Moreover, one of the ironies of the book is that, for any of the youngest participants, the whole ghastly episode might have been regarded, even to the end, as little more than an exciting (if bewildering) romp on a desert island. It is this limited attitude toward reality, without benefit of adult insinuation, which Stevenson sought to capture in *Treasure Island.* His extraordinary success depended largely on his early conviction that, with respect to certain areas of experience, the child's amoral view was perfectly valid.

In "A Gossip on Romance" Stevenson wrote:

> There is a vast deal in life and letters . . . which is not immoral, but simply a-moral; which either does not regard the human will at all, or deals with it in obvious and healthy relations; where the interest turns, not upon what a man shall choose to do, but on how he manages

> to do it; not on passionate slips and hesitations of the conscience, but on the problems of the body and of the practical intelligence, in clean, open-air adventure, the shock of arms or the diplomacy of life. (XIII, 329)

It is devotion to this principle of "clean" adventure virtually unblemished by good or evil which produces the novels that may be placed in the category of boy's daydream, including *The Black Arrow, Kidnapped, David Balfour,* and *St. Ives.*

3

Kidnapped (1886) and its sequel *David Balfour,* published as *Catriona* seven years later, are usually taken as though they belonged in an altogether different category from *Treasure Island.* Both novels admit details of geographical locale and historical time which are obviously missing from the earlier book, in which chronology is presented through the highly omissive mind of a child and an island is a place where treasure is buried, not an actual piece of land a given number of miles off the coast of England. There is also the difference in the ages of the heroes. Jim Hawkins is only a boy (though Stevenson, in keeping with his avoidance of particulars in *Treasure Island,* does not give his precise age) whereas David Balfour, we are informed on page three of *Kidnapped,* is a youth of seventeen when he first sets out on his adventures.

But in spite of these admittedly important differences, the basic impulse evident in the two later books, their primary value and interest to the reader, as well as Stevenson's apparent pleasure in writing them, places them with *Treasure Island* in the category of adventure fiction as boy's dream. At the center of the two books lies not psychology, or morality, or politics, or patriotism, or history, or geography, or romantic love, but "the problems of the body and of the practical intelligence, in clean, open-air adventure." Both *Kidnapped* and *David Balfour* are essentially amoral novels, aimless, hectic, and almost totally devoid of characters complex enough to experience the pleasures or pains of maturity.

Kidnapped, like *Treasure Island,* begins with the death of the young hero's father, and his departure from the familiar comforts and limitations of home to sections of Scotland previously unknown to him. The departure from home and the release from the conventional moral restraints associated with paternal authority is stated in the first sentence of the novel with almost scriptural economy as David recalls "the year of grace 1751, when I took the key for the last time out of the door of my father's house." David, like Jim Hawkins, is not plunged immediately into the unfamiliar world of buccaneers and Highland outlaws, but is given a hint of it by the eccentric and treacherous ways of parsimonious Uncle Ebenezer, his closest living kinsman, to whom he goes to claim a rightful inheritance. But Ebenezer, for all his wickedness (he makes several covert attempts on David's life and is eventually the cause of his being kidnapped), is physically vulnerable, like Blind Pew, the apoplectic Captain Flint, and one-legged John Silver.

When David returns alive from a supposedly fatal errand on which he was sent by his uncle up an unsafe staircase, in the dark, Ebenezer suffers a mild stroke. But neither in *Kidnapped* nor in *Treasure Island* is physical weakness necessarily an outer sign of inner moral decay as we often find it to be in Hawthorne and Melville. Nor does Stevenson, for all his borrowings from the Gothic, use physical deformity as Poe does, primarily as a macabre sign of insane depravity. Though the abnormalities of Pew, Silver, and Ebenezer obviously have in them elements of the grotesque, Stevenson generally insists upon employing them in their least symbolic and most literal sense. If an unnatural appearance frightens the boy-hero, it also gives him evidence of physical frailty in his enemy. In a genre which turns on "the problems of the body and the practical intelligence," that is a grave disadvantage indeed.

The weakness of the villain—or, more accurately, would-be villain since the skulduggery is rarely if ever carried out successfully—prevents evil from taking a permanent hold in the book. It should be remembered that in spite of the unexpected reserves of strength possessed by Pew and Silver their disabilities finally do them in. Pew is unable to see the horses bearing down upon him and Silver at his moment of humiliation is without a crutch and forced to crawl "hand over hand" like an infant. Nor does Stevenson really humanize his villains by making them vulnerable. It is simply his way of dissipating the threat of wickedness, of nipping evil in the bud, by reducing its physical power. Ebenezer Balfour is a bogieman like Bones and Pew and Silver, who can be depended upon to fall with a half-comic, half-pathetic, but very loud thud at the appropriate moment.

Uncle Ebenezer has sufficient strength and treachery, however, to have his nephew shanghaied by a disreputable crew of slave-traders under the leadership of the next potential "badman" of the story, Captain Elias Hoseason. After hearing several frightening tales of the captain from Ransome, the cabin-boy, David finally sees him. He turns out to be a "fine, tall figure with a manly bearing," which causes David to wonder "if it was possible that Ransome's stories could be true . . . they fitted so ill with the man's looks." Stevenson does not leave us very long with this puzzle, but offers an already familiar explanation:

> . . . indeed, he was neither so good as I supposed him,

> nor quite so bad as Ransome did; for, in fact, he was two men, and left the better one behind as soon as he set foot on board his vessel. (V, 45)

Here again, as in the case of John Silver, we have a character ready to play two roles, shedding one and assuming the other as the situation requires. Stevenson does not use the dual nature as an excuse to raise a subtle question of morality or to complicate the conscience of the captain, but rather as a way of neutralizing his character and sidestepping moral judgment of it altogether. By treating human nature as a kind of nonorganic particle in which positive and negative charges cancel each other, Stevenson denies that imbalance of properties which is the perennial source of moral conflict.

Even the natural landscape, for all its atmospheric importance in *Kidnapped,* is not permitted to pose an ultimate threat to the characters. Like Uncle Ebenezer and Captain Hoseason, it may *seem* frightening at first, but that is only because of imperfect perception on the part of David, and, as Stevenson has often explained, it is precisely this faultiness of vision which allows the child to become involved in adventures not possible for the more observant adult. Once the inadequate view has been corrected, the danger disappears and the young hero is able to control and toy with topography just as, with the help of Alan Breck, he overcomes Hoseason and his entire crew aboard the *Covenant,* and plays a practical joke at the end of the book on old Ebenezer.

One of the most interesting of David's various encounters with nature is his being washed ashore on the Isle of Earraid after the wreck of the *Covenant.* The episode is a kind of miniature *Robinson Crusoe* in the midst of a novel which is mostly set on the Scottish mainland. We enjoy observing the ingenuity by which David keeps himself alive on a diet of limpets and finds partial shelter between two boulders, but the incident reaches a most un-Defoe-like conclusion when two fishermen sail by and indicate to David that all along it had been possible for him to walk to the mainland.

> Earraid . . . [was] what they call a tidal islet, and except in the bottom of the neaps, can be entered and left twice in every twenty-four hours, either dry-shod, or at the most by wading . . . The wonder was . . . that [the fishermen] had ever guessed my pitiful illusion. (V, 120)

The island is not a real island any more than Ebenezer and Hoseason are real villains. It, like its human counterparts, creates an *illusion* of danger until the hero is finally able to see all around it, and then it becomes innocuous, almost cooperative with the will of the protagonist. Even nature, then, has two selves, an illusive one which is unfriendly and threatening, and a "real" one which is bland and malleable.

For all the fatigue and discomforts caused by the rough terrain and the fickle Scotch climate during their flight in the heather, David and Alan have a rather whimsical time of it, whistling and joking and treating the dangers of man and nature with an air of casual disregard. Throughout their flight, while hotly pursued by semi-barbarous Campbells out for revenge, and troops of red-coats with a warrant for their arrest, the two heroes insist upon acting like vacationers on a walking tour of the Highlands:

> With a rivalry that much amused us, we spent a great part of our days at the waterside, stripped to the waist and groping about or (as they say) guddling for . . . fish . . . They were of good flesh and flavour, and when broiled upon the coals, lacked only a little salt to be delicious. (V, 182)

A holiday mood of rough-and-tumble masculine playfulness pervades much of the novel. Near the end of the supposedly exhausting and harrowing journey, while plotting to trick the maid of an inn into giving them a boat, Alan turns to his friend:

> "Ye have a fine, hang-dog, rag-and-tatter, clappermaclaw kind of look to ye, as if ye had stolen the coat from a potato-bogle . . ." I followed him, laughing. "David Balfour," said he, "ye're a very funny gentleman by your way of it, and this is a very funny employ for ye, no doubt." (V, 240)

Alan is referring to the immediate trickery at hand, but he might as well be speaking of the entire adventure.

Kidnapped, we soon come to realize, is a "very funny employ" indeed, another game not so very different in spirit from *Treasure Island.* As in all games, at least two sides are required, though neither has a profound moral advantage over the other. We are, of course, expected to root for David and his Highland companion, Alan; we hear the story told from their point of view, and as a result, they seem to be friendlier company than Ebenezer, Hoseason, and the redcoats. But we are often reminded that the members of the opposition have their better sides along with their weaknesses, and although for the duration we agree to notice only their meanness, there is always the possibility that in some future skirmish they might make fairly respectable allies. "Our criminals are a most pleasant crew, and leave the dock with scarce a stain upon their character," wrote Stevenson in 1891. And though the specific reference is to *The Wrecker,* it is applicable to a great many of his adventures.

One reason *Kidnapped* has been taken more seriously than *Treasure Island* is that the alignment of opponents is more complex than in the earlier book. We begin with David Balfour alone against Uncle Ebenezer; then David, who is a Whig Lowlander, and Alan Breck, a Tory Highlander, are against Hoseason and his pirates; then David and Alan flee through the Highlands from the wrathful Campbells and the King's redcoats. The infiltration into the game of ancient rivalry between Highland and Lowland Scots and the historical enmity between Jacobite and Whig give the novel more weight than *Treasure Island,* and a point beyond the immediate conflict of characters engaged in tricking, battling, and escaping one another. But historical and geographical divisions, like the two halves of Hoseason's personality, also serve to accelerate and maintain motion, balancing each other with approximately equal resources, until one side eventually peters out, and gives the advantage to the other.

Stevenson set out to write a richer and more serious book than *Treasure Island* when he began *Kidnapped.* In many ways he succeeded. But if there is a tendency to expand the field of adventure and to complicate the action with historical and geographical association, there is, I think, a simultaneous and stronger tendency to remain in the relatively simple and limited world of child's dream.

Kidnapped has an authenticity which could not be claimed for *Treasure Island,* but when that authenticity threatens to intrude on the relatively carefree adventure with serious ethical and political questions, Stevenson withdraws from it. Undoubtedly his approval of the inclusion of a map of David's travels in the first edition of *Kidnapped* was a way of calling attention to the nationalistic and topographical flavor of the story. But *Treasure Island* started with a map too, and it is difficult to read what Stevenson wrote about that cartographical invention without suspecting him of similar sentiments toward the genuine chart in *Kidnapped:*

> It contained harbours that pleased me like sonnets . . . I am told there are people who do not care for maps, and find it hard to believe. The names, the shapes of the woodlands, the courses of the roads and rivers . . . the mills and the ruins . . . here is an inexhaustible fund of interest for any man with eyes to see, or twopence worth of imagination to understand with. (II, xii)

If the map at the front of *Kidnapped* is an aesthetic ornament even while it is serving as a fairly reliable guide to the Highlands, then it is a good symbol of the use to which Stevenson puts topography and political history in the novel. He takes them seriously enough to make the adventure turn on clan warfare between the north and south of Scotland, but not so seriously as to let them divert him from "the problems of the body and of the practical intelligence."

The quarrel between David and Alan is a typical example of the extent to which history colors and intensifies a private conflict without ultimately lifting it above the level of an adolescent skirmish. During their flight through the Highlands the two heroes, who in spite of their friendship represent opposing political factions, have a falling out. Alan, at one point, whistles a Jacobite ditty which mocks David's Whiggery. They argue and each stands ready to duel, but the two friends do not cross swords; David is too tired, and Alan too sympathetic toward his young companion. The political differences between them are in no way resolved or evaluated by Stevenson. The quarrel amounts to little more than an entertaining interval of name-calling, the Viking messenger berating Byrtnoth before the Battle of Maldon or Unferth ridiculing Beowulf at the feast, with the important difference that in *Kidnapped* the name-calling is not a prelude to epic struggle.

David Daiches suggests that the reader of *Kidnapped* "provide himself with sufficient background information to enable him to find some satisfaction in the historical and topographical elements in the novel."[9] His advice is good. It is true that much that at first appears to be obscure local color makes better sense in the context of Scottish history. Nevertheless, it remains a fact that *Kidnapped* has continued to be popular with young readers who probably know almost nothing about clan warfare in eighteenth-century Scotland. This does not mean that the historical setting is not important in the novel, but that it remains peculiarly detachable from the action in the foreground. In reading *Kidnapped* a child can quite easily leave "the bulk of the book unrealized," but fix on the rest and live it. That is not true of the history and topography in *The Master of Ballantrae* or *Weir of Hermiston;* and neither book has ever been highly favored by Stevenson's younger admirers. The surface of *Kidnapped* reveals an attempt by Stevenson to move away from the self-contained world of *Treasure Island,* but the internal logic of the narrative discloses again and again his compelling need to prolong that inconsequential dream.

4

David Balfour was one of Stevenson's last complete works, published under the title of *Catriona* in 1893, the year before he died of a cerebral hemorrhage at Vailima. In many ways it is a more sophisticated novel than either *Treasure Island* or *Kidnapped,* and, although it is avowedly a sequel to the latter book, critics have been hesitant for a variety of reasons to consider the two together. *David Balfour,* like *Kidnapped,* is narrated in the first person by the young hero, but in parts it comes closer to being a "domestic and usual novel" than anything else Stevenson wrote because it deals with Barbara Grant's attempts at turning David into a gentleman and with the love affair between David and Catriona Drummond. It differs from *Kidnapped,* too, in its comparative paucity of visual imagery. Whereas *Kidnapped,* with a much simpler plot, seems visually a cluttered book, full of gloomy lairs, somber estates, complicated moorland topography, tartans and plaids and significant silver buttons, *David Balfour,* with a more intricate plot, becomes barer and barer as the story progresses. "It subjects my visual sense, my *seeing* imagination," complained Henry James in a letter to Stevenson, "to an almost painful underfeeding."[10]

Still, notwithstanding these differences, *David Balfour* provides an interesting and fitting conclusion to a study of Stevenson's adventure fiction as youthful dream. Like *Treasure Island* and *Kidnapped,* its basic impulse is play. Its incidents are without serious moral implications, its characters without psyches, its politics without issue, and its history without consequence. There is a tone in the book which suggests that Stevenson was at last beginning to find the game stale, was becoming disillusioned with the efficacy of dream, but for all that, it does represent one last fling, even during a time when his imagination was probing other and more serious prospects of adventure.

David Balfour is the closest Stevenson ever came to writing an eighteenth-century novel. Other books, *Treasure Island* and *Kidnapped* included, were set in that century, but in no other work does he contribute, along with Scott, Dickens, and Thackeray, to that body of nineteenth-century fiction deliberately imitative of the style and spirit of the preceding era. The note he strikes is a modified English picaresque in the tradition of Fielding and Smollett, only without the humor. The hero and heroine are generalized types whose even features and open expressions reflect pure spirits and essentially good natures. Their faces, like their personalities, undergo no development in the course of the narrative, but are caught in an attitude early in the book which is statically maintained throughout. David's first glimpse of Catriona fixes her mask in the mind of the reader as it does in his own, and whether she pouts, weeps, or shouts invective, the basic expression somehow never changes.

David himself is a country boy, healthy, durable, well-knit, naturally intelligent, but unspoiled by the affectations of the city. As a physical type he might easily change places with Tom Jones or Roderick Random. We learn little about his looks beyond the description in the warrant for his arrest: "A tall strong lad of about eighteen . . . speaks like a Lowlander and has no beard." Although taught to dress and speak properly by Miss Grant, so that he will look a "pretty gentleman" during a stay with the Lord Advocate in Glasgow, David retains the heart and face of a country schoolmaster's son. Nevertheless, in spite of his humble upbringing, Balfour, like Jones, Joseph Andrews and Random, has true claims to wealth and name. When his Uncle Ebenezer dies, David is left heir to the House of Shaws. In the good eighteenth-century tradition, middle-class virtues tend to bear noble fruits.

The secondary characters of the novel have as familiar a ring as the hero and heroine do. David, like his eighteenth-century prototypes, is provided with a paternal benefactor, experienced, wise, and rich. The villains who pursue him are even more vacuous and vulnerable than those of *Treasure Island* and *Kidnapped,* and are exceeded only by the entertaining incompetence of the bad men of Fielding's two great comic novels. Lieutenant Hector Duncansby, described as a "gawky, leering Highland boy," who has been commissioned to slay David, melts before the "defenceless" courage of his victim. David's kidnappers on the Isle of Bass are so gentle with him that he is prompted to call them "my three Highlanders (I call them mine, although it was the other way about)," and so ineffectual that when he downs one, he captures all.

Catriona's father, who in some ways is the worst villain of the piece—dishonest, unreliable, hypocritical—is a dual character in the amoral tradition of Long John Silver and Elias Hoseason. He alternates between bravery and cowardice, personal charm and total dissipation. But, as in the earlier books, Stevenson does not ask us to judge the man, and scrupulously avoids doing so himself. In the intermediate manuscript of the novel, written in Stevenson's hand, most of the deletions and corrections reveal a disinclination to conjecture about the ethical or psychological nature of James Moore Drummond's character. "He was perfectly selfish, with a perfect innocency in the same" is scored in manuscript and eliminated from the final text. When Drummond dies "in a kind of odour of affectionate sanctity," Stevenson again deletes from the manuscript a reference to his "extraordinary fund of innocence."[11] David's remarks at this point in the revised version beg nicely the question of innocence or guilt and reflect Stevenson's reluctance to adopt a moral point of view: "I had him buried; but what to put upon his tomb was quite beyond me, till at last I considered the date would look best alone."

Aside from some of the familiar conventions of characterization, *David Balfour* bears other earmarks of eighteenth-century romance. There is the pretense, especially suggestive of Defoe, that what is being related is historically true. But although names, places, and incidents are borrowed from Scottish history, and the intricacies of political intrigue are probed at some length, Stevenson makes an attempt, in the proper spirit of neoclassicism, to avoid particularization of character and locale. James's visual sense was starved partly because in *David Balfour* we see no more of Glasgow, Bass, Leyden, or Dunkirk than in *Tom Jones* we see of Somersetshire or London.

Despite its impressive and authentic touches of the eighteenth century, *David Balfour* remains an unmistakably Victorian novel. It is not a lusty story, and David, for all his youthfulness, is not a lusty hero. The most obvious, though certainly not the single sign of this, is Stevenson's treatment of David's relationship with Catriona. One does not expect the breezy sexuality of *Moll Flanders* or *Tom Jones,* which is typical of only one kind of eighteenth-century romance in any case, but there is an almost bleak solemnity in the love affair between David and Catriona which appears peculiarly Stevensonian and Victorian. When sex was taken up at all by one of the major eighteenth-century novelists, it was taken not like a medicine out of duty, but usually out of genuine interest. If chastity and promiscuity are not treated comically and satirically by Richardson as they are by Defoe, Swift, Smollett, Fielding, and Sterne, he at least demonstrates a prurient concern which, though unhealthy, is not dispassionate.

When David finds himself living alone with Catriona in Leyden, her only friend and protector, he rigorously honors her virtue while inwardly struggling against his own passion. Stevenson's way of portraying this supposedly unbearable tension between respect and desire is to have David read his law books while Catriona sits in a corner biting her lip; or to have them take long silent walks through the city, or, more often, to have them quarrel over trivia. Since the subjects of their disagreements are her clothes, her housekeeping, or her father, they suggest the bickering of a middle-aged married couple more than the passionate flare-ups of young lovers. When David does for a moment break out of his self-imposed restraint and embrace Catriona, it is he rather than the girl who nearly faints: "I raised her face to mine, I kissed it, and she bowed her brow upon my bosom, clasping me tight. I sat in a mere whirl like a man drunken" (VI, 283).

Loving a woman unmans David Balfour, but not in the chivalrous, courtly sense in which the lover humbles himself to obtain his lady's favor. David is continually apologetic for the grossness of his feelings and he struggles to turn them into purer sentiments akin to a son's love for his mother. Catriona, like so many Victorian heroines, does not turn her man into an animal but into a child. She takes on the role of strength—maternal, authoritarian, and mature—while David is constantly forced to play the naughty boy, chastised for wanting things he is not supposed to have and, in fact, is all but powerless to get. In this sense, not only is Stevenson's dream of adventure boyish, but also his dream of love.

On the boat trip to Holland, Catriona becomes angry and silent over a letter from Miss Grant to David, advising him to kiss Catriona without asking permission. David's reaction to his beloved's cold fury is characteristically "like an angry boy's."

Once settled in Leyden, although Catriona is the weak female supposedly under the protection of the sturdy hero, she gains power over David until she is able alternately to entice and mortify him, acting with a duplicity not altogether unlike that of Silver and Hoseason. Stevenson manages to turn even love into a contest which depends much more heavily on an assumed position within a rigid framework than on the unruly responses of the human heart to another creature imperfectly understood. Upon arrival in Leyden, David had bought Catriona some clothes until her own luggage should arrive. When it does, she has two costume changes, two real as well as metaphorical guises; and then the tournament can really begin:

> There was one point in particular on which our warfare turned, and of all things, this was the question of her clothes. She had now, as it were, two wardrobes; and it grew to be understood between us . . . that when she was friendly she would wear my clothes, and when otherwise her own. It was meant for a buffet, and . . . the renunciation of her gratitude; and I felt it so in my bosom. (VI, 278)

In the "warfare" of their relationship David is invariably on the losing side. Catriona alternately denounces him and pleads with him to care for her in her isolation; she calls him a brute and a brother, a coward and her dearest friend. David's reaction to both moods is guilty and apologetic. When she wears her own clothes and is abrupt and unfriendly with him, he becomes uncivil in return and then tortures himself for the "wretched boyishness" of his response. When she wears his clothes, and is fragile and dependent, luring him to embrace or kiss her and then bursting into tears, he is tormented with remorse for his momentary brutishness.

One might be prompted to place Catriona in the large category of man-destroying Victorian females along with Becky Sharp, Rosamond Vincy, and Sue Bridehead if

Stevenson had treated her with even the slightest ironic detachment. But he does not. He allows her to retain her "other" role—the doll-faced heroine in distress, her bright eyes still shining "like stars," her lips still "a trifle open"—unchanged by, almost unconscious of, the recurring appearances of the angry harridan. As much as her behavior may sound at first like feminine caprice, it alternates with such awful regularity that it seems hardly human, let alone womanly.

The clue to Catriona's character as well as to the difficulty in her love affair is contained in an early speech of hers which also provides an excellent summation of the novel's basic mood. David has just related to Catriona the episode in the park in which he was challenged to a duel by the gawky Highlander, Lieutenant Duncansby. Having been raised by a peace-loving father, David has never learned to use a sword. He stands up bravely to the challenge, but when the Highlander realizes his victim is unable to draw a proper sword, he lets him go. Catriona's reaction to the story is revealing:

> "I should have been a man child. In my own thoughts it is so I am always; and I go on telling myself about this thing that is to befall and that. Then it comes to the place of the fighting, and it comes over me that I am only a girl at all events, and cannot hold a sword or give one good blow; and then I have to twist my story round about, so that the fighting is to stop, and yet me have the best of it, just like you and the lieutenant; and I am the boy that makes the fine speeches all through, like Mr. David Balfour." (VI, 101-102)

Catriona's dream is an avowed case of sex envy, the female desiring to play the male role, which she eventually does as David's querulous partner in adventure. David's inability to use the sword, insofar as it too may be taken as a sign of underdeveloped masculinity, corresponds symbolically with his immature treatment of Catriona as sister, mother, fellow-adventurer, and only rarely and timidly as lover. The usefulness of this interpretation is in what it tells us of Stevenson's apparently unconscious desire to keep the story in the realm of boy's adventure in spite of the presence of a grown heroine and a hero past puberty. It is Stevenson, who, once he has her in the book, seems to wish Catriona were "a man child" and finally treats her almost as though she were; and it is Stevenson who provides his young hero with a mistress and then makes him behave like a little boy before her.

In this adolescent game of adventure, Stevenson does with the love affair what in *Treasure Island* and *Kidnapped* he had done with history, time, and morals: he sacrifices it to the cause of action and conflict for their own sake. Catriona as an object of love is mechanical and dull, but Catriona as an excuse for travel and adventure serves her purpose fairly well. David guides her through the dingy waterfront of Helvoet in search of her father, and from there by "rattel-waggon" to Rotterdam, and finally takes her with him to Leyden. When her father does eventually turn up, David is immediately plunged into intrigue with him, follows father and daughter to Dunkirk, where old Drummond's treachery causes a close call with a ship full of redcoats, and stops Alan Breck from killing the old man in a duel just in the nick of time.

And all this because of Catriona. In fact, Catriona's best reason for existing in the novel is not so that David can make love to her (which he hardly ever gets a chance to do), but so that all this excitement may occur. Stevenson's original impulse to include a heroine in his book may have been a sign of growing pains, but the use to which he finally puts her shows him reverting incorrigibly to old tricks. "Pure dispassionate" adventure is still his mill, and Catriona, like the map of Treasure Island, the Uprising of '45, the Appin murder, Earraid and Bass and Pilrig and Prestongrange, is so much grist for the grinding.

The obvious parallel between Catriona's remembering in the middle of her daydream that she is "only a girl . . . and cannot hold a sword" and David's encounter with Duncansby in the park suggests that for Stevenson as well as for his heroine it was becoming more and more difficult to imagine a romantic conclusion without admitting along the way some of the frustrations and failures inevitable in the waking world.

For all the intrigue, kidnapping, border-crossing, spying, and sword-play, David Balfour, without being Shandean, is an impotent hero, and without being Quixotic, is one of the most inactive and inept heroes in the noncomic literature of adventure. While excitement and peril rage around him, he spends most of the novel *not* being able to do what he wants to. He cannot duel in the park with Duncansby; he cannot join Alan in his flight across the channel; he is kidnapped and cannot attend the Appin murder trial until the last day in session, and then cannot testify when he gets there; he cannot be told where Catriona is hiding in Glasgow and can see her for only a moment through a window; he cannot make love to her when he lives alone with her in Leyden; he cannot repel her father even when he knows he is a villain; and finally he cannot even break the seal of a letter when he knows it contains the instructions for a plot on the life of his best friend.

Daiches calls David "a more active hero throughout the book than the hero of any other of Stevenson's adventure stories, the master of his own destiny rather than someone acted upon,"[12] but I find this difficult to accept. There is action enough in the book, and there may be the illusion that David is in the midst of it, whereas in fact he is rarely the initiator of or an active participant in any of it. If he is in the middle at all, he stands in the eye of the storm, inactive, observant, relatively undisturbed. In *Treasure Island* the contrary is true of Jim Hawkins, who boasts to Silver:

> "I was in the apple barrel the night we sighted land, and I heard you [plot mutiny] . . . and told every word you said before the hour was out. And as for the schooner, it was I who cut her cable, and it was I that killed the men you had aboard of her, and it was I who brought her where you'll never see her more." (II, 213)

When he adds, "I've had the top of this business from the first," he is absolutely right. *Treasure Island* is Jim's story in every way. He responds resourcefully to trouble throughout the adventure and is actively embroiled in dangerous exploits from beginning to end. How is it that little Jim Hawkins, an innkeeper's son, is deft with two pistols against Israel Hands and can sail a schooner by himself while his fictional big brother cannot duel in the park because his schoolmaster father never taught him the principles of fencing? It would seem that the boy's dream is breaking up, being intruded upon by the consciousness of the limitations of the world in which training, physique, age, and balance of odds have direct bearing on the possibilities of active heroism. The process of casting off, so airily begun in *Treasure Island,* has become less easy for Stevenson to accomplish and less convincing to himself when he tries it.

He is tempted more than ever to step into the childish fantasy as an adult and to make judgments derived from maturity. In manuscript he has David end the story (supposedly told to his and Catriona's children) with an apology for himself and his deceased father-in-law: "If your father was something of a simpleton, and grandfather not better than a rogue, no harm that you should know it." But Stevenson reconsidered the effect of these sentiments, probably recognizing an asperity in them which might have allowed accuracy to triumph over whimsy, and struck them out of his final text.

The dream continues in *David Balfour,* even if some of the magic of the ritual is gone because the celebrants are no longer able to cast off their old ordinary selves and assume new identities without being reminded from time to time that the change is make-believe. There are signs of Stevenson's decreasing confidence in the enchanting power of the "assumed role," but he has not in this novel provided us with any substantial alternative. The disguise of the "superchild" is growing thin and transparent, but we must look to others of his books to discover what is emerging behind it.

5

In the boyish adventures following *Treasure Island* we find only a Jim Hawkins in decline—a hero with all the vulnerability and most of the limitations of youth without its protective and audacious fancy. If Jim is the perfect image of the dream hero in a child's game, capable of everything, and David in *David Balfour* is an adolescent plagued by his own inadequacy, David in *Kidnapped,* one year younger, is an interesting cross between the two. He is less inept than his later self but there are signs even in *Kidnapped* that the hero is not dauntless. Although at times he is energetic and active, he also has a way of falling dazed or unconscious at moments of crisis requiring physical resistance or endurance. The blow upon his head when he is first taken aboard the *Covenant* keeps him sick and helpless for days until even his captors feel pity for him and treat him like an invalid.

David also proves a rather sickly companion for Alan Breck in an otherwise jaunty flight through the heather. His recurring fever and fatigue hamper the "walking tour" much more consistently than the Campbells or the redcoats. At a stopover in a Highland hideaway called Cluny's Cage, David falls into a delirium—"a kind of trance in which I continued almost the whole of our stay"—which prevents him from taking part in a good deal of scheming and intrigue. It is also David's weakness which arrests the quarrel between him and Alan when they are at the point of drawing swords.

Unlike Stevenson's sickly villains, the ailing hero is neither cowardly nor ultimately ineffectual, but becomes rather an effective innocent, a peacemaker, a potential martyr. Although he may be physically incapable of defending himself, he still *thinks* and *talks* like a hero—is loyal to friends, unwilling to yield on a point of honor, unafraid to die. When heroic action is called for, the protagonist's flesh sometimes proves weak, but his spirit is usually willing. Stevenson turns David's frailty to his advantage in *Kidnapped* just as in *David Balfour* he makes his lack of skill and inability to act, in love and war, inverse signs of honor and heroism.

What happens between *Treasure Island* and *David Balfour,* then, resembles in miniature what happened between Homer and Tennyson: the idea of bravery has been separated from the act. In the age of Homeric epic, a brave man is a man who acts bravely. In the mercantile age of nineteenth-century England a man may be considered heroic for thinking bravely and not acting at all. We are presented with the brooding and victimized heroes of Byron. We find an increasing number of elegiac poems glorifying men like Chatterton and Hallam as much for unaccomplished feats as for what they had lived to do. "'Tis not what man Does which exalts him," wrote Browning in *Saul,* "but what man would do!"[13]

The theme of unfulfilled (or unfulfillable) heroic intention produces heroes like Pip, Pendennis, and Phineas Finn, whose capacity for looking pathetic or foolish depends on the degree to which their dreams exceed their ability to see what is at hand and to act upon it. These Victorian heroes anticipate in one sense the tragic protagonists of the later nineteenth and early twentieth centuries, the ironically viewed hero *manqué* of Eliot, Hardy, and Conrad—the Lydgates, the Judes, the Lord Jims, all romantic dreamers who wreck their lives with impossible visions of themselves which the world cannot let them fulfill.

The curious thing about Stevenson is that although, by the time he wrote *David Balfour,* he seemed to be growing more conscious of the inadequacy of child's play as a way of art and of the ultimate self-deception inherent in daydreaming as a way of life, he continues to treat his protagonists without irony. *Treasure Island, Kidnapped,* and *David Balfour* are not tragic or comic books because in them there is no moral or philosophical ideal not reached. And that, of course, is because in narrative terms there is none implied. Taken together, however, as part of a creative experiment, there is in the three books an artistic ideal attempted: the reintegration through fiction of mind and body into heroic action. "I have been after an adventure all my life," wrote Stevenson in *Travels with a Donkey,* "a pure dispassionate adventure, such as befell early and heroic voyagers."

The difficulty is that, as soon as he leaves the uncomplicated and limited world of childhood behind, the intrusions of the adult world only widen the gap between wishing and being. By the time he comes to write *David Balfour,* he seems to be admitting in various ways throughout the book that intent may be heroic but only a dream, while action is real but rarely heroic. What separates Stevenson from Hardy and Conrad is that, although in *Kidnapped* and *David Balfour* he begins to show signs of dissatisfaction and bewilderment over his vision of a "pure dispassionate adventure," he still shares the fault with his own characters and clings almost apologetically to a dream in which he has already begun to disbelieve.

There is little question that in the years between 1881 and 1892 Stevenson's imagination underwent considerable change or that *Kidnapped* and *David Balfour,* with their sometimes bulky authenticity, show evidences of that change. But his best inclination as a writer of fiction, in spite of a not altogether undeserved reputation for stylistic ornateness, is economy. His growth from the ingenuous vigor of *Treasure Island* to the spare power of *The Master of Ballantrae* and *Weir of Hermiston* is a development in narrative simplicity. "There is but one art," he wrote in 1883 to his cousin, Robert, "to omit! O if I knew how to omit, I would ask no other knowledge. A man who knew how to omit would make an Iliad of a daily paper . . . He learns it in the crystallization of daydreams; in changing, not in copying, fact" (*Letters,* II, 173-174).

It would of course be misleading to speak of *Treasure Island, Kidnapped,* and *David Balfour* as though they were written on a single track or in a compartment sealed off from the rest of Stevenson's works. His development as an artist was even more erratic than that of most novelists and is further complicated by the fact that he often worked on two or three books at the same time. In keeping with his adventurer's spirit, he was an experimenter in art, willing to try almost anything once. The frivolity of some individual results plus the patchwork quality this procedure made out of his career have led to accusations of dilettantism. But Stevenson's apparent lack of direction is in itself a kind of direction, and his refusal to be philosophical while indulging in his boyish daydreams is itself a philosophy. "His appreciation of [youth] amounts to a passion," wrote Henry James, "and a passion, in the age in which we live, strikes us, on the whole, as a sufficient philosophy."[14]

The importance of the three novels discussed thus far lies not alone in their individual literary excellence, though each has considerable merit, and *Treasure Island,* within its limits, is a small masterwork, but also in the chart they provide of a Victorian mind rejecting the present. Stevenson seeks order for his art in the personal past of his childhood and in the public past of the Scottish nation. He turns away from the world and into the self, hoping to cultivate there a diminutive garden with a pattern and formality the universe seems no longer to possess. In the apparent absence of a single permanent goal, Stevenson tries to squint his eyes and recapture the imperfect vision of a child so that he may enjoy the journey and damn the destination. His adventure fiction, as a result, tends to be contractive rather than expansive, more concerned with closing in and shutting out than with diving headlong into the chaos.

Writers of highly fanciful fiction and poetry have often, especially since the nineteenth century, questioned the moral relevance and even the sanity of their creative habits. Joseph Conrad, who labored with such careful genius to keep his exotic tales "true," understood better than most the temptations which beset the romantic dreamer. His famous description of the artist as Don Quixote serves as a peculiarly apt summary of Stevenson's literary character in its earliest phase:

> His was a very noble, a very unselfish fantasy, fit for nothing except to raise the envy of baser mortals. But there is more than one aspect to the charm of that exalted and dangerous figure. He, too, had his frailties. After reading so many romances he desired naively to escape with his very body from the intolerable reality of things . . . O amiable and natural weakness! O blessed simplicity of a gentle heart without guile! Who would not succumb to such a consoling temptation? Nevertheless it was a form of self-indulgence, and the ingenious hidalgo of La Mancha was not a good citizen.[15]

Stevenson did not create civic disorder, but his ethic, like that of Don Quixote, became for a time a cultivated form of self-indulgence. His attempts to avoid commitment on moral issues by resorting to the "freedom" of childish fantasies led him to self-involvement and a curiously unconscious effeteness. During the very years he was writing of "Buccaneers and Buried Gold," he came precariously close to literary decadence. And nowhere is that proximity revealed more clearly than in two collections of seemingly frivolous satires to which critics have never paid much serious attention.

* * * * * * *

A fool is generally the wisest person out. The wise man must shut his eyes to all the perils and horrors that lie around him; but the cap and bells can go bobbing along the most slippery ledges and the bauble will not stir up sleeping lions. Hurray! for motley, for a good sound *insouciance,* for a healthy philosophic carelessness!

—*Letters* (I, 59)

* * * * * * *

III

ADVENTURE AS COMIC SATIRE

Stevenson did not seem to have many of the traits of a true satirist. He was not furious or bitter enough, not witty or boisterous, not unusually observant or avowedly pessimistic, not sufficiently detached and idealistic to look at life with a genuinely critical eye. We normally think of the comic satirist as one who mocks the partial for not being whole, whereas Stevenson, as we have seen, seeks comfort and sanity in the deliberate curtailment of imaginative perception, partly out of fear of uncontrollable possibility and ultimate madness for the perceiver, but primarily out of the anxiety that in the farther reaches of his mind he will stumble into vacancy. His danger is barrenness. "Never, please, let yourself imagine that I am fertile," he wrote to Colvin in 1874; "I am constipated in the brains" (*Letters,* I, 173).

In the decade of the seventies and on into the early eighties, Stevenson's favorite way of skirting his fear of creative deficiency was deliberately to avoid writing with a predetermined point—moral, philosophical, or aesthetic—which might inhibit his imaginative impulse by placing demands on it he feared he could not fulfill. This is not to say he was not didactic, for obviously in his early essays he often was, and even in some of his early fiction it is not uncommon for a lesson to appear in conclusion. What he refused was a coherent plan with a thematic or formal objective which would control or, as he evidently feared, might stifle the creative flow at its source by implying a goal beyond his reach.

In the same letter to Colvin quoted above, he discusses a proposed series of essays, which never were written, and firmly rejects any thematic commitment. "The Essays must fall from me, Essay by Essay, as they ripen . . . I should feel myself . . . at liberty to write as I please, and not bound to drag in a tag about Art every time to make it suitable." As a result of this attitude, many of Stevenson's essays not only shift aimlessly in tone from nostalgia to pedantry, from the anecdotal to the whimsical to the ponderous, but they are thematically difficult to categorize.

His own titles are only a partial help. *Virginibus Puerisque,* with its observations on romantic love, marriage, and death, is not really for boys and girls at all; "Ordered South," initially a meditation on travel for the sake of health, includes a long digression on the creative imagination; and in a piece called "Victor Hugo's Romances," Stevenson devotes more time to Fielding and Scott than one is led to expect from the title. His essays, like most of his novels, lack proportion. And they lack proportion because they lack design in the fullest sense of the word. With the exception of *Treasure Island* and the *Weir of Hermiston* fragment, the prevailing theme and tone of most of his longer works of fiction are as difficult to establish as they are in the essays. Many novels have been given two titles, but it is something of a literary phenomenon that *Catriona* might just as well be known as *David Balfour,* since the identity of the main character depends largely on which part of the book you are reading.

For much of his career, then, writing meant to Stevenson immersion in the craft for its own sake without very much advance concern for over-all structure or "total" meaning. The result of this, especially in the early years, was often a highly polished and professional form of literary doodling, which is not what normally constitutes satire; unless, as in the case of Laurence Sterne, the rationalistic system of describing experience is under attack. But Stevenson was no Sterne. He was not ridiculing reason. With the temperament of a chronically sick man guarding a small reserve of health, he jealously kept his imagination from the potential strain of predetermined commitment to a strict literary form or a consistent moral, philosophical, or social aim.

Insofar as satire is by definition one of the most pointed of literary forms, we might despair of ever finding it in Stevenson at all. He continually stresses writing as a craft first, and only secondarily as a channel through which ideas or morals may be communicated. In 1882 he wrote that the best thing a writer can do is "to forget sentiment, to think of his material and nothing else . . . for art is, first of all and last of all, a trade. The love of words and . . . the love of form . . . mark the vocation of the writer and the painter. The arabesque . . . even in literature, is the first fancy of the artist" (XV, 173). In 1883 he advises an aspiring young writer to "bow your head over technique . . . Forget purposes in the meanwhile; get to love technical processes" (*Letters,* II, 148).

Stevenson, surprisingly enough, follows his own advice, at least in the beginning, forgetting purpose to the point where one is sometimes compelled while reading his fiction or nonfiction to wonder just what it is he has on his mind. Even in a good many of his critical and moral essays the point is blurred or lost altogether in an excess of digression, rhetoric, and whimsy. We need only recall almost any one of Dr. Johnson's short essays to realize that it is Stevenson, not Johnson, who is the rambler. He toys with words and ideas, often fruitfully and well, but his is not a mind which proceeds according to any logical system, or pursues a series of assumptions in an attempt to reach a conclusion. He wrote in 1878 that "to travel successfully is better than to arrive"; and we might very well take this as the literary motto of his early career.

In his longer fiction, as well as in the expository prose, he has a habit of shifting emphasis in the middle of things. He may suddenly focus attention on a fresh set of circumstances which change the direction of the narrative, artificially prolong the tale, and avoid the conclusion suggested by the original series of events. *Kidnapped, David Balfour,* and *The Wrecker* would be the most obvious and outstanding cases in point. Stevenson enjoys getting his characters into trouble, but generally refuses to let them face the consequences. Fate is avoided with an arabesque, which means more often than not that the villains as well as the heroes get off scot-free. It is a kind of leniency appropriate to boys' adventures, but it shows little promise as satire.

Even when he writes something that begins to look like satire he can become so engaged in the technique and excitement of his own invention that he seems to lose sight of the object. It is true that the great English satirists, particularly Swift and Dickens, could become sufficiently enchanted by their own rage or laughter that their critical aim could be temporarily forgotten; but Stevenson hardly ever seems concerned enough with the object of his satire to let it distract him from the pleasures of ridicule. The irony of this, and one reason why his satire has so little sting to it, is that ridicule depends upon an object external to itself and upon the writer's ability to hold that object constantly, if distortedly, in view.

Swift saw satire as an "unmasking," the "art of exposing weak sides," and in his effort to tell the truth he attacked deception of every kind, including what he regarded as the illusion of human happiness, or the "perpetual possession of being well deceived." To make men wiser and possibly better, Swift took what he considered the necessary risk of making them unhappy. Stevenson's position could hardly be more at odds with that of the great eighteenth-century satirist. "There is an idea abroad among moral people that they should make their neighbours good. One person I have to make good: myself. But my duty to my neighbour is much more nearly expressed by saying that I have to make him happy—if I may" (XV, 305). The desire to make others happy at almost any cost is at the center of Stevenson's morality, certainly through the seventies and eighties, and is the one consistent and unchanging justification of the way he practiced his craft during that period. His distaste for Zola, his impatience with George Eliot ("a high—but may we not add?—a rather dry lady"), his dislike of literary realism and philosophic pessimism, can be explained by a straightforward statement included in a letter to William Archer in 1885: "I believe that literature should give joy" (*Letters,* II, 301).

If we take comic satire in its broadest sense to mean the exposure of folly by ridicule, as a genre it would seem ill-adapted to Stevenson's literary credo of giving joy. But before we dismiss him as a satirist altogether, it is worthwhile to look at those works which bear at least the superficial earmarks of satire (including diminution, exaggeration, and the juxtaposition of incongruities) to see whether there is something more than satiric atmosphere in his comic tales. Is he simply toying with the *idea* of satire without having a serious object in mind, or does he, in spite of himself and his professed scorn for discomforting purpose, have a target about which he feels strongly enough to heckle and scoff?

2

In 1878, three years before the serialization of *Treasure Island,* Stevenson published in the magazine *London* a series of interconnected tales called *Latter-Day Arabian Nights* (printed together in book form under the title *New Arabian Nights* in 1882). The structure of the series was to be in imitation of the old *Thousand and One Nights* frame-story, and the tales themselves a parody of popular adventure fiction of the day. They are curious, often downright silly stories, which have provoked a good deal of critical comment, but seem to have defied serious analysis and classification. William Archer, writing for the *New Review* of January 1895, sums up the contemporary opinion: "[Stevenson] never wrote anything more consummate in their kind than the *New Arabian Nights;* yet one is glad to think that these exercises in blood-curdling humour came at the beginning of his career."[1]

New Arabian Nights consists of two divisions, "The Suicide Club," based on an idea of Stevenson's cousin Robert, and "The Rajah's Diamond," each of which contains three linked episodes with, for the most part, a fresh set of characters. "The Suicide Club" opens with an introduction of Prince Florizel of Bohemia, the one constant figure in all the tales. When he tires of the high social life of London, he disguises himself and his confidant, Colonel Geraldine, in order to gain admission into "strange societies," and hopefully to take part in an adventure which will temporarily interrupt the monotony of existence. We find that, like the characters in *Treasure Island,* Florizel has no substantial or basic personality (other than the fact that he is a foreign prince), but takes on the traits called for by the peculiarities of the adventure at hand.

In the first episode, Geraldine and the Prince gain entrance to a secret and exclusive society of disillusioned young men who meet nightly in formal dress to drink champagne, discuss death, and play a game of cards to determine which member will be next to depart and which his gentle executioner. "A feverish hilarity reigned with sudden and rather ghastly pauses." The company is all male, young, and sensitive—"people in the prime of youth, with every show of intelligence and sensibility in their appearance, but with little promise of strength or the quality that makes success. Few were much above thirty and not a few were still in their teens." It soon becomes evident that the tale is not a fragment of foolishness for its own sake, but a rather broad and amusing "spoof" at the expense of the professional pessimists and aesthetes of the seventies and eighties: the exquisite and morbid young men portrayed and epitomized by Swinburne and Oscar Wilde, with whom Stevenson, in the most public of his various moods, had so little patience.

If we stop a moment and recall the fashionable literary currents of the years during which Stevenson wrote and published *New Arabian Nights,* the general target of his satire becomes clear, even though he refrained from ridiculing specific personages. Pater had collected his *Studies in the History of the Renaissance* by 1873, and in 1885 was to publish *Marius the Epicurean.* In 1881 Rossetti's volume of *Ballads and Sonnets* was published, and, like him, Stevenson's young friends Andrew Lang and Edmund Gosse were imitating early French verse in the manner of Villon and Charles D'Orléans. In 1878 Swinburne's *Poems and Ballads, Second Series,* appeared; his reputation had been established in 1866 when his *First Series* was attacked by scandalized London critics. It was in 1881 that Wilde's book of *Poems* was published and went through five editions; and it was in that same year that Gilbert and Sullivan's *Patience,* a farcical operatic satire at the expense of the melancholy aesthetes, opened in London with immense popular success.

Read as a joke on the aesthetic mentality as it was on the verge of overripening into decadence, "The Suicide Club" reveals elements of irony and casual scorn which we are not accustomed to in Stevenson. The one old character in the story, Mr. Malthus, calls the Club a "temple of intoxication" because it provides its members with the luxury of tasting forbidden sensations solely for the sake of savoring them. He explains to Colonel Geraldine that

> ". . . it requires all the sense of duty engendered by a long habit of ill-health and careful regimen, to keep me from excess in this, which is, I may say, my last dissipation. I have tried them all, sir . . . and . . . there is not one of them that has not been grossly and untruthfully overrated. People trifle with love. Now, I deny that love is a strong passion. Fear is the strong passion; it is with fear that you must trifle, if you wish to taste the intense joys of living." (I, 27-28)

Stevenson describes the general atmosphere and conversation of the society with deliberate simplicity and naive curiosity:

> There was little decency among the members of the club . . . There was a tacit understanding against moral judgments; and whoever passed the club doors enjoyed already some of the immunities of the tomb . . . They compared and developed their different views of death—
>
> "For my part," said [one], "I wish no more than a

bandage for my eyes and cotton for my ears. Only they have no cotton thick enough in this world."

. . . and [another] professed that he would never have joined the club, if he had not been induced to believe in Mr. Darwin.

"I could not bear," said this remarkable suicide, "to be descended from an ape."

Altogether, the Prince was disappointed by the bearing and conversation of the members.

"It does not seem to me," he thought, "a matter for so much disturbance. If a man has made up his mind to kill himself, let him do it, in God's name, like a gentleman. This flutter and big talk is out of place." (I, 25)

In the speech of Prince Florizel we hear the voice of Stevenson the essayist, the popular moralist, who is irritated by the whining of those whose lot in life does not seem half-bad from an invalid's couch. Stevenson was always ready to admit that his optimism was deliberate and forced, but this only convinced him all the more that the pessimism of his contemporaries was itself a conscious and carefully designed pose. "Can you conceive how irritated I am by the opposite affectation to my own," he asked William Archer in 1885, "when I see strong men and rich men bleating about their sorrows and the burthen of life, in a world full of 'cancerous paupers,' and poor sick children, and the fatally bereaved, ay, and even down to such happy creatures as myself?" (*Letters,* II, 292)

This final touch of self-pity betrays the limitation of Stevenson's resignation and the fragility of his optimism. Stevenson was a professed optimist who never got over the feeling that he had a *right* to be pessimistic. It is a frame of mind which makes dabbling, even satirically, with the morbid and unhealthy aspects of aestheticism somewhat dangerous because of the possibility that one may come to scoff and remain to indulge. And this is precisely what Stevenson repeatedly does in the *New Arabian Nights*. He begins with sophisticated detachment, smirking and mocking, playing an amusing game; then his satire begins to splinter and turn on itself, until everything becomes dreamlike and absurd, leaving no rational foothold, not even the previously clearheaded commentary of Prince Florizel; and, finally, satire and fantasy give way to melodrama, which has about it the same "feverish hilarity" Stevenson had attributed to the young members of the Suicide Club because it too is a thin surface covering over a tendency which is unwholesome and potentially self-destructive.

We cannot hope to understand the peculiar nature of Stevenson's satire (not to say his optimistic philosophy and his obsession for "clean, open-air adventure") unless we see that morbidity and effeteness were temptations he wanted scrupulously to avoid. He did avoid them, too, most of the time, in spite of the long hair and velvet jacket; but perhaps occasionally and only half-consciously he entered the "temple of intoxication." Stevenson's "long habit of ill-health and careful regimen," while making him prone to self-pity and morbid fantasies, kept him, like Mr. Malthus, from conscious excess in this form of "dissipation."

The pointed satire of "The Suicide Club" begins to disintegrate when Florizel provides funds and jobs for several of the most discouraged members, and dispatches Colonel Geraldine's younger brother to Paris to duel with the scoundrel who had been president and lived on the members' dues. The events of this second episode are seen through the eyes of the rich Silas Q. Scuddamore, "a young American of simple and harmless disposition," who divides his time between counting his money and peeping through a hole in his wall at his neighbor, a worldly *femme fatale* named Madame Zephyrine. Through an involved series of contrived episodes Silas remains the *voyeur,* gratifying himself with titillating glimpses of robust and mysterious older women, and delicate, pale young men: Madame's "admirable foot and ankle," spied briefly on the staircase; Geraldine's brother, "a very handsome young fellow" with long "blond locks," admired from a distance at the Carnival Ball.

When Silas is approached by "a lady cast in a very large mould and with somewhat stately features," he is at once "overwhelmed by [her] size and attractions," and makes a love-tryst with her that night at the Luxembourg Gardens. It is, of course, in keeping with Silas's role as observer rather than participator that the lady not appear. And it is with something halfway between reluctance and relief that he returns alone to his furnished room. What he finds waiting in bed for him there comes as little surprise to a reader with a good Freudian intuition. It is the handsome young fellow with the long blond locks. He is dead. In fact, he has been murdered, which again relieves Silas from having to do anything more than stand aside and gasp. It is at this moment of crisis that Stevenson rushes in with the slap-dash, helter-skelter melodrama of crating the body, shipping it to Florizel, and having him swear revenge on the president of the Suicide Club, who obviously was responsible for the death of Geraldine's ambiguous younger brother.

The reader, like Silas, has been prepared for a strange love scene, which he half suspects will never take place. (The large woman and the slight young man seem equally curious and, for different reasons, unthinkable companions for Silas.) But perhaps the preparations are too elaborate and the possibilities they suggest too intriguing to be taken as just another inconsequential device in an amusing story. The point of drawing attention to them at all is not to cast dark inferences on Stevenson, or even to prove that the tale is essentially unwholesome and prurient. It is simply to show that the satiric interest, which was clear and strong in the first forty pages, has begun to blur and give way to impulses, rarely so pronounced in Stevenson's other work, which eventually make sustained satire impossible. Apparently unable to preserve his comic detachment—unable, that is, to separate himself from the half-imaginary follies of his own characters—he retreats from satire into fantasy, and from there blunders noisily into the protective excesses of farce and melodrama.

3

The third and final section of "The Suicide Club" introduces as protagonist Lieutenant Brackenbury Rich, a minor military hero alone on leave in London, strolling the streets at night in search of adventure. Very soon he is invited into a hansom cab and mysteriously driven to a brilliantly lighted villa, whereupon the driver announces that there is a party inside for which he "was hired to kidnap single gentlemen in evening dress."

Upon entering the house we find very much the same atmosphere described earlier at the meeting of the Suicide Club, with the important difference that here is no gathering of despondent weaklings to be observed with detachment and despised for their elaborate affectations of self-pity. On the contrary, the hero of this episode eagerly enters the scene of overripe elegance, and if the absence of irony in the prose is an indication of acquiescence, Stevenson himself has yielded to the intoxication:

> A young man, slender and singularly handsome, came

> forward and greeted him with an air at once courtly and affectionate. Hundreds of candles, of the finest wax, lit up a room that was perfumed, like the staircase, with a profusion of rare and beautiful flowering shrubs. A side-table was loaded with tempting viands. Several servants went to and fro with fruits and goblets of champagne. The company was perhaps sixteen in number, all men, few beyond the prime of life, and with hardly an exception, of a dashing and capable exterior. (I, 80-81)

Brackenbury is intrigued but mystified by his host. Yet suspicious though he is, "and though he chid himself for the weakness he was unable to resist a sort of friendly attraction for Mr. Morris's person and character." It passes through Brackenbury's mind that he may be at the threshold of hell, and Morris the devil, luring souls into tasting pleasures that will corrupt them for eternity. Indeed, Stevenson does speak of Brackenbury's attraction to Morris as a "weakness," and it is partly the awareness of something dark and foreboding beneath the polished surface which gives the gathering as well as its host a decadent appeal. Brackenbury "followed Mr. Morris in all his movements; and although the man had a ready smile, he seemed to perceive, as it were under a mask, a haggard, careworn, and preoccupied spirit" (I, 82).

One by one, Morris ushers out most of the guests, explaining politely that the invitations they received must have been for another party because he does not know them. When all but a few have gone, Morris increases his elaborate attentions, going "from person to person with looks of the readiest sympathy and the most pertinent and pleasing talk; he was not so much like a host as like a hostess, and there was a feminine coquetry and condescension in his manner which charmed the hearts of all" (I, 85).

It is at this point of accumulated insinuation that the story must finally take a turn, choose a direction, and follow it through to some kind of conclusion, however disreputable and inconclusive that may be. If the choice were Oscar Wilde's, he might have prolonged the dubious pleasures of the party with witty dialogue and, for a finale, thrust his characters into hell with a moral epigram. Hawthorne would surely have singled out the allegorical possibilities, only hinted at by Stevenson, and permitted Morris to play out his diabolical role, eventually revealing the black and destructive force beneath the veneer. Poe, of course, would have chosen the way of nightmare, allowing the incipient absurdity of the situation and the eccentricities of the host to swell into utter depravity.

But Stevenson, in this story, looks not to wit, morality, or the grotesque. Instead, item by item, he carefully dismantles his well-wrought dream, and turns its suggestive distortions into the preposterous, but clearly perceived, details of melodrama. The dismantling process is not subtle. The reader, like Lieutenant Rich, passing through the entrance hall in search of fresh air, is

> brought to a dead halt by a discovery of the most surprising nature. The flowering shrubs had disappeared from the staircase; the servants were busy dismantling the house upon all sides; and some of them had already donned their great-coats and were preparing to depart . . . First, the guests, who were no real guests after all, had been dismissed; and now the servants, who could hardly be genuine servants, were actively dispersing.
>
> "Was the whole establishment a sham?" he asked himself. (I, 85)

Yes, Lieutenant Rich, the whole establishment was indeed a sham, and so, in a sense, is the story. Not that Stevenson creates greater illusions with his tales than most other artists. On the contrary, he insists upon presenting an illusion, often a very compelling one, and then turning to the reader and saying, "This is a fraud. Not one word of it is true." He is the magician who stops in the middle of his most convincing act to show his audience where the trap door is; or, what is more unthinkable, the priest who announces at the moment of consecration that he does not believe in transubstantiation. This characteristic, incidentally, is one of the marked differences between Stevenson and Edgar Allan Poe, to whom he is often compared as a writer of short stories. Poe, with some obvious exceptions, tends to work in the reverse way, beginning with absurd contraptions and melodramatic coincidences, but gradually distorting character and incident into permanent nightmare.

The distinction should also be made between what Stevenson does in these stories and what is a common pattern in those fairy tales in which the hero breaks a spell, wakes from a dream, or returns from a magic land to discover the mundane realities of life still with him. Stevenson refuses to leave even the trace of a possibility that dream, magic, or obscure powers of the will may have been at work in shaping the weird worlds into which his heroes wander. There is only one way to distort dull reality, and that is by faking. The president of the Suicide Club and the stately lady who missed her appointment at the Luxembourg Gardens are engaged in an intricate and deliberate hoax.

The house in the third episode is being dismantled because Mr. Morris is Colonel Geraldine, Florizel's companion, who has given the mysterious reception in a villa rented for the night in order to attract and observe adventurous gentlemen. Out of the company he intends to select two to serve as seconds in a duel between the Prince and the recalcitrant former president of the defunct Suicide Club. Once this discovery is made, the story grinds mechanically and predictably on, until the parties concerned can come together in a dark place where the duel may be fought, the former president slain, and the two supernumeraries thanked and dismissed. The superfluousness of Lieutenant Rich at the duel is further indication that the melodramatic conclusion is a contraption, a device to stop a dream with, rather than an integral and final part growing out of an organic whole.

"The Suicide Club" teaches us some interesting lessons about Stevenson as a satirist and as a writer of fiction. In the first place, we learn how strong his tendency was even this early to question his own faith in the inherent romance of things; but, what seems more serious, to doubt the artist's ability to endow an inert and unpoetic world with more than a flimsy semblance of mystery. In 1886 he dedicated a poem to his cousin Robert, lamenting the incapacity even of a rare imagination to reanimate the dead gods of poetry and love. One hears in the closing stanza not only an indictment of the era but a kind of sad apology for the fraudulent heroes and heroines of *New Arabian Nights:*

> That, that was not Apollo, not the god.
> This was not Venus, though she Venus seemed
> A moment. And though fair yon river move,
> She, all the way, from disenchanted fount
> To seas unhallowed runs; the gods forsook
> Long since her trembling rushes; from her plains
> Disconsolate, long since adventure fled;
> And now although the inviting river flows,
> And every poplared cape, and every bend
> Or willowy islet, win upon thy soul
> And to thy hopeful shallop whisper speed;

> Yet hope not thou at all; hope is no more;
> And O, long since the golden groves are dead
> The faery cities vanished from the land![2]

The second lesson "The Suicide Club" teaches us is that although, rationally, Stevenson disapproved of the sensuous indulgence, the affectation, the tendency to amorality and self-pity associated with the aesthetes, temperamentally he was in closer sympathy with them than is usually recognized. As a young man he often embarrassed his more conventional friends with his intentionally odd mannerisms and bizarre dress. There is a story told of his meeting Andrew Lang one day on Bond Street. Stevenson was wearing a black shirt, red tie, black brigand coat, and velvet smoking cap. "No, no; go away, Louis, go away!" cried Lang. "My character will stand a great deal, but it won't stand being seen talking to a 'thing' like you in Bond Street!"[3] His intermittently Bohemian habits as a young law student may not mean very much by themselves, but his attitude toward art as a craft sufficient to itself does coincide in several important respects with the familiar theories of Pater and Wilde.

As for prolonged expressions of self-pity, his letters are full enough of those, including self-consciously "artful" references to contemplation of his own death, not unlike those he ridicules in the members of the Suicide Club. In 1873, at the age of twenty-three, he wrote: "I am a man of seventy: O Medea, kill me, or make me young again!" In 1875 he courts death like an eager youngster panting after the ultimate adventure:

> Only to go out forever by sunny day and grey day, by bright night and foul, by high-way and by-way, town and hamlet, until somewhere by a roadside or in some clean inn clean death opened his arms to me and took me to his quiet heart forever. (*Letters,* I, 102, 230)

It must be remembered that, regardless of what can be detected in his correspondence, Stevenson rarely wanted his private anguish to become the undisguised material of his art. Insofar as it is justifiable to regard the ways in which he seems most to resemble the aesthetes—the literary preciousness, the cavalier pose, the morbid self-involvement and concern with death—as compatible with, if not attributable to, the psychology of an invalid, we can begin to understand his attitude toward them, not only as temptations and weaknesses, but as infirmities which he was trying to overcome. Even at the period in his life when he seemed most the ailing and sensitive dilettante, there was something in Stevenson which despised that tendency in himself and struggled to be rid of it. William Archer once called Stevenson an "athletico-aesthete," which implied that he somehow united the muscular Christianity of Charles Kingsley with the blue-china delicacy of Oscar Wilde. But a hyphenated label cannot convey what an unsatisfactory, even torturous, combination that was. As satire, "The Suicide Club" is uneven and incomplete, but it is peculiarly instructive as a reflection of an artist's mind in turmoil.

4

The more we read in *New Arabian Nights* and in *The Dynamiter* a similar set of connected tales, published in collaboration with his wife in 1885,[4] the more convinced we become that Stevenson's experiments in satire almost invariably break down because, although he may try to maintain comic distance from the intended object of ridicule, sooner or later he begins talking about himself. He ridicules his personal weaknesses, his profession, and his attachment to adventure, almost to the point of self-flagellation; he recites a public and, at times, nearly hysterical *mea culpa* obscured by rhetorical artifice and outrageous narrative coincidence.

Partly because of the age into which he had been born, partly because of his middle-class Scotch Calvinist upbringing, and partly because of serious doubts about his own talents, Stevenson took a lifetime to get over the feeling that art is essentially ornamental and frivolous, a trick played on the public, its practitioners shams, and he the biggest fraud of them all. As late as 1888 he wrote an essay "To a Young Gentleman Who Proposes to Embrace the Career of Art," in which he observes only half-jokingly that, in some ways, an artist is a kind of prostitute because he chooses "his trade to please himself, gains his livelihood by pleasing others, and has parted with some of the sterner dignity of man" (XV, 285).

This statement cannot be shrugged off entirely as a playful attempt to discourage an overly eager, aspiring young artist, even though on the surface that is what it is. There seems never to have been any doubt for Stevenson, or for the other insistently virile writers of the period, that the active life carries with it elements of truth and beauty which the imagination can counterfeit but not excel. He describes himself in 1886 to an American reviewer as "being a person who prefers life to art, and who knows it is a far finer thing to be in love, or to risk a danger, than to paint the finest picture or write the noblest book" (*Letters,* II, 336). Not only does he speak of art as a trade, but as one which a large and gifted man, after the model of Fielding, Scott, or Montaigne, ought to be able to combine with some more utilitarian occupation.

> Why the artist can *do nothing else?* is [a problem] that continually exercises myself . . . *David Balfour* is a nice little book, and very artistic and just the thing to occupy

> the leisure of a busy man; but for the top flower of a man's life it seems to me inadequate. Small is the word; it is a small age, and I am of it. I could have wished to be otherwise busy in this world. I ought to have been able to build lighthouses and write *David Balfour* too. (*Letters,* IV, 284)

One reason *New Arabian Nights* and *The Dynamiter* are not quite successful as satire or fantasy is that they were written with a sense of their own smallness. Stevenson continually reveals his lack of confidence in his art's ability to sustain ironic detachment or suspend disbelief. Repeatedly he admits midway through a tale, as he does during the dismantling of Mr. Morris's villa, that the foundation of the plot and the source of the reader's interest have been nothing but artificial contrivances.

Most of the adventures which the characters relate to one another in *The Dynamiter* are eventually explained away as deceptions. The laughing lady, who recounts a macabre and almost surrealistic tale of life among Mormon pioneers in the American West, is forced to admit finally that the whole narrative was pure fabrication from beginning to end. The heroine-narrator of "The Story of the Fair Cuban" tells a tale which includes an account of a "Hoodoo" ritual, involving nude celebrants and writhing serpents, which, with a kind of adolescent sensationalism, is more openly erotic and orgiastic than anything Stevenson ever wrote. But the speaker turns out to be Clara Luxmore, the same feminine deceiver of the Mormon hoax, who has this time painted herself brown and posed as a mulatto, until once again she must face a moment of truth:

> And raising the veil, she showed him a countenance from which every trace of colour had fled, eyes marred with weeping . . . "Harry," she began, "I am not what

> I seem . . . I was never nearer Cuba than Penzance. From first to last I have cheated and played with you."
> (III, 242)

Even granting the convention he is parodying, we get the uncomfortable sense that Stevenson is almost compulsive about forcing his various narrators in these tales to plead guilty to telling lies. In a way he seems to feel the guilt is his as well as theirs. Not only did most of the adventures not happen, but those who told them are posers and triflers. By repeating this pattern of deception followed by remorse, he implicitly casts aspersions on the validity of certain kinds of narrative art, especially adventure fiction, and on the integrity of artists like himself who write it.

It has been suggested that Stevenson identifies with Prince Florizel, the arch-manipulator and solver of every character's problems.[5] If that is true, so much the worse for Stevenson. Florizel is a sham like all the rest. In fact, he is a double sham. We have already been told that he possessed a "singular facility in disguise," and are not surprised halfway through *New Arabian Nights* to find him, after a "revolution in Bohemia," reduced to running a cigar store under the alias of Thomas Godall (whose omnipotence extends no further than his last name). In a book so full of deception there is no reason not to believe that Prince Florizel has all along been Thomas Godall, cigar salesman, posing as a prince who enjoys wearing false whiskers and adhesive eyebrows.

But if Stevenson has populated his tales with caricatures of himself, we can find better likenesses than Florizel. Throughout *New Arabian Nights* and *The Dynamiter,* which consists of three fairly distinct adventures, Stevenson introduces protagonists after the pattern of Silas Q.

Scuddamore. They are exaggerated imitations of the young R.L.S.—physically weak, hypersensitive, impractical, mildly effeminate *observers* of life who are inclined toward the arts, but become ridiculous the moment they attempt to take an active part in an adventure. In the first section of "The Rajah's Diamond" we are presented with Harry Hartley, the private secretary and fashion consultant of Lady Vandeleur:

> For all active and industrious pursuits, Harry was unfitted alike by nature and training. He could sing romantic ditties, and accompany himself with discretion on the piano; he was a graceful though a timid cavalier . . . He had an air of agreeable tenderness and melancholy, and the most submissive and caressing manners. (I, 105)

After a series of episodes during which the priceless diamond passes from hand to hand, we meet another in the long line of incompetent heroes. Francis Scrymgeour is a twenty-five-year-old clerk in the Bank of Scotland "of a docile and affectionate disposition," whose major pastime in the evenings is to "play upon the flute to amuse his father." Francis is lured by a mysterious note to Paris, where he spends most of his time—like his prototype, Silas Q. Scuddamore—observing the private lives of his neighbors. Instead of a hole in his wall, he looks through "the window of his new apartment [which] commanded a complete view into the garden of the house with the green blinds." Francis not only observes his neighbors at home, but since they are implicated in the note which brought him to Paris in the first place, he follows them everywhere, attempting to overhear bits of their conversation. He is fated, however, to experience the frustration which is something like a trademark of the Stevensonian hero—"not able to interfere, not able even to follow the debate, but condemned to sit and suffer where he was, in impotent anxiety."

When unable to restrain himself any longer, Francis, "casting open the shutters . . . closed his eyes and threw himself with outstretched arms into the foliage of the chestnut," and from there onto the terrace of his neighbor. As soon as the weakling hero insists upon being more than an onlooker, is dissatisfied with catching an unclear glimpse here and overhearing a fragment of conversation there, and blunders into the midst of the mystery, demanding to know all, he discovers, and so does the reader, that everything has a moderately rational explanation. The whole adventure is a kind of misunderstanding, a hoax perpetrated on the hero partially by others, but essentially by the dimness of his own powers of perception. Like David Balfour stranded on the Isle of Earraid, the incompetent hero sustains the illusion of adventure by means of his own temporary blindness, and destroys it at the instant of intelligent contact.

The three protagonists of *The Dynamiter* are so much like the Scuddamore-Hartley-Scrymgeour brand of fool that it is unnecessary to examine their characters in detail. The personalities of these mock-heroes, most of whom are dabblers in one of the arts, each with a large imagination and "small capacity for action," not only present a self-caricature of certain aspects of Stevenson's temperament, but in their characteristic attitudes as spectators in the lives and adventures of other people, crystallize his anxieties about himself as an artist. "I am supposed to be an *esprit observateur!*" he wrote to his mother in 1874 with a tone of brittle mockery. "À mon age, c'est étonnant comme je suis observateur!" (*Letters,* I, 129) And a few months later, in a letter to Colvin, he describes himself without false modesty, "as a person with a poetic character and no poetic talent." An artist dissatisfied with his role as observer and troubled with genuine doubts about his gifts does not usually make the best satirist, especially if he is so self-conscious as to keep involving himself in his own ridicule.

In the rare instances when Stevenson is able to project his derision on an object other than a thinly veiled version of himself, his satire becomes firm, consistent, and often extraordinarily effective. The one episode in *The Dynamiter* which is thought to be totally of his own invention is a twelve-page narrative called "Zero's Tale of the Explosive Bomb," an extremely amusing burlesque of political violence and anarchy. The almost frighteningly absurd atmosphere of grotesque comedy, incompetent anarchists racing around London, and a fanatical professor inventing bombs he calls his "infernal machines," anticipates Conrad's satiric masterpiece on a similar theme, *The Secret Agent.*

Stevenson, like Conrad, was opposed to sudden or violent social change; he put into the mouths of his rebellious characters the kind of rhythmic and insane rambling we find twenty-two years later in the passionate and obscure dialogues of Conrad's conspirators. The object of the dynamiters' first stroke against civilization, even more absurd than the observatory selected by Conrad's anarchists, is the statue of Shakespeare in Leicester Square. It is, according to Zero, the chief subversive,

> a spot . . . admirably chosen; not only for the sake of the dramatist, still very foolishly claimed as a glory by the English race, in spite of his disgusting political opinions; but from the fact that the seats in the immediate neighborhood are often thronged by children, errand-boys, unfortunate young ladies of the poorer class and infirm old men—all classes making a direct appeal to public

a frivolous disguise for boredom or timidity, rather than as a meaningful allegory of the human condition. He seems glad also to comfort himself and his reader that all is well and sane, after all, and that the world is not really full of effete decadents, maniacal Hoodoos, and Mormon spies. The threat vanishes along with the lure; and if there are men and women with tendencies toward suicide, seduction, murder, thievery, madness, and anarchy, most of them are silly, ineffectual people who have to tell lies and wear false whiskers in order to bolster up their own absurd image of themselves. Within the limits of the story, the alternative which Stevenson offers to the fantasy world of degenerate gentlemen, sensual Cubans, and mad bombers is an equally unlikely one of impossibly silly prigs, meddling old ladies, and chronic practical-jokers. The shift from deception to revelation takes us no closer to reality than we had been from the beginning. The delusion is different, but no less artificial.

The ambiguous attitude toward adventure shows the kind of confusion between the artist and his material which often precedes development and clarification, if not profound change. Stevenson was to be a good many years trying to settle for himself whether adventure was essentially a state of mind, a daydream like the story of Treasure Island, in which excitement and danger are generated by means of a cerebral machine which eliminates vast areas of concrete reality; or whether it was a physical and spiritual actuality, a possible way of living close enough to nature to have to respond to its moods (the way a sailor must, for example, or a foot-soldier, or an explorer) and thereby to encounter essential truths about the self which may be obscured by the evasions of polite society. Stevenson was enough of a Romantic to recognize that all forms of experience involve an interplay between the mind and external reality, so that every human version of truth is a half-perceived and half-created blending of ego and object. But it is one thing to understand a theory, and another to find in one's self the proper equipoise between absorption and invention necessary to the successful practice of an art.

5

Stevenson's own physical attempts at open-air adventure previous to the serialization of *Latter-Day Arabian Nights* in 1878 and through the publication of *The Dynamiter* in 1885 were fairly disillusioning to him. His *idea* of adventure was of a way of life cleaner, simpler, purer, freer, than the routine existence within the stifling confines of Victorian society. He begins his account of *An Inland Voyage* (published in 1878 about a trip taken in 1876) hopefully describing the experience of setting out in a canoe under sail as "a venture into the regions of the unknown." But after a few damp, uncomfortable, and relatively uneventful weeks of rain, bad food, and inhospitable French innkeepers, he concludes his journal with a brave moral, which does little to conceal the fact that he had had an unpleasant, and, what is more significant, an unexciting trip:

> You may paddle all day long; but it is when you come back at nightfall, and look in at the familiar room, that you find Love or Death awaiting you beside the stove; and the most beautiful adventures are not those we go to seek. (XII, 135)

The concluding sentiment of *An Inland Voyage* notwithstanding, Stevenson's taste for rugged travel in unlikely places was not entirely dulled. Two years later he was ready to set out again, this time alone with a donkey on a walking trip through the Cevennes. Once again he begins optimistically, seeking to clear away the cobwebs of Victorian Britain and to face life head-on:

> The great affair is to move; to feel the needs and hitches of our life more nearly; to come down off this featherbed of civilization, and to find the globe granite under foot and strewn with cutting flints. (XII, 186)

Although he fares somewhat better on this trip than on the previous one, if the irritations were slight, so apparently were the pleasures. After beginning a hardy travel journal full of weather reports and detailed descriptions of the local terrain, apparently bored with the blandness of his adventure, he turns to a discussion of the history of the Protestant-Catholic conflicts in the part of France through which he is walking. Like so many of his works, the piece breaks in two. It begins as a travel diary and concludes as a historical commentary.

The big adventure of Stevenson's early life was his first trip to America by steamer in August of 1879, and across the continent by train to California to claim his American bride. His comment on emigration as a shipboard experience, in contrast with his imaginative anticipation of it, repeats the pattern of his previous "real life" adventures: "There is nothing more agreeable to picture and nothing more pathetic to behold. The abstract idea as conceived at home, is hopeful and adventurous . . . [but] the more I saw of my fellow passengers, the less I was tempted to the lyric note."

But once on land it seemed Stevenson at last would have his opportunity to escape the confines of European civilization and to luxuriate in the unsettled expanses of the American West:

> For many years America was to me a sort of promised

> land . . . It seems . . . as if, out west, the war of life was still conducted in the open air, and on free barbaric terms; as if it had not yet been narrowed into parlours, nor begun to be conducted, like some unjust and dreary arbitration, by compromise, costume, forms of procedure, and sad, senseless self-denial. (XV, 86-87)

But once again his optimism, partly because it expects so much, is disappointed. In *The Amateur Emigrant* it had not been the Atlantic Ocean, but the hot, crowded steamer and its pathetic passengers that had engaged him. Once in the American West, it was not the vast plains and ranges of rugged mountains, but "that long, narrow wooden box, like a flat-roofed Noah's ark, with a stove and a convenience, one at either end, a passage down the middle, and transverse benches upon either hand," that occupied his imagination. What Stevenson does experience of life at sea or of rough living in the wide-open spaces is through a porthole or a train window, intrigued but a little frightened by what he sees, like the comic-pathetic heroes of his satires, or simply too sick and weak to care very much what is passing by.

The idea of physical hardship and spaciousness of terrain appeals to Stevenson, but the actuality is more than he is constitutionally or emotionally able to endure. When he is not made physically ill by the discomforts of nineteenth-century travel, his mind recoils from the strangeness, novelty, and immense territorial range of the New World. He gives us upon landing in New York City, for example, not the size and confusion of a great port, but narrow rainy sidestreets, a detailed description of the cozy room in his hotel, and a welcome meeting with two Scots lads who, like himself, had recently arrived from abroad. When he is confronted with the vast sweep of the Wyoming desert, his imagination is oppressed, and turns back again and again to the mean but familiar comforts of the railroad.

Stevenson's travels seem to involve the constant defeat of hope by experience. In fact, during his American journey he wrote that "sight-seeing is the art of disappointment," and proceeded to compose a jingle on the subject:

> There's nothing under the heaven so blue,
> That's fairly worth the travelling to. (XV, 329)

To complete his long series of disappointments, minor catastrophes, and endless days of tedium, when he reached Monterey he suffered a total physical collapse which brought him closer to death than he had ever been before.

It perhaps appears surprising after so much misadventure that upon his return to England Stevenson would continue to write adventure fiction at all, even in the form of a boy's daydream of buried treasure or a sequel to *New Arabian Nights*. But it is one of the most persistent characteristics of his mentality, particularly in the years preceding his departure for Samoa, to deny disillusioning experience access to his creative imagination. Unlike Dr. Johnson, who regarded the discomforts of travel as a good antidote for the excesses of the imagination, Stevenson preferred to sustain his illusions without admitting too many dampening interruptions from the world of concrete experience. While Johnson does not often include specific references to private disappointments in his work, it is usually with a keen philosophical sense of *all* personal experience, even of the most painful nature, that he composes his moral and critical essays.

Stevenson, on the contrary, in the early fiction as well as the early essays, tends to ignore, simplify, or sentimentalize all evidence of human anguish. If he has returned from a disastrous and abortive journey or recovered from a nearly fatal illness, it may show in his letters and journals, but he will go to any length to exclude it from his fiction. "You are very right about my voluntary aversion from the painful sides of life," he wrote William Archer in 1885. "My childhood in reality was a very mixed experience, full of fever, nightmare, insomnia, painful days and interminable nights . . . But to what end should we renew these sorrows?" Eight months later he wrote in a letter to the same correspondent: "I would as soon drag my [sickness] under the eyes of my readers as I would mention a pimple I might chance to have on my posteriors. What does it prove? What does it change?" (*Letters,* II, 280, 302)

In this century of James Joyce, D. H. Lawrence, and Henry Miller (which is to say in this post-Freudian age), Stevenson's analogy may seem naive and his question hardly rhetorical. What he refers to as "these unimportant privacies," by which he implies a good deal more than physical disease, are generally acknowledged in the twentieth century to prove and change much. Stevenson was by no means alone in regarding the particulars of disease and sexual desire as unfit subjects for fiction. Whatever the attitude may reveal of his own character, it also reflects a fairly common antirealist position of the period. Sexuality and serious illness, while not necessarily to be despised, were conditions to be quietly endured. Even if no longer considered direct consequences of sin, both remained morally disconcerting. They did not enhance man's ideal of himself. Hence, one's strength of character increased in proportion to his ability to deal with them without seeming to. Andrew Lang makes a typical association of "unhealthy" subject matter in a fictitious letter to Alexander Dumas:

To you, who can amuse the world—to you who offer

it the fresh air of the highway, the battlefield, and the sea—the world must always return: escaping gladly from the boudoirs and the *bouges,* from the surgeries and hospitals, and dead rooms, of M. Daudet and M. Zola and of the wearisome De Goncourt.[6]

What Stevenson took a long time to understand is that it is possible for an artist to admit the importance of the privacies of the body, mind, and soul, and give up trying to fence them out of the realm of the creative imagination, without necessarily dealing with them autobiographically in his fiction. For all his enlightened rejection of the perverse moral effects of Puritan repression, his attitude as an artist toward human suffering and human desire is not unlike that of an old-school Scotch Calvinist toward sin. But try as he may, no artist can successfully seal off in one compartment of his being all the tiresome, humiliating, disappointing, and painful aspects of experience, and call that portion of himself "creative" which pretends not to know they exist.

The point is not that we may dredge up unpleasant details of Stevenson's private life in order to prove that they figure in his fiction after all, but rather to show that what he was trying to do was impossible once he left the fictional realm of pure boyish fancy. "Unimportant privacies" in the form of morbid obsessions, erotic fantasies, thinly veiled expressions of self-pity, misgivings about art and artists, uncertainty about the nature and value of adventure, crop up unexpectedly and baldly in *New Arabian Nights* and *The Dynamiter* as they do in no other of his works; because at no other time in his career was he so rigorously trying to keep his "posteriors," the private and "painful sides of life," out of sight, where they seemed to him to belong. In none of his fiction, save the strictly juvenile pieces, does Stevenson seem so bent upon being frivolous, aimless, gay, and irreverent as in these two collections of tales. Yet in few of his works before *The Master of Ballantrae* (including *Dr. Jekyll and Mr. Hyde* and *Markheim*) does he inadvertently reveal so much darkness of spirit. It casts forth its shadow abruptly, inconsequentially, artlessly. Because he has so vehemently and consciously denied to his art whole areas of psychic experience, they emerge all the more arbitrarily and uncontrollably, unrefined, almost undistorted, by the imagination.

As the satire or fantasy verges closer and closer on the forbidden and the painful, Stevenson dives onto stage center in his own "public" person, makes a few bad jokes, offers a hurried explanation for the plot's sake, and abruptly closes the curtain. As long as he treats adventure indirectly and evasively, through the imperfect memory of a small boy or through the amused detachment of a comic-opera prince, it has qualities of vitality, suggestiveness, and coherence which it immediately loses when R.L.S., Scotsman, amateur historian, professional artist, and invalid, breaks in and decides that he wants to play.

In the satirical episodes it is as though Swift, in the middle of Book IV, suddenly had Gulliver romping with the Yahoos and discovering that they were not such ugly things after all; or Pope were to begin writing love lyrics to Lady Mary Wortley Montagu and serious panegyric to Colley Cibber. The satire would be demolished, leaving behind it, as in "The Suicide Club," a fantastic indulgence in the very follies which were being ridiculed.

But if Stevenson spoils satire by moving into it in his own person (or a thinly disguised version thereof), he spoils his adventurous fantasy in much the same way. Like his own incorrigible heroes who invariably leave their posts of observation, leaping into the midst of other people's back terraces, he leaves his detached vantage point as artist-dreamer and, in an apparent attempt to uncover the secret source of the intrigue, succeeds instead in revealing that the tale had been held together by patches and wire. In the end the reader is left without satire and without illusion. But the question that lingers in his mind is whether the impertinent (and unconvincing) dénouement stems as much from lack of invention as it does from lack of nerve. The bauble which Stevenson had asserted would "not stir up sleeping lions" has come precariously close to doing just that.

It is easy to say that Stevenson was temperamentally a child, wanting to play adventurous games with his own characters, but it is important to add that whenever he changes his point of view from detached spectator to involved participant—feeling sorry for the characters, looking into their bankbooks, charting their gains and losses as he would his own—he displays not only the boyish impulse to jump into the midst of things, but also the adult tendency to rationalize play in terms outside itself. He enters the game as much to *explain* it as to enjoy it. If his explanations often seem maddeningly irrelevant and mechanical, it may be that, contrary to the prevailing critical opinion, he did not at this point in his career see the vital relationship between playing a game and living a life. Make-believe was a form of cheating which he was a little ashamed of loving. Unlike Ben Jonson, Laurence Sterne, or Lewis Carroll, he did not quite believe that play could be a way of approaching the truth. The harder he tries to believe it, the more clearly his skepticism is revealed.

When he was only twenty-two years old, Stevenson wrote his mother from Frankfurt:

> An opera is far more *real* than real life to me. It seems as if stage illusion, and particularly this hardest to swallow and most conventional illusion of them all—an opera—would never stale upon me. I wish that life was an opera. I should like to *live* in one. (*Letters,* I, 51-52)

This self-defeating wish to exist in "conventional illusion," when to do so would eliminate the distance which produces the enchantment, characterizes the mood of Stevenson's comic-satiric tales better than anything that might be quoted from them.

As part of a narrative pattern the extravagance of light opera ought to be funny; and undoubtedly Stevenson hoped it would be taken that way. But, instead, his satiric tales are reminders of the folly of turning "impotent anxiety" into disappointed hope; they are, in a sense, demonstrations of disenchantment and unfulfilled desire. And these are not subjects, however decoratively tricked out, to provoke so comfortable or so simple a response as unmixed amusement or derision. The curious combination of charm and downright awkwardness in *New Arabian Nights* and *The Dynamiter* resembles that of adolescence. The childish young men spend all their time watching grown-ups play their adult games, and yearning to join them. When at last they do, they find so much of the mystery diminished by proximity that they look around in bewilderment for the enchantment they thought to enter, and begin wondering, like Stevenson, whether they had left it behind in their youth.

✲ ✲ ✲ ✲ ✲ ✲ ✲

I should like to rise and go
Where the golden apples grow;—
Where below another sky
Parrot islands anchored lie.

—Travel

✲ ✲ ✲ ✲ ✲ ✲ ✲

IV

ADVENTURE AS FABLE OF FARAWAY PLACES

* * * * * * *

Stevenson found it necessary in his early career to reject the readymade forms provided for him by his parents, the state, and the Scottish Church by creating a child's vision into which their morality would not penetrate. He gradually awoke from that evasive dream and took the necessary risk of looking at more of himself and the world around him than either a child or an invalid is ordinarily capable of doing. His works of fiction set in exotic places reflect an attempt to stay alive (by moving to a tropical climate) with an effort to find out what cultures not yet fixed into Victorian molds could tell him about himself and the nature of man generally. They might properly be regarded as adventures with undetermined destinations, fables in search of a moral.

Ten years after the serialization of *Latter-Day Arabian Nights,* Stevenson, at the peak of his popular success, embarked with his American wife, his stepson, his fifty-nine-year-old mother, and the family servant, upon a voyage to the South Pacific aboard the schooner *S.S. Casco.* The date was the twenty-eighth of June 1888. On this first cruise, the ship sailed to Nuka-hiva, navigated the coral atolls of the Paumotus, anchored for several weeks offshore at Tahiti, and reached Oahu, the capital island of the Hawaiian chain, by Christmas. After two more years of voyages in the Pacific, which took them to the Gilbert, Samoan, and Marshall Islands, as well as to Australia, the

Stevensons decided to remain indefinitely in the South Seas. They bought property in Samoa, constructed a large frame house in a clearing on a hill, and stayed there until Stevenson's sudden death in 1894.

Stevenson's South Sea journey took him closer than he had ever dreamed to the undomesticated heart of human anguish and to an idea of evil he had labored for a long time to disavow. It is a rarely paid tribute to his integrity that, at a time in his life when it must have been extraordinarily difficult, he acknowledged a philosophical burden he had for years been trying to set down and deny.

Often in discussing a writer whose temperament and personal history seem almost too conveniently to complement his work there is a tendency to pay either too much or too little attention to the relationship between biographical "externals" and the interior development of the creative mind. In Stevenson's case, a partial improvement in physical well-being and a radical change in geographical surroundings have been variously blamed for a decline in his creative powers, acclaimed as the source of a new artistic maturity, or disregarded altogether as having had no effect whatever on his imaginative development after 1888. If the letters of the period can be regarded as a reliable indication, there is little doubt that the South Sea years were in some ways among the happiest in Stevenson's life; and there is no doubt at all that in a relative sense they were physically his hardiest and most active.

Without attempting the impossible task of establishing a direct causal relationship between his life and his work, one must begin by admitting that for a writer like Stevenson, devoted from early childhood to the fiction of faraway places, to have set out on a long and hazardous expedition of his own could have been a matter of profound consequence to his inner as well as his outer life. Because of a childhood and youth of hushed sickrooms, monotonous routine, raw, damp Edinburgh streets, somber Sabbaths, and endless hours in the kirk, he developed the fixed idea that to live was to be out of all these things—out of the sickbed, out of church, out of the city, out of Scotland. Strength, health, physical vigor, fresh gusts of wind over tropical seas, became not only metaphorical terms for moral well-being, but literal requisites for a kind of wholeness in which the spirit, the mind, *and* the body are in perfect equipoise.

Artists in every age, like most human beings with an imagination, have spent a good part of their conscious lives wishing they were somewhere else. But this persistent desire, insofar as it is essentially poetic—that is, serious and permanent rather than occasional and curable—is normally associated with a transcendental state which may be reached through and by the world, but not in it. The Christian poet longs for heaven, the Platonist for ideal beauty, and the Romantic genius, in the words of Coleridge, is body "striving to become mind." A great many Victorians, R.L.S. among them, with a weakened faith in heaven, philosophy, and the supreme powers of the imagination, began taking the signs of their "divine unrest" in the only way left to them—literally and concretely—looking for a haven in the world, not like the Greeks because they were so much at home here, but because they were not at home anywhere else.

Three characteristics of the literature of the Victorian search for an earthly Utopia (variously known by actual place names like Mandalay, Zanzibar, Tahiti, Timbuktu) distinguish it from previous literary concepts of exploration. In the first place, though the British Empire may play an important historical role, national interests are not usually of *primary* dramatic concern. The novelist may be openly and honestly patriotic, like Captain Marryat or Charles Kingsley; or he may be indifferent, and even skeptical, like Stevenson. But in either case, the state of the nation is not altered in the course of the narrative. The British Empire is a "given," which various authors may choose to praise or blame as they tell their story. But they do not undertake to explain it in terms of their characters' actions. One does not normally get from reading a nineteenth-century English adventure novel an Old Testament, Homeric, or Virgilian sense of nationhood as the sum of the temperaments, hopes, and sufferings of a whole people. Great Britain is never an effect, always a cause. It is not a living organism which can be explained in terms of its parts. It is a fact and a principle, like gravity, which has considerable influence within the natural order, without, under the usual conditions, being itself subject to alteration.

For those like Stevenson who were not convinced that the Empire had been ordained by God, the political and military quest for a "perfect" state on earth was, like all other adventures after an ideal, a contradiction in terms. Even Kipling and Haggard, certainly more sympathetic to the claims of Empire than Stevenson, occasionally recognized that there was irony in employing ethical and ideal terms to describe an enterprise which was essentially economic and political. Yet Stevenson, while aware of the shortcomings of the Empire, was not vigorously opposed to colonization. With a mixture of bitterness and sympathetic resignation he saw imperialism's hyperbolic justification of itself, as repeating on a massive political scale what was necessary on a personal level: to describe the confused, not always generous, occasionally desperate, response to human unrest in heroic, even supernatural, terms. The moral failure of the Empire to live up to the ideals it set for itself was, in Stevenson's eyes, no more or less reprehensible than the same inevitable shortcoming in individuals.

A second general characteristic of the Victorian fictional quest for faraway places is that, unlike great epic literature, it tends not to identify its heroes with a significant tribal or national cause. Amyas Leigh, the hero of Charles Kingsley's *Westward Ho!,* is said to epitomize the adventurous spirit of Elizabethan England.[1] It is true that his escapades borrow prestige and authenticity from association with Sir Francis Drake and encounters with the Spanish Armada, but they do not explain history in mythic or symbolic terms. Leigh participates in the heroic English past; he does not embody or shape it. Rudyard Kipling's protagonists are natives and roustabouts almost as often as they are reputable Englishmen; and although Rider Haggard's heroes are usually proper Anglo-Saxons, they are not conquerors, founders, or breeders so much as cultivated men on holiday. They enjoy the bizarre contrast of seeing themselves in a strange world, but find one of their greatest pleasures in the contemplation of returning home.

The confrontation in the heart of Africa between Leo Vincey, lately of Cambridge, and She, exotic queen of a subterranean kingdom, is a masterpiece in the personification of British national pride, without a trace of epic vitality:

> It was a pretty sight to see her veiled form gliding toward the sturdy young Englishman, dressed in his grey flannel suit; for . . . Leo is one of the most English-looking men I ever saw. He is very tall and broad-chested

> . . . and his head is set upon him in such a fashion as to give him a proud and vigorous air, which was well described by his . . . name of "Lion."[2]

If Leo Vincey is the "conquering lion," he has been copied too faithfully from a coat of arms, and not from the king of beasts. In this scene he is all but inanimate. For long stretches of time he quite literally does not move. The reader hardly objects to hearing that Leo's "head is set upon him" in such and such a fashion because we have long since grown accustomed to thinking of him as a monument. In this type of non-epic adventure, the hero may be very English, may even be a kind of emblem, but his feat is one of confrontation and observation rather than of possession, absorption, or assimilation. The anxiety reflected here and in so much Victorian adventure is that if the type of young English manhood sets out on an epic mission of love or war, he is likely to lose some of his tribal purity in the climactic encounter. In fictional terms, to an even greater degree than what seems to have been the historical case, one sort of English adventurer can never achieve heroic stature because he travels in a moral enclosure which gives him a brief look at the mysterious enemy or strange lover but prevents a consequential exchange of any kind.

Stevenson does create an occasional character of this kind (most notably Attwater in *The Ebb Tide*), but more often his protagonists in the exotic tales have little more association with the motherland than a mild feeling of nostalgia. He did not choose to link the destinies of the heroes of his South Sea stories with that of the state. Three of them are not even British (Loudon Dodd is an American, and Keawe and Keola are both Hawaiians); and the two who are British—Wiltshire and Herrick—

are disreputable and godless renegades, totally cut off from any formal contact with the Crown.

The common choice in creating a hero, within the convention of nineteenth-century adventure fiction, was either to build an immobile effigy of empire or to invent a slightly tarnished creature who moves along the edges of the established order. Stevenson often took the latter course. It is a choice between personification and a form of characterization almost as formalized as that which it is trying to avoid. But if the tension is not between simple allegory and complex realism, it is between degrees of conventionality, and therefore reveals a healthy protest against rigidity. In the early and middle years, Stevenson, like Marryat, Kingsley, and Haggard, often alternates in one book between presenting the same character as an emblem and as an individual, which never quite get together. (Alan Breck in *Kidnapped* is probably the best example.) More and more often after 1888, he strove to fuse the abstract and the concrete, the general and specific. And as he did so, he began to unify and transcend the divided convention in which he wrote.

The third and perhaps most significant characteristic of the Victorian quest for paradise is that it shifts uneasily and awkwardly back and forth between the ideal and the real. If we take a symbol to be that which both signifies *and* participates in a truth, simultaneously meaning and being, then Victorian adventure rarely can be called symbolic. There is a thin line between believing in an ideal which can never be attained, rationally, imaginatively, spiritually, or in any other way, and not believing in an ideal at all. Stevenson, like a good many of his contemporaries, wavered back and forth on that line, preaching with momentary sincerity that the "best adventures are not those we go to seek" and that fortune "is not to be found in foreign lands, but in the heart itself," while he had his eye on some very real islands not only for reasons of physical health, but as a possible cure for the less tangible "sickness of maturity."

When Keats writes of having traveled much in "the realms of gold," he is speaking in metaphorical terms of an imaginative flight inspired by the actual experience of reading books. Stevenson proceeds in quite another way, beginning with unreal fantasies of distant travel which he then goes on to try to enact, to participate in physically. In attempting to "make his dreams come true," he succeeds only in convincing himself and his readers, in the literal terms he insists upon using, that they must be false. We have seen the pattern already in the boys' adventures and in the comic satires. The important question is whether the final disillusionment, accompanied by the mixed blessing of his healthy but isolated life in the South Seas, maims the entertaining and fanciful child or whether it gives birth to a mature artist with a new breadth of vision.

There is little doubt that for many years Stevenson worked within the tradition of popular Victorian adventure fiction. In his alternation between the emblematic and the unique, in his attitude toward the hero and the nation, he was not at first an innovator. *Treasure Island* is the perfection of a convention. But there were hints, even in the beginning, that profound changes were in the offing.

2

Stevenson's first story *about* far-off adventure was not, strictly speaking, an adventure story at all. Its hero does not go anywhere; he does not display unusual physical prowess or extraordinary moral courage; he does not risk his personal safety by attempting to perform difficult tasks or to reach out after distant objectives; and, in fact, he dies quietly of natural causes at an advanced age. Yet "Will o' the Mill" has adventure as its theme and center. It is about a man who never goes on one. First published in *The Cornhill Magazine* in January of 1878, it precedes the writing of all of Stevenson's major works of fiction, including *Latter-Day Arabian Nights* and *Treasure Island.* It is not only one of his finest short stories, but it serves as a splendid apology for the romances written in the decade between 1878 and 1888, and as an instructive preface to the tales written in the South Seas during the last six years of his life.

On the surface the plot is simple enough. It tells of the adopted son of an innkeeper-miller in a remote mountain valley who watches the river disappear into the plains below and dreams of the gorgeous cities through which it runs and of the great sea into which it empties. Until the age of sixteen young Will is nearly sick with the desire to leave home and explore the world beyond the valley. He feels with all mariners, colonists, pilgrims, and adventurers "that divine unrest, that old stinging trouble of humanity." But his father will not permit him to leave home. Finally, Will confides in one of the inn's guests, a jolly fat young man, who advises him to stay where he is and enjoy his dreams because the plains below are not all he imagines; in fact, they are filled with people who wish they were in the mountains.

Will seems to have learned the lesson of Rasselas without the trouble of a long journey. But he has learned it too easily and perhaps too well. He follows the guest's advice so completely that after his parents' death he runs the inn by himself and refuses to marry the parson's daughter, whom he loves, because he convinces himself that he can be happier thinking about her than being with her. He prefers not to spoil his pure idea with reality. Three years later the girl marries someone else and dies shortly after, leaving Will alone with his philosophy and his dreams. He grows old serenely and even in the great cities of the plains becomes famous for his stoicism. Eventually, when his hair is white and his cheeks ruddy, death comes in the guise of a stranger and takes him in his carriage on the way to his first and last adventure.

The usual way to read the story is as a kind of fable with an antistoical moral. Will's life of noninvolvement becomes a living death, which he himself admits in his old age: "I am a dead man now: I have lived and died already." And he concludes with a most un-Stevensonian moral: "But that is the object of long living, that man should cease to care about life." Though this may resemble a noble statement of Christian resignation, it is for Stevenson an admission of the first deadly sin. When Will meets death's personification, he is like a resigned Faustus almost relieved by the appearance of the Mephistopheles with whom he had made an agreement years before. He has wrested from death some of its sting by accepting it emotionally while still a young man. But the price he paid for the "comfort" of being numb to death was life itself. He has grown as insensible to pleasure as to pain. For an author without faith in the immortal soul of the Christians or full comprehension of the imagination of the Romantics, this story comes as close as possible to being an allegory of damnation. If life is the soul, death is the devil, resignation the sin, and going down to the grave without ever having lived is the eternal punishment.

But, having made this comparison, it is important to emphasize that this is an earthly rather than a spiritual fable. Stevenson does not use natural terms to describe a supernatural state, but he does employ sacred, quasi-religious terminology to evoke concrete nature. The language of the story is deliberately scriptural, as are the abrupt transitions of tone and incident. There is also an occasional echo from a fairy tale, primarily because of the naive and subjective observations of the boyish protagonist. Phrases like "a great conspiracy of things animate and inanimate" and "posting downward to the unknown world" seem to hint at the existence of some transcendent reality beyond the physical surface of things being described. But Stevenson's philosophy, insofar as he can be said to have any, is materialistic. When he speaks of an "unknown world," he means actual parts of the natural world not known to his hero; the mystery lies not in an independent spirit of nature, but in the effect natural processes have on the human heart: "Everything that went that way, were it cloud or carriage, bird or brown water in the stream, [Will] felt his heart flow out after it in an ecstasy of longing" (VII, 73).

Stevenson knew only too well that the human urge to participate imaginatively in the "free movement" of nature, when not nourished and balanced by sensuous contact with objective reality, could develop into a kind of self-deceptive illusion which ultimately separates the individual from life and turns his visions into pipe dreams. From the earliest years of his writing career it seems to have been a tendency he alternately cultivated and questioned in himself. It is also one source of his uneasy fascination with the Romantic poets, especially Wordsworth.

It seems likely, in fact, that Stevenson had Wordsworth in mind when he composed his tale about a passionate young lover of nature named Will who in later life becomes renowned as a sage and stoic, placidly receiving visitors in his mountain retreat. Stevenson's attitude toward Wordsworth is not simple. He is unable to decide whether the lyrical, passionate young poet or the serene philosopher is the better model; whether it is preferable to join "the great conspiracy of things animate and inanimate," or to hold back and let them pass. In "Aes Triplex," an essay published three months after "Will o' the Mill," Stevenson quite emphatically casts his lot with passionate involvement. In his conclusion to the essay he turns a familiar Wordsworthian sentiment on its head by echoing a phrase from the "Ode on Intimations of Immortality" in a reference to death rather than birth. The ideal and heroic way to die, he explains, is in the midst of "full-blooded" activity, with a kind of athletic leap into the grave rather than a gradual and silent settling:

> In the hot-fit of life, a tip-toe on the highest point of being, he passes at a bound on to the other side. The noise of the mallet and chisel is scarcely quenched, the trumpets are hardly done blowing, when, *trailing clouds of glory,* this happy-starred, full-blooded spirit shoots into the spiritual land. (XIII, 105)

This is the kind of gymnastic prose, with its enthusiastic conglomeration of metaphors, that makes Stevenson an embarrassment to those who try to defend him in a relatively serious way. But it is nonetheless a good antidote for those who would read his early yearnings after adventure as a symbolic expression of transcendental unrest or a kind of Victorian religious allegory. Stevenson's glorious clouds, unlike Wordsworth's, do not come from heaven—not even one created in the mind—but from earth. They are the attendants of hard work and hard living, signs of active participation in the business of the world, which follow a man, if only through reputation, even beyond the grave.

Still, Stevenson was capable, partly because of his temperament and partly out of physical necessity, of being stoical. His letters are frequently filled with expressions of detachment and resignation. Where his moods of stoicism differ from the later Wordsworth's is in the fact that they *were* moods—erratic, temporary, inconsistent—rather than a gradual hardening of mind. Stevenson borrowed his stoicism, as he did so many of his fragments of philosophy, as a stay against dereliction in prolonged periods of physical weakness. He gladly threw it over at the first sign of a clear sky and a steady pulse.

Stevenson was a man in search of a cure. He took philosophy as a temporary palliative, but had almost no faith at all in its remedial powers. This helps to explain how he could write one of his most complacent and bourgeois homilies, admonishing man to be satisfied with his lot, however modest it may be, to be content to "earn a little and to spend a little less . . . to renounce when that shall be necessary," only a few months before investing almost his entire savings in a schooner-yacht and embarking with his family on an impractical and dangerous expedition to the South Seas. In these years Stevenson was not a hypocrite, but an invalid, emotionally as well as physically. He saw his own suffering as a peculiar problem rather than as one manifestation of the universal human condition, and philosophy as a doctor which could be discarded once the cure was temporarily attained.

Stevenson was so obsessed with his own physical health that for many years it dominated all other consideration, mental and spiritual, and eventually became inseparable from them. He made the mistake of the chronically sick man who believes that to heal himself is to save himself.

It may be true that Proust molded his frailty into art—manipulated, savored, and in a sense, triumphed over it—but that is not true of the young Stevenson. His sickbed overwhelmed him even when he was out of it. With rare exceptions he was unable to regard artistic, moral, or emotional problems without a subjective physiological referent.

Stevenson describes Will's yearning for travel and adventure in terms which, like those in the Psalms, seem to define the soul by means of the body:

> If he could only go far enough out there, he felt as if his eyesight would be purged and clarified, as if his hearing would grow more delicate, and his very breath would come and go with luxury. He was transplanted and withering where he was; he lay in a strange country and was sick for home. (VII, 74)

The intensity of feeling, the almost morbid concern for the sick body, combined with a persistent desire for health, parallels the yearning of the sinful man for purification and admission into heaven. But in this story the two states of mind are never more than parallel; they do not meet at any point. Will is obviously looking for more than a rest cure at a health resort. His *need* for release, for deliverance from monotony and unrest, is pervasive and deeply human. He seeks salvation, but he seeks it, like Stevenson, from the earth. Will's sense of being away from "home" has relatively little to do with the concept of the Christian soul dwelling, since the Fall, out of perfect communion with God.

The language which at the beginning of the story suggested travel as a physical "cure" is at the conclusion applied to the strange visitor who personifies death.

> "You are a doctor?" quavered Will.

> "The best there ever was," replied the other; "for I cure both mind and body with the same prescription. I take away all pain and I forgive all sins; and where my patients have gone wrong in life, I smooth out all complications and set them free upon their feet." (VII, 102)

That the "curative" allusions to death resemble the language applied to the beneficial effects of outdoor adventure indicates the uncertainty in Stevenson's mind. The active life may or may not be restorative, whereas death cures effectively by taking away. Passive resignation to non-being before the event of one's death is a kind of moral amputation, a lobotomy at the source and center of life. Still, Stevenson seems to acknowledge the fact that there are painful cases sufficiently serious to warrant a cutting away of the diseased members as the only stay against unbearable suffering.

The question which plagues him in his uncertainty is whether the "painful cases" are accidental and isolated, or whether instead they represent the common fate of man in an irresponsible universe. If the world of external reality is meaningless, ugly, and vacant, a place where the permanent and successful accomplishment of any human endeavor is not possible, then perhaps the best solution is to remove one's self from it, either by physical suicide or by existing as painlessly as possible in an invention of the mind. (Whether it is a systematic philosophy or a childish dream makes little difference.) "We are in a rat-trap," Will admits to the fat guest at one point in the story. "Something of that size," agrees his counselor. "Did you ever see a squirrel turning in his cage? and another squirrel sitting philosopically over his nuts? I needn't ask you which of them looked more a fool."

The answer to this apparently simple rhetorical question is not easy for Stevenson to give. His dilemma, especially during the time when he was writing "Will o' the Mill," was that, for all his admiration of the practical and active life and his rejection of stoical resignation, he was in no physical condition to act upon the vigorous moral of his own fable. Obviously sensing this, he tempers the satire on Wordsworth's resolution and the antistoical parable with a kind of sympathy which, though it may not appreciably alter the narrative sense of the piece, does leave a great many more unanswered questions than are allowed by the direct simplicity of most moral fables.

3

Stevenson spent most of his lifetime trying to convince himself and others that the "trap" was not a permanent fact of the universe, urging effort in the face of failure, praising agitation and damning passivity. But underlying his optimism, just as it underlies the moral of "Will o' the Mill," is the sick man's spirit—weary, weak, sometimes willing with the resigned hero of the story to seek his cure elsewhere when the remedy prescribed by an active life seems too bitter and outrageous.

But if Stevenson's sickness occasionally brought him to the edge of despair, it also prevented him from crossing it. One way to combat the demoralizing suspicion that pain is a permanent element of being is to fix upon a source for it which is accidental, external, and readily localized. Though he protests to William Archer in 1885 that "the medicine bottles on my chimney and the blood on my handkerchief are accidents [which] do not colour my view of life," Stevenson repeatedly holds his physical infirmity responsible for anxiety, depression, irritability, moral and emotional capriciousness, and loss of creative power. Up to a point he was undoubtedly justified in doing so. There is little question that poor physical health affected his disposition as well as his creative imagination. But there is no particular reason to believe, as at bottom he did, that to recover the soundness of his body would have purified his spirit and improved his writing.

He embarked for the South Seas in search of a physical cure, but he hoped that the torments of his mind and soul would fade with the external symptoms of disease. The comparatively comfortable state of health he eventually attained in Vailima was to put an end to this persistent dream. The disillusionment was all the greater because at the beginning of the adventure the fantasy seemed to be coming true. Happy because in the South Seas his mind was at first full of "external and physical things," rather than the "rot about a fellow's behaviour," he began to assume that he was more and more alive as his Victorian conscience was less and less active. What was to be looked for, then, were places or situations in which that moral conscience was least called upon to act. Only then could the individual behave as a whole and healthy creature, undivided by the conflicts of the civilized and the damned.

That same tendency of mind which made him limit and crystallize the causes of his own personal weakness led him to isolate and externalize the ills of the world. His habit, unlike Thomas Hardy's, was to blame injustice on the nineteenth century and the peculiar turn of Western civilization, rather than on an inherent indifference in the universe and inadequacy in man. He speaks of the Victorian era as an age devoted to the ugly; he writes to Henry James from Samoa that "my nineteenth century strikes here, and lies alongside of something beautiful and ancient." He confesses to W. H. Low that he prefers the Polynesian way of life to the European because "this civilisation of ours is a dingy, ungentlemanly business; it drops out too much of man, and too much of that very beauty of the poor beast; who has his beauties in spite of Zola and Co." (*Letters,* III, 128-129, 142-143). He consistently places the blame for lack of nobility, beauty, and justice on a specific time and place which he hopes to leave behind by means of a long sea voyage.

As we have already seen, Stevenson has a habit of conducting his romantic quests in a relentlessly dogged and literal-minded way. He is not comfortable for long in the realm of pure imagination. Unlike most English Romantics, who tend to move from the concrete to the imagined world, he invariably jumps out of his dream, and roams the globe trying to make it come true. The treatment of boys' adventure, as it is modified after *Treasure Island,* establishes a pattern which recurs, as he sets out imaginatively and actually in search of man's purest and most essential self. This time his objective is not the man-child, but the race-child, the semiprimitive inhabitants of the Pacific islands, "the trunk and aboriginal taproot of the race" (XIII, 238).

One of the most profound manifestations of Stevenson's reaction against the Victorian manners and Calvinistic morals of his childhood is his belief that the submerged self, the hidden and natural man within, is not tainted or depraved, but on the contrary is the source of all that is genuine and pure. The outer self, which has been conditioned and shaped by public morality and social law, is the corrupter of clean passions and the destroyer of life. We have heard this before in various keys from Rousseau and later French and English Romantics; we have heard it sung by Blake and shouted by Hemingway. We hear it again and again in the twentieth century from writers like Lawrence and Gide, for whom the symbol of self-discovery and self-liberation is not the savage, the rustic, the idiot, or the orphan, but the sexual man at peace with his libido.

Neither his time nor his temperament enabled Stevenson to deal with the problem of locating and liberating the private self in sexual terms, though he does admit at the end of his career that if he had had his life to begin again, he would "try to honour Sex more religiously." Still, the self Stevenson seeks in the South Seas, the one for which the natives are expected to set the example, is physical, if not specifically sexual, and its enemies are the excesses of social habit, moral conscience, and an overactive intellect.

In *The Wrecker,* Stevenson's first South Sea novel, Loudon Dodd, the narrator-hero, sails for Midway Island in search of a wrecked cargo ship. The exhilaration of hard physical labor with his fellow crewmen makes him look back with shame on his former life as "a dweller under roofs: the gull of that which we call civilisation."

In his initial encounter with sailoring in the South Seas the hero senses that he has caught a glimpse of something permanent, a kind of immortality: "the eternal life of man, spent under sun and rain and in rude physical effort . . . scarce changed since the beginning." Dodd, like Stevenson, hopes to find the hard core of existence, naked being stripped of historical and regional distinction. They seek "pure" life in the Pacific, but the irony is that both author and hero become most obviously British and Victorian the more vehemently they attempt to express their release from time and place. Stevenson rarely conjures up his era so well as when he is shouting it down. In several passages in the novel we can hardly hear the narrator's voice for the passionate intrusions of the author.

> I would I could have carried along with me to Midway Island all the writers and prating artists of my time. Day after day of hope deferred, of heat, of unremitting toil; night after night of aching limbs, bruised hands, and a mind obscured with the grateful vacancy of physical fatigue . . . the rugged speech and faces of my fellow-toilers, the glare of the day on deck, the stinking twilight in the bilge . . . above all, the sense of our immitigable isolation from the world and from the current epoch;—keeping another time, some eras old; the new day heralded by no daily paper, only by the rising of the sun; and the State, the churches, the peopled empires, war, and the rumours of war, and the voices of the arts, all gone silent as in the days ere they were yet invented. Such were the conditions of my new experience in life, of which (if I had been able) I would have had all my confreres and contemporaries to partake: forgetting, for that while, the orthodoxies of the moment, and devoted to a single and material purpose under the eye of heaven. (X, 271-272)

Dodd's wish to carry all the "writers and prating artists" of his time with him to the Pacific comes closer to being realized by Stevenson than he suspected. For if he did not take with him a shipload of contemporary observers, he did take a headful of Victorian preconceptions about semiprimitive societies. The more emphatically he insists that life on Samoa or Tahiti is in every way the reverse of life in nineteenth-century Britain (simple where it is chaotic, happy where it is sad, picturesque where it is ugly, natural where it is artificial), the more he marks himself as a man of his time, almost incapable of conceiving of anything foreign without automatically placing it in opposition to what he already knows. The result in the South Sea journals and in the island fiction is a splendid Victorian clutter, a crowded sepia-tone with an outlandish frame.

Among Stevenson's best writing on the Pacific islands is a collection of travel memoirs entitled *In the South Seas,* a work much admired by Joseph Conrad. The famous account of the first landfall of the voyage is a characteristic example of his tendency to describe scenes of fresh natural beauty by introducing images from the urbanized civilization he was bent on forgetting. He recalls his first glimpse of the mountains of Nuka-hiva rising against the horizon:

> . . . like pinnacles of some ornate and monstrous church, they stood there, in the sparkling brightness of the morning, the fit sign-board of a world of wonders . . . The land heaved up in peaks and rising vales; it fell in cliffs and buttresses . . . the isle and its unsubstantial canopy rose and shimmered before us like a single mass. There was no beacon, no smoke of towns to be expected . . . The only sea-mark given [was] a certain headland . . . distinguished by two colossal figures, the gross statuary of nature. (XIX, 3-4)

With the analogies to a church, a signboard, buttresses, a canopy, and statuary, as well as the negative mention of smoky towns, the picture of a virgin island is confused, almost blurred. The passage brings to mind Dr. Johnson's criticism of "velvet green" in Gray's "The Progress of Poesy": "An epithet or metaphor drawn from Nature ennobles Art: an epithet or metaphor drawn from Art degrades Nature."[3] Stevenson may not degrade nature with his artificial imagery, but he plainly distorts a South Sea island to fit into a European mold:

> The trees, from our distance, might have been hazel; the beach might have been in Europe; the mountain forms behind modelled in little from the Alps, and the forests which clustered on their ramparts a growth no more considerable than our Scottish heath. (XIX, 4)

Even granting that these journals were written as a kind of travelogue for publication in Britain and America, there is an atmosphere of closeness, a combined fascination and bewilderment with new sights, a need to describe by constant comparison with what is known and perhaps missed, which is surprising in a writer of so-called "escape" literature.

More than forty years earlier the young Herman Melville also recorded his first impression of Nuka-hiva in the opening chapter of *Typee*. His prose conveys unadorned enthusiasm as he recalls "short glimpses of blooming valleys, deep glens, waterfalls, and waving groves, hidden here and there by projecting and rocky headlands, every moment opening to the view some new and startling scene of beauty." The simple diction and breathless phrasing offer a telling contrast to Stevenson's visualization, which seems to have Victorian Edinburgh, London, and parts of continental Europe impressed indelibly upon it. Even some of the *Songs of Travel,* written by Stevenson in the South Seas ostensibly about the South Seas, are poetic excuses for conjuring up images of home:

> The tropics vanish, and meseems that I,
> From Halkerside, from topmost Allermuir,
> Or steep Caerketton, dreaming gaze again.
> Far set in fields and woods, the town I see
> Spring gallant from the shallows of her smoke,
> Cragged, spired, and turreted, her virgin fort
> Beflagged. About, on seaward-drooping hills,
> New folds of city glitter. Last, the Forth
> Wheels ample waters set with sacred isles,
> And populous Fife smokes with a score of towns.[4]

Another "travel" song, dedicated to Sidney Colvin, begins with a night stroll on tropic sands but turns quickly—again reversing a Wordsworthian pattern—to a recollection of urban pleasures shared with an urbane friend:

> To other lands and nights my fancy turned—
> To London first, and chiefly to your house,
> The many-pillared and the well-beloved.
> There yearning fancy lighted . . .
> . . . I beheld again
> Lamps vainly brighten the dispeopled street;
> Again I longed for the returning morn,
> The awaking traffic, the bestirring birds.[5]

It quickly becomes clear that the pleasure in reading *Songs of Travel, In the South Seas, Island Nights' Entertainments, The Wrecker,* and *The Ebb Tide* is rarely that of sensing the oppressive heat, the presence of luxuriant vegetation pressing along the banks of slow brown rivers, or the illusion of involvement in the unfamiliar rhythms of native life. It is not, in other words, even superficially Melvillean. The pleasure is in observing the author-narrator touring the South Seas, often without shoes and wearing a funny hat, but always accompanied by a picturesque if cumbersome bundle of Victorian keepsakes.

4

The Beach of Falesá,[6] published in 1892 and later included in *Island Nights' Entertainments,* was regarded by Stevenson as containing the "essence" of the South Seas. It might have been more accurate if he had said that it contains the essence of himself and his epoch in the South Seas. The tropical island of Falesá to which John Wiltshire comes as a new white trader is described as a world "all new painted," with grass smooth as on Fiddler's Green, full of children who "looked like figures on a chimney-piece," and pious old women who moan like "Dissenters in their chapels at the sermon."

Wiltshire himself is described as "sick" for new companions and fresh experience after having spent several years on an obscure trading outpost. He feels his blood "renewed" on first seeing his new home, but is soon warned that his predecessor died of a mysterious "sickness." The island itself is "healthy" enough, but a rival white trader named Case turns out to be the cause of irritation, disease, and occasional disappearances among potential business competitors. He was ugly, "yellow and smallish," but "splendidly educated," could speak "when he chose, fit for a drawing-room," and, most damning of all, "would have passed muster in a city." If the source of evil in the story is educated and city-bred, Wiltshire's good angel is his native wife, Uma, physically beautiful, intuitively loyal and generous, "so like a child or a kind dog," that she throws herself at her master's feet, exclaiming that she belongs to him "all-e same pig!" Not only is Uma like an unspoiled child or tame pet, but so, according to Wiltshire, are most natives. "Just go back to yourself anyway around from ten to fifteen years old, and there's an average Kanaka." Wiltshire explains at another point in the narration that the natives do not have "any real government or any real law," presumably because they are too irresponsible to maintain them and too innocent to require them.

Before half the story is over, then, a series of oversimplifications and romantic daydreams are passed off as the truth about Falesá and its inhabitants. Of course, Wiltshire, not Stevenson, is the narrator. But although his poor English, his blunt observations, and his plain sentiments give superficial evidence of his lack of sophistication as an observer, Stevenson deliberately or unconsciously shares in that naiveté by failing to introduce even the faintest irony in the tale. Wiltshire's insensitive and condescending observations are thoroughly borne out by the behavior of the characters. Uma and the other natives *do* act and speak like children, and the white trader Case, with his city manners and greed, *is* the cause of "sickness" on the island, which returns at once to its Arcadian state when he is eliminated. Also, if the man with the splendid education and drawing-room manners is a villain partly because of the corrupting effect civilization has had on his natural spirits, then Wiltshire's simplicity and roughness have positive value. Even obtuseness, insofar as it is the opposite of cunning, can be a form of moral superiority. Wiltshire, along with the natives he is describing, may be in the good Romantic tradition of the unsophisticated hero with a wisdom deeper than reason.

Stevenson's problem is that he learned most of his Romantic lessons from books rather than from nature. His respect for the unlearned mind was learned, and he carried it to the South Seas a little too certain that he would find there one of the last flourishing outposts of natural man, untainted by the trappings of civilization. Wiltshire is obtuse all right, not with the innocence of Blake's lamb, nor of Stevenson's own childish savages, but, notwithstanding the shabbiness of his dress and grammar, with some of the civilized myopia of a benevolent British colonial. He tramps happily through the tropics, finding the climate sweet, the scenery picturesque, the populace beautiful, innocent, and inferior.

In fairness to Stevenson it should be pointed out that, though in the first year or two in the Pacific he may have shared some of these oversimplified notions with his protagonist, once he settled among the people of Samoa the stereotype began quickly to deteriorate. In a letter to Colvin in 1891 he calls *The Beach of Falesá* "really very fetching," "a little gem," but "a hallucination I have outlived." Still, by taking the Romantic idea of the noble simplicity of primitive man and turning it into a formal and literal doctrine, he made it difficult for himself at first to perceive new aspects of reality.

The source of the villainous Case's hold over the native population of Falesá is a mysterious shrine in the heart of the jungle, where he is reported to hold traffic with devils.[7] Upon investigating the devil-work one day for himself, Wiltshire discovers that the wailing voices are produced by Aeolian harps (which he calls "Tyrolean") attached to the branches of trees, and that the grotesquely glowing figures are masks coated with luminous paint. Right at that point in the story when Case seems most dangerous and the native fear of evil spirits most potent, the whole matter is reduced to the level of child's play. Wiltshire muses:

> I remember a boy I was at school with at home who played the Case business. He didn't know anything, that boy; he couldn't do anything; he had no luminous paint and no Tyrolean harps; he just boldly said he was a sorcerer, and frightened us out of our boots, and we loved it. And then it came to my mind how the master had once flogged that boy, and the surprise we were all in to see the sorcerer catch it and hum like anybody else . . . I must find some way of fixing it so for Master Case. (IV, 314)

Later, Wiltshire has his native wife explain to one of the chieftains that the devil shrine is just so much harmless artifice: "Tell him the place is a blooming toy-shop! Tell him in England we give these things to the kids to play with."

It would be a mistake to assume that Stevenson diminishes the potential evil purely for convenience. The tendency to reduce a serious threat to the level of child's play goes deeper than the need to find a device which will supply a "rational" explanation for the mystery. Stevenson not only makes the instruments of evil foolish artifacts, but he turns their manipulator into *Master* Case, a bully and a bad boy, who deserves a good flogging. He derives most of his power not from internal resources, but from the fear, morbidity, and ignorance of the natives.

Before leaving for the South Seas, Stevenson wrote an essay in which he severely criticized any moral system which places too much emphasis on interdiction, damnation, and sin because of the corrupting effect it inevitably has on a frightened and vulnerable populace.

> It is certain we all think too much of sin . . . To make our idea of morality center on forbidden acts is to defile the imagination and to introduce into our judgments of our fellow-men a secret element of gusto. If a thing is wrong for us, we should not dwell upon the thought of it; or we shall soon dwell upon it with inverted pleasure. (XV, 301)

By forcing the natives of Falesá to concentrate upon "forbidden acts" (taboos), devilish curses, and black magic, Case plays upon their weakness and fear, and paralyzes them so that he can move about doing as he likes without interference. Stevenson leaves little doubt that the situation he has created in Falesá (which means "sacred house," or "church," in Samoan) resembles in miniature another taboo-ethic he hoped to have left behind him in Scotland. Wiltshire describes the superstition of the natives as a religious fear which finds some comfort in numbers:

> I saw that Case had plenty of disciples . . . A young man scarce reckoned himself grown till he had . . . seen Case's devils . . . This is mighty like Kanakas: but, if you look at it another way, it's mighty like white folks too. (IV, 312)

It is not necessary to turn the story into allegory to see

that the methods and effects of Case's devil-work, if not the deliberate treachery of his motives, have a parallel in the negative and sin-centered morality of the Scottish Church as Stevenson conceived of it. Wiltshire's struggle with Case is not so much a conflict between good and evil as a struggle between the natural and the artificial; a quarrel, not with the devil, but with an *idea* of the devil, which both Wiltshire and Stevenson refuse to accept.

Stevenson had still not worked out the question of evil to his own satisfaction, and his encounter with life in the South Seas began to complicate it more than ever. It may be sound psychology to say that excessive concern with sin is unhealthy and can lead to morbid pleasure, but it does not necessarily follow that a deliberate attempt not to think of sin will make it go away. Whether sin has an existence absolute and real in a divinely ordered creation or whether it is an idea in the mind of man, inventing his own law in a lawless universe, makes less difference psychologically than many Victorians who "freed" themselves from the orthodoxies of Christianity had at first assumed. Stevenson (like Joyce and Lawrence after him) might liberate himself from the acceptance of religious myth as literal truth; it was another question altogether whether he could liberate himself from mental habits formed by the Church in his youth, or whether any man can escape some of the realities of the human condition which invariably lie behind formalized religious creeds.

It would be extreme to assert that *The Beach of Falesá* is a kind of *Faerie Queen* in reverse, with Wiltshire, the Redcrosse Knight, battling the dragon, and Case as the demonic invention of Scotch Calvinism. But it does seem fair to say that some of the uncertain and ambiguous feelings Stevenson had for the Kirk's doctrine of sin and the nature of evil come to bear on Wiltshire's last skirmish with Case. It is during crises of this kind that Stevenson must decide, if only in the simplest narrative terms, what evil is and how an ordinary man with moderate resources of strength and courage can deal with it.

During the hand-to-hand fight between Wiltshire and Case, Stevenson offers three answers which he intermingles indiscriminately. One we have already encountered in the tale, and that is that evil is hocus-pocus, "kid's stuff," the impetuous projection of undisciplined and uninformed emotion into inanimate matter or innocuous persons. The extension of this attitude makes the conflict with evil a simple and amoral matter of entertaining agitation, which cannot possibly have a serious consequence since it is conducted entirely between the individual and a creation of his own fancy and can be dismissed as quickly as it was summoned. This is the evil, or substitute for evil, we have found in *Treasure Island* and all the fiction of boys' daydream. In *The Beach of Falesá* it appears in the form of "Tyrolean" harps and luminous paint. Case himself becomes for a moment a boy's plaything without character or independent existence when Wiltshire holds him down and thrusts a knife into him: "His body kicked under me like a spring sofa . . . The blood came over my hands, I remember, hot as tea." Tea and a sofa seem to be inappropriate analogies in a life-and-death struggle, until we recall that, for the moment, Stevenson has Wiltshire engaged in a game. As he explains in his essay on "Child's Play," when the boy's "story comes to the fighting, he must rise, get something by way of a sword and have a set-to with a piece of furniture, until he is out of breath" (XIII, 140).

The second answer to the question is that evil, inasmuch as it is a name given to acts not sanctioned by needlessly severe man-made law, is desirable and pleasing in direct proportion to the discomfort produced by the artificial rigidity of that law. "If your morals make you dreary," Stevenson wrote in 1888, "depend upon it they are wrong. I do not say 'give them up,' for they may be all you have; but conceal them like a vice, lest they should spoil the lives of better and simpler people" (XV, 303-304). Unlike Blake before him and his admirer Gide after him, Stevenson did not follow through the full implications of this theory, turning hell into heaven, and making a bold and deliberate breach of the conventional moral code a symbolic expression of virtue. Still, the distance between treating some repressive morality *as though* it were a vice, and coming right out and calling repressive morality vicious, is not so great.

Stevenson often referred bitterly to the atmosphere of "sad, senseless self-denial" in which he had been raised. And he toyed curiously with the lure of "high-flying vice" in much of his fiction, but there is in Wiltshire's fight-to-the-death with Case an unexpectedly strong element of sadistic pleasure, felt by the protagonist and perhaps partially shared by the author. Not only is Case compared with a woman, easier and pleasanter to subdue than Wiltshire had anticipated, but with each thrust of the knife there is an increasing particularization of brutality which is rarely found in Stevenson's writing. The passage conveys an immoderate and orgastic sense of release in the outrageous violation of one human being by another:

> I'm a pretty strong man anyway, but I never knew what strength was till I got hold of Case. He . . . threw up his hands together . . . like a frightened woman, so that I caught both of them with my left. This wakened him up, and he fastened his teeth in my forearm . . . I drew my knife and got it in the place.

> "Now," said I, "I've got you; and you're gone up, and a good job too! Do you feel the point of that? That's for Underhill! And there's for Adams! And now here's for Uma, and that's going to knock your blooming soul right out of you!"
>
> With that, I gave him the cold steel for all I was worth . . . He gave a dreadful kind of a long moan, and lay still . . . I tried to draw the knife out to give it him again. The blood came over my hands, I remember, hot as tea; and with that I fainted clean away, and fell with my head on the man's mouth.
>
> When I came to myself . . . the first thing I attended to was to give him the knife again a half a dozen times up to the handle. I believe he was dead already, but it did him no harm and did me good. (IV, 331-332)

The renewal of strength, the "good" feeling, and the high-spirited banter, while they appear to stem from sheer sensual pleasure, may also be justified as the joys of righteousness in the heat of moral triumph. Inasmuch as this would be the explanation of Wiltshire's satisfaction in murdering Case according to the narrative surface of the tale, it provides the third answer to the question of evil and man's response to it. That is the Judeo-Christian concept of the deliberate transgression of the divine will (expressed through the community will), which, for the safety of the soul (and the common body), must be impeded and extinguished. The intensity of emotion and energy expended is not, according to this interpretation, a result of physical stimulation, but rather an indication of the enormity of the threat and of the extraordinary effort necessary to subdue it.

The trouble is that the three tentative notions of evil do not converge in Case's character, but remain as three distinct possibilities, leaving him equally unsuccessful as a clown, a serious villain, or a sympathetic personality. Stevenson, once again, cannot make up his mind about one of his own characters, and still he is unwilling to accept this state of indecision as appropriate in a mature novelist. Rather than use evasive methods of characterization, he jumps aboard in the most direct way possible, introducing his characters with the picturesque clarity of a Dickensian caricature.

Case, we are told on the fourth page of the tale, is "yellow and smallish, had a hawk's nose to his face, pale eyes, and his beard trimmed with scissors." After a few more lines about his city-breeding, smooth talk, and capacity for blasphemy, there seems no doubt that he is to be a villain in the popular, uncomplicated sense of the word. Yet, before the story is out, he has been called "rat," "lion," "Yankee boatswain," "a good Christian," "parasite," "fly," "a square and hearty man," "devil," "sorcerer," "a prank-playing child," "louse," "a frightened woman," "a spring sofa," and "a soul damned to hell." The problem is that his many forms are clearly defined and carefully outlined, each leaving very little room for the possibility of another.

Stevenson uses the apparatus of external and static characterization in an attempt to achieve complexity. Instead, he creates in Case a kind of multiple personality which is different from Silver, Hoseason, and Hyde largely because it has more than two parts. Few readers can be expected to take very seriously the fate of Case's soul or the pain inflicted on his body when in the throes of death he is described as a spring-sofa being jumped upon by a rambunctious child. On the other hand, the intensity of Wiltshire's rage, combined with the almost ecstatic satisfaction he takes in plunging a knife into his enemy, goes beyond the innocent pleasures of child's play. If evil is a cheap mask, a figment of the imagination, why become so excited about it? Or is there something behind the luminous paint even worse than the ugly exterior suggests? Is it possible that man's fetishes intimidate in order to protect him?

These may very well be questions Stevenson asked himself. The brittle surface of popular adventure—the picturesque locale as backdrop, the simple hero pitted against the caricature villain, the mysterious evil explained by mechanical trickery—is under a serious strain in his later South Sea fiction. The Victorian veneer was bound to buckle and crack when laid over the moral and physical topography of the tropics. Even in *The Beach of Falesá,* with its conventional happy ending (Wiltshire lives happily ever after with Uma), the exotic fable discloses moral complications which threaten to shatter its own simple frame.

5

One of the last books Stevenson wrote—and the last to deal with the South Seas—is a novel called *The Ebb Tide.* It was published in August 1894, four months before his death. He collaborated on the work with his stepson Lloyd Osbourne, but became so interested midway through that he took over its completion totally on his own. "You can't get into *The Ebb Tide* until after the first hundred pages," wrote André Gide in 1905, "but suddenly it becomes excellent and remains so almost to the end."[8] The book as a whole is uneven but it contains passages which show a quite radically changed attitude toward the tropics and an increased emphasis on the relationship between morality and adventure. Stevenson begins to imply that the distinction between "behavior" and "action" is not so great as he had once assumed;

that man does not necessarily escape difficult problems of conscience by engaging in intense physical activity, by going to sea or exploring an island; that the "problems of the body and the practical intelligence," contrary to his dream of ten years before, are seldom obvious and simple, and, for a responsible man, never amoral.

The narrative deals with three white outcasts—a drunken American sea captain named Davis, a snivelling and unscrupulous Cockney clerk named Huish, and an Oxford graduate called Herrick who has an underdeveloped will and a penchant for Virgil. Stranded penniless and hungry on the beach of Papeete, they are offered the opportunity to take a cargo ship loaded with champagne to Australia. The previous captain and first mate have died of smallpox, and no reputable mariner will take the risk of going aboard so soon. Once out at sea, the three decide to hijack the ship, take it to Peru, sell it complete with cargo, and keep the profits for themselves. But after the first few days Huish and Davis have broken into the champagne, and remain drunk or asleep, while Herrick, without previous experience at sea, navigates the vessel and commands the small native crew. Within a relatively short period the ship has floundered off course and is beginning to run dangerously low on supplies.

Up to this point Stevenson has succeeded in making the story come as close as possible to his early definition of "open-air adventure" in which the immediate demands of self-preservation subordinate and simplify the problems of the will. But when the ship comes to a small island, and the three find living on it an educated English gentleman named Attwater, with a taste for good food, an evangelical zeal, and a ten-year accumulation of priceless pearls, the whole mood of the novel changes. The simple problem of self-preservation, for Herrick at least, becomes complicated with questions of divided loyalties: pity and understanding for the weaknesses of Davis and Huish contrasted with respect for the civilized ways of a fellow gentleman.

One of the most curious things about the story, for all its South Seas trappings, is that it is an urban daydream, an expression of nostalgia for civilization. In the middle of the Pacific Ocean Stevenson creates a strip of Britain. Earlier in the novel, each of the three renegades had dreamt about going home (which, for two of them, means London), hearing again the bustle of traffic, tasting good food, seeing familiar faces. Stevenson does his best, especially for Herrick, right on New Island, for Attwater makes him feel at home as soon as he hears his Oxford accent.

The three renegades are invited ashore for dinner, and although the food is native, it is prepared and served in the most civilized manner, in "a glittering of crystal and the fluttering of white napery," and accompanied by a plentiful supply of sherry, hock, and claret. The physical description of the island, too, has more than the usual number of imported images: the sand is "noiseless as . . . newfallen snow"; the ground "bore marks of having been weeded like a garden alley at home"; the sound of the breakers had earlier been compared with that of a train; and it is noted that the noise of the Trade Winds in the palm trees "contributed a humming bass, like the roar of cities."

But the primary reminder of Victorian Britain is Attwater himself. Not only is he a cultivated product of Trinity Hall, but, more important, he is a man of strict principle, a Protestant Christian, a "dark apostle." In the first few pages after introducing Attwater, Stevenson quickly establishes the extent of his Puritanism. In the first place, he is a businessman as well as a missionary, one who equates industry, thrift, and ambition with the heavenly virtues, and regards worldly success as a sign of God's blessing:

> "I was a man of the world before I was a Christian; I'm a man of the world still, and I made my mission pay . . . A man has to stand up in God's sight and work up to his weight avoirdupois." (XI, 334)

Secondly, Attwater mistrusts women. He regards sex as an annoying temptation which can incur God's wrath and ruin one's business prospects by spoiling the chance for a profitable marriage in the future. To avoid falling into sexual sin he has the one pretty native girl on his island married off to a servant against her will.

Finally, Attwater has a rigidly determined and relentless sense of justice, which transcends all considerations of compassion for human weakness. He relates a story of two servants, one of whom was blamed for a series of petty offenses and banished from the household. He is found the next day hanging from a tree, having taken his own life out of shame. Attwater discovers too late that the second native was in fact responsible for the transgressions. He cannot save the first man's life, but he can punish the true offender. Attwater describes his retribution with the impersonality and dispassion of a man who regards himself as an instrument of a transcendent will. He refers to himself throughout as "one."

> "One told him to go up the tree [where the first native was still hanging]. He stared a bit, looked at one with a trouble in his eye, and had a rather sickly smile, but went. He was obedient to the last; he had all the pretty virtues, but the truth was not in him. So soon as he was up, he looked down, and there was the rifle covering him; and

> at that he gave a whimper like a dog . . . He was obedient to the last, recited his crime, recommended his soul to God. And then—" . . . "And then?" said the breathless captain.
>
> "Shot," said Attwater. "They came to ground together." (XI, 354)

Stevenson has created in the self-righteous Attwater an exaggerated personification of everything he most feared and despised in the religion of his father. Yet if we take for granted that he has introduced Attwater as a simple object of disdain, we are in for a surprise. When Huish and Davis plan to kill the pious gentleman and make off with his pearls, Herrick is left with a choice more complicated than the one which faced young Will o' the Mill. Total rejection of responsibility or involvement in the lives of others, which in the end is Will's choice, occurs to Herrick as one possibility when he contemplates drowning himself. But unable to yield up his life, he must decide whether to warn Attwater of the plot, and thereby save a man whose adherence to stern religious principles appalls and frightens him, or, by his silence, to become the accomplice of murderers and thieves.

The choice is not the old familiar one—between airless rooms and wide-open spaces, sickness and health, reading the Shorter Catechism and dreaming of one-legged pirates. It has neither the moral irrelevance of childish games nor the moral clarity of pure good versus pure evil. Someone is bound to be killed, whatever Herrick decides; and each of the parties has something to be said in his favor despite an accumulation of obvious flaws.

The way in which Stevenson describes Herrick's dilemma indicates that it has taken on a significance for him beyond the immediate and melodramatic working out of an action story with an exotic setting. It is a decision which ultimately involves the hero in a division of allegiance between the good-natured outlaw (even Huish has his charms) and the bloodless lawmaker; the renegade and the man of principles; the weak, undisciplined, sentimental, and disorderly men who have put themselves outside society, and the strong, civilized, ruthless man who is the embodiment of a social and moral order.

> Herrick . . . revolved and resisted an immense temptation, to go up, touch [Attwater] on the arm, and breathe a word in his ear: "Beware, they are going to murder you." There would be one life spared; but what of the two others? . . . He considered the men. Attwater intrigued, puzzled, dazzled, enchanted, and revolted him. Alive, he seemed but a doubtful good; and the thought of him lying dead was so unwelcome that it pursued him, like a vision . . . Incessantly he had before him the image of that great mass of man, stricken down . . . He heard the click of the trigger . . . he saw the blood flow. And this building-up of circumstance was like a consecration of the man, till he seemed to walk in sacrificial fillets. Next he considered Davis, with his thick-fingered . . . commonness of nature; his . . . valour and mirth in the old days of their starvation; the endearing blend of his faults and virtues . . . And even Huish shared a little in that sacredness . . . there was an implied bond of loyalty in their . . . past miseries, to which Herrick must be a little true or wholly dishonoured . . . There was no hesitation possible; it must be Attwater. (XI, 339-340)

In the end it is not Attwater who is sacrificed, but Huish, the meanest and least well-bred of the three possible victims. The responsibility is Herrick's; he has swum ashore in the night and warned Attwater that he is in danger. Stevenson, as well as his protagonist, seems curiously intrigued, dazzled, and enchanted by the "dark apostle," the "angel of God's wrath," "that great mass of man," who, when his life is threatened, "seemed to walk in sacrificial fillets." The story trails off ironically and inconclusively. Huish has been shot by Attwater; Davis has undergone a religious conversion and is last seen trying to persuade Herrick to "come to Jesus"; Herrick looks out to sea in expectation of an approaching ship upon which he intends to sail home; and Attwater, still in possession of his island and his pearls, remains undefeated and unchanged.

Stevenson quite rightly calls the last two chapters of the novel "ugly and cynical." The mood is so pervasive that it drenches every aspect of the tale, every character, every incident, to a point where nothing is salient. Once again the atmosphere and even some details remind us of Conrad—especially of *Victory,* with its three renegades in search of another man's "wealth" on a God-forsaken island. Everything is dampened and rendered shapeless by disillusionment. If *The Ebb Tide* were all that Stevenson had written in the South Seas, it might be taken as a testimony to the wisdom of Will o' the Mill's stoic decision to stay home and dream about the active life.

While the mood of one novel cannot be regarded as the full reflection of Stevenson's state of mind in this period, it is an indication of an increasing pessimism and, what is more important, a willingness or necessity to deal in fictional terms with that pessimism. Stevenson's reaction to the South Seas is obviously not the single cause of his disenchantment. Nor is it by itself significant except as the most concrete and easily described factor in a gradual process of maturation through preconception, observation, disappointment, and reformulation.

What Stevenson found in the tropics was his same old self, a bit hardier physically, but still subject to fever, insomnia, neurasthenia; still wishing he were somewhere else, still wishing he were writing better books, or not writing books at all, but building lighthouses, commanding armies, or tending sheep.[9] And all around him he found men in the South Seas very much as he had left them in Edinburgh, Davos, Braemar, and Monterey—no healthier or cleaner or happier. If anything, they were less orderly, less powerful, less able to cope with the hardships of existence than the members of the civilization he had left behind.

When one recalls the boyish eagerness with which Stevenson looked forward to the health, simplicity, and natural morality of the Pacific islands it is not surprising that he was profoundly disillusioned, almost staggered, by his first-hand sight of leprosy, influenza, and smallpox; appalled by the realities of cannibalism, devil worship, fetishism, sexual license; and revolted by the natural phenomenon of life feeding upon life in the very coral rock which supported him. Stevenson's earliest recorded reference to the South Seas is in a letter to Mrs. Sitwell, dated June 1875. His family had been visited by the former Secretary to the Customs and Marine Department of New Zealand, who spent considerable time "telling us all about the South Sea Islands till I was sick with desire to go there; beautiful places, green forever; perfect climate; perfect shapes of men and women, with red flowers in their hair; and nothing to do but to study oratory and etiquette, sit in the sun, and pick up the fruits as they fall. Navigator's Island is the place; absolute balm for the weary" (*Letters,* I, 218).

It should be noted that, like many commentators on the Pacific, Stevenson placed heavy blame for corruption and hardship on white settlers. He was well aware, for example, that several deadly and contagious diseases had been introduced to the islands by colonials, free-traders, and missionaries; that, because of them, whole village populations were threatened with extinction. *A Footnote to History,* or *Eight Years of Trouble in Samoa,* is his most detailed protest against white exploitation of the islanders. But it is important to see that he quickly disabused himself of the oversimplified notion of a totally harmful civilization tainting a native Eden. He devoted much of his time in the South Seas to defending Christian missionaries and government officials as well as the rights of the island populace. His "Open Letter to the Reverend Dr. Hyde of Honolulu," in defense of Father Damien, the Catholic missionary to the lepers of Molokai, is the most famous and passionate of his testimonies on behalf of Christian missions in the Pacific.

If he was shocked by the destructive aspects of Western colonization, he was equally conscious of and horrified by the indigenous miseries and ugliness of native life. In the Marquesas he is sickened by the sight of a cannibal feasting place, and the thought of the chiefs coming away from it "heavy with their beastly food."

> There are certain sentiments which we call emphatically human—denying the honour of that name to those who lack them. In such feasts—particularly where the victim had been slain at home, and men banqueted on . . . a comrade with whom they had played in infancy, or a woman whose favours they had shared—the whole body of these sentiments is outraged. To consider it too closely is to understand, if not to excuse, these fervours of self-righteous old ship-captains, who would man their guns, and open fire in passing, on a cannibal island.[10]

In the Paumotus he is disgusted and overwhelmed by the thought that in the most innocent and apparently inanimate matter, the blind and relentless life process of growth and disintegration is being carried on:

> It adds a last touch of horror to the thought of this precarious annular gangway in the sea, that even what there is of it is not of honest rock, but organic, part alive, part putrescent; even the clean sea and the bright fish about it poisoned, the most stubborn boulder burrowed in by worms, the lightest dust venomous as an apothecary's drugs. (XIX, 170)

And finally, on the Gilbert Islands, the same Stevenson who had once damned the superficiality of a civilization which did not touch the natural man, the "trunk and taproot of the race," has seen the "noble savage" for himself and awakened from his Romantic dream:

> Crime, pestilence, and death are in the day's work; the imagination readily accepts them. It instinctively rejects, on the contrary, whatever shall call up the image of our race upon its lowest terms, as the partner of beasts, beastly itself, dwelling pell-mell and hugger-mugger, hairy man with hairy woman in the caves of old. (XIX, 258)

Even in his disillusionment Stevenson retained a real affection for the islands, but it is an affection derived from sympathy and understanding rather than from wish fulfillment. There is poverty and a cold wind on the beach of Tahiti where *The Ebb Tide* opens. The exotic veneer of the tropics has worn thin just as it has for the other stock ingredients of this potentially commonplace adventure story. The three renegades from society, the hijacking of a ship, the storm at sea, even the discovery of a mysterious island, seem almost deliberately to have been turned sour by Stevenson.

What Herrick discovers on the mysterious island is so

familiar and real as to be almost dazzling in its combined power to enchant and revolt in the midst of a tale littered with the fragments of cardboard characters and broken images of the South Seas left over from a romantic vision of faraway places. What is discovered on the island is something like a whole man, admirable, almost majestic, but with blackness rooted to his soul like the eye in his socket. It is a vision of man which both Herrick and Stevenson had been trying to run away from. Insofar as he permits his protagonist to face it, Stevenson may be said to have run head-on into it himself. Finally strong, curious, and mature enough to stare hard at what he had averted his eyes from in his father, his friends, and himself, he personifies evil, not as a grotesque aberration, as in Mr. Hyde, nor as a temporary failure of vision, as in Deacon Brodie, nor as a glamorous vice, as in the Master of Ballantrae, but as an integral part of the human organism. Attwater may seem more vicious than the other three characters in *The Ebb Tide,* but it is primarily because he is larger than they in all ways. None of the four central figures of the novel avoids the taint of cowardice, envy, and potential depravity.

That Stevenson reached a conclusion naturally and empirically which his church had taught with the authority of revelation does not mean he underwent, at this late date, a religious reconversion. Still, Attwater is both an example and a minister of the doctrine of original sin, and as such he comes as close as any character created by Stevenson to symbolizing the wrathful God projected to him as a boy through and by his father and his mid-Victorian Edinburgh environment. "[Attwater] knows all," says Herrick. "He sees through all. We only make him laugh with our pretenses—he looks at us, and laughs like God." It is an idea of a deity marked, like his own creation, by a fascination with sin, a love of vengeance, and a knowledge of evil.

When Herrick crawls from the sea, in which he had intended to drown himself, and places himself at the disposal of Attwater, his language is not unlike that of one emerging from a joyless baptism into a new life:

> "I have nothing left that I believe in, except my living horror of myself. Why do I come to you? I don't know. You are cold, cruel, hateful; and I hate you, or I think I hate you. But . . . I put myself helpless in your hands. What must I do? If I can't do anything, be merciful . . ."
> (XI, 370)

Herrick's consignment of his destiny to Attwater is hardly cheerful, yet it does have an intensity and an inevitability which give it a suggestive power beyond that merely of the weak character yielding to the strong. If Herrick abdicates his will to Attwater, without really accepting his evangelical doctrines, he does so because he has lost faith in everything else. He had been lured to the Pacific originally in the hope that there the air would blow cleaner, that he might change his name (which he does), and eradicate his past, his conscience, and his weakness (which he does not). When he comes dripping from the sea and a close encounter with suicide, his false dreams have been washed away. His baptism is incomplete, however. It may have succeeded in removing old illusions, but Herrick is left barren rather than purified for a new faith.

On his first visit to Attwater he had passed the figurehead of an old sailing ship installed at the pier's end, and had thought of it as a goddess in some outworn religion in which he can no longer believe:

> She seemed a defiant deity from the island, coming forth to its threshold with a rush as of one about to fly, and perpetuated in that dashing attitude. Herrick looked up at her . . . with singular feelings of curiosity and romance . . . So long she had been the blind conductress of a ship among the waves; so long she had stood here idle in the violent sun . . . and was even this the end of so many adventures, he wondered, or was more behind? And he could have found it in his heart to regret that she was not a goddess, nor yet he a pagan, that he might have bowed down before her in that hour of difficulty. (XI, 329)

This divinity, this emblem of high adventure, retains some of her former appeal, but she is a fallen and powerless deity. It seems no coincidence that Huish, the one member of the crew who retains his faith in the goddess of adventure and chance, is destroyed by his own credulity. On his way to murder Attwater, "the clerk turned . . . toward the figure-head, as though he were about to address to it his devotions." In a matter of minutes he lies dead on the beach. The wooden deity has proved incapable of rewarding his momentary homage.

There is no need to turn Herrick into Stevenson to see that the author shares with his shabby hero a general disillusionment with the efficacy of open-air adventure in distant lands as a healthy, heroic, or even interesting way of life. Foreign travel has not finally proved to be a very successful means of escape. If anything, it makes one even more aware of human folly by eliminating some of the defenses of habit.

That the fictional expression of this disenchantment should be in covert (and occasionally obvious) religious terminology is not surprising if we remember that Stevenson had carefully constructed an elaborate, if somewhat fragile, morality of optimism largely in reaction against the severities of Victorian society and the repressive traditions of the Scottish Church. Among the islands of the South Seas, save in various trading and missionary centers, neither Christianity nor the nineteenth century could be wholly blamed for social abuses, devil-worship, and a proscriptive ethic. The old standards, which he had so long regarded as the errors of the opposition, began to look like distasteful particles of a larger truth than he had cared to imagine.

It is a mark of the quality and depth of Stevenson's love for Samoa that it did not remain for long that of a foreign traveler in search of the picturesque. He found during his years in the Pacific, with its superstition, taboos, fear of death, envy, pride, lust, petty contentions, that the whole range of human wretchedness and human folly is neither the peculiar product nor the peculiar property of an anglicized Christian civilization in the nineteenth century, but perhaps the perennial and universal condition of man.

A few months before Stevenson died, S. R. Lysaght, a friend of George Meredith's, visited Samoa and later recorded a conversation with Stevenson which reflects this change in attitude:

> In a conversation on his own writings I alluded, perhaps injudiciously, to a fear expressed by George Meredith that his banishment from the great world of men, his inability to keep in touch with the social development of the time, might be a disadvantage to his work. He showed in reply an unexpected warmth which suggested that he really felt the burden of his exile but refused to admit it. "It is all the better for a man's work if he wants it to be good and not merely popular," he said, "to be removed from these London influences. Human nature is always the same,

and you see and understand it better when you are standing outside the crowd."[11]

Aside from revealing the tactlessness of Meredith's friend and Stevenson's deep longing for home, the incident shows an important change in Stevenson's idea of human nature. By 1894, from the distant perspective of Vailima, he was beginning to see the religion and society in which he was raised not as a unique and perverse inversion of the natural law, but as all too accurate a reflection of it.

In a Blakean poem called "The Woodman" Stevenson uses the Samoan forest as a symbol of nature, infected, in all its variety, with the need to destroy in order to survive:

> For in the groins of branches, lo!
> The cancers of the orchid grow.
> . . . The rose on roses feeds; the lark
> On larks. The sedentary clerk
> All morning with a diligent pen
> Murders the babes of other men;
> And like the beasts of wood and park,
> Protects his whelps, defends his den.[12]

This may be second-hand Darwinism and sing-song poetry; but it is also an assertion nurtured in experience and a ditty sung in a very different key from the travel lyric of parrot islands "where the golden apples grow."

✵ ✵ ✵ ✵ ✵ ✵ ✵

In the highest achievements of the art of words, the dramatic and the pictorial, the moral and romantic interest, rise and fall together by a common and organic law. Situation is animated with passion, passion clothed upon with situation. Neither exists for itself, but each inheres indissolubly with the other. This is high art; and not only the highest art possible in words, but the highest art of all, since it combines the greatest mass and diversity of the elements of truth and pleasure. Such are epics, and the few prose tales that have the epic weight.

—*A Gossip on Romance*

✵ ✵ ✵ ✵ ✵ ✵ ✵

V

ADVENTURE AS MODERN EPIC

* * * * * * *

Stevenson's peculiar position in the late eighties and the early nineties is that of the voluntary exile thoroughly saturated by the modes of thought, the rhythms of speech, and the habits of invention of the homeland, yet profoundly convinced that the possibilities of heroic and creative achievement lie outside it. The move to Samoa, though it was brought about primarily by considerations of health, disturbed his conscience because it seemed to bear out the accusations that, having spent a Frenchified youth, married an American wife, and lived much of his early middle age in England, he was not as faithful to Scotland as he might have been.

Still guilty in America and Vailima about his youthful estrangement from his father and his rejection of the Scottish Church and, at the same time, suffering from a genuine sickness for home (a chronic ailment with Stevenson), he faced himself in 1887 and again in 1893 with the task of writing a fictional valediction to Scotland. Among his motives must surely have been the hope that he might resolve his personal concept of "renegade" heroism with a conscience still pricked by the sterner communal virtues of loyalty, obedience, and perseverance.

Stevenson's two most serious and moving works of fiction are Scottish novels written out of Scotland. *The Master of Ballantrae* and *Weir of Hermiston* both involve protagonists who achieve a kind of heroic stature through an almost demonic refusal to submit, which at once sets them above family and state while it identifies them with the national spirit of recalcitrance. Still, there is no epic struggle because Ballantrae and Hermiston are born into a world populated by "small" people—simpering, pious, effeminate members of a watered-down race, unwilling and unable to stand up to them with the physical and emotional force they demand. With a puny opposition, all the old heroic virtues dwindle into cowardice and vice. Bravery turns to recklessness, strength to brutality, perseverance to inflexibility, and justice to persecution. In each book the protagonist seems a throwback from an older, more heroic time, who by an accident of birth has been cast into a tribe of pygmies which provides no natural outlet for his extraordinary potential. Instead, its little members taint and corrupt his ancient virility with their own meanness.

Ballantrae and Hermiston are of the darkly masculine race of nineteenth-century demon-heroes: Manfred, Melmoth, Rochester, perhaps Michael Henchard, but, above all, Heathcliff. When Catherine shouts at Linton, "Heathcliff would as soon lift a finger at you as the king would march his army against a colony of mice," she articulates the outrage of all power frustrated by frailty. Heathcliff has aptly been called the id personified, but the sexual emphasis should not obscure the symbolic relevance of this character type to an artistic anxiety which was felt with particular acuteness in the nineteenth century. To have a large imagination—or large imaginative ambition—without comparable energy or cultural conditions which permit its full expression is to dwell apprehensively with the impossible.

In both novels Stevenson presents a myth of a lost giant in an uncongenial world. It is a symbolic predicament which fuses his private feelings about himself and his family and the artist in a bourgeois society with the national dilemma of Highland Tory versus Lowland Whig and a rude, rural Scotland versus a cultivated, industrialized England. The point in common among the rebellious son, the artist, the Jacobite, and the nationalistic Scot is that, gigantic though their wills may be, they, like Gulliver in Lilliput, are frustrated and made monstrous by the predominance of littleness around them. The myth has universal implications as well as personal and national ones. The ancient hero, turned villain by the strange society into which he has been born, is also the natural man at ease with his own instincts, as opposed to the civilized man who has dulled his capacity to love along with his ability to hate. Stevenson treats sexuality in these novels with a directness and seriousness we do not find elsewhere in his writing. It generally serves as a symbol of wholeness, an indication of the degree to which psychological, physical, and spiritual resources are in balance.

The two books dramatize and epitomize what might be called epic-envy. In them we find traces of the romantic nostalgia of Scott and hints of the mythic reformulation and mock-heroics of Joyce. But essentially they represent a characteristically literal-minded attempt on Stevenson's part to re-create a barely civilized warrior out of Homer and to thrust him under the polite nose of the nineteenth century.

In describing the genesis of *The Master of Ballantrae,* Stevenson admits to having been inspired by Captain Marryat's *The Phantom Ship:*[1]

> "Come," said I to my engine, "let us make a tale, a story of many years and countries, of the sea and the land, savagery, and civilisation; a story that shall have the

> same large features, and may be treated in the same summary elliptic method as the book you have been reading and admiring" . . . I saw that Marryat, not less than Homer, Milton, and Virgil, profited by the choice of a familiar and legendary subject.[2]

He goes on to describe how he decided to weave familiar legends into his story, and concludes that for the protagonist "I had to create a kind of evil genius."

James, the young Master of Ballantrae, is usually seen by the reader at one remove—a large and obscure figure, imperfectly described, full of contradictions, set apart from the ordinary and more clearly perceived characters. He is never shown, as the other members of the household are, performing commonplace domestic tasks. As we hear of Heathcliff largely from Nelly Dean, Ballantrae is presented from the beginning through the eyes of Mackellar, the prudent family servant, who hates him and regards him as a practicer of "black dissimulation," a man both "popular and wild." We are told that he "sat late at wine, later at the cards; had a name in the country of 'an unco man for the lasses.'"

Tempted to discount Mackellar's prudery, we may at first take Ballantrae's "blackness" as roguishness in the glamorous Jacobite tradition of Alan Breck. But there are early hints of a cold and mechanical relentlessness which jar that simple convention. "He had always vaunted himself quite implacable, and was taken at his word; so that he had the addition among his neighbours of 'an ill man to cross.'" And later when Mackellar begs him to turn back from the path on the way to the house he has come to disrupt, he answers coldly, "You waste your breath on me . . . I go my own way with inevitable motion."

The reader's vision of Ballantrae is so distorted by Mackellar's puritanical prejudices, which themselves are obscured by gossip and legend, that he seems large partly by virtue of the variety of incongruous things which may be said of him. Much of Mackellar's commentary reflects the local consensus rather than direct observation, and is regularly interspersed with "He had the name in the country of . . ." or he "enhanced his reputation [by] . . ." The most damning evidence against the Master is hearsay that is never fully explained.

Occasionally, something like a clear visual image of Ballantrae burns for an instant through country legend and the subjective encrustations of Mackellar. When he returns to Durrisdeer after his first absence, he has been rowed across the bay in a small boat. The sun has already set, but he is observed from a distance by Mackellar:

> . . . standing alone upon the point of a rock, a tall slender figure of a gentleman, habited in black, with a sword by his side and a walking cane upon his wrist.

He is conceived of as a Byronic monument, tall and motionless, on the point of a rock. But as the mists fall away from him he is no less impressive:

> . . . a very handsome figure and countenance, swarthy, lean, long, with a quick, alert, black look, as of one who was a fighter and accustomed to command; upon one cheek he had a mole, not unbecoming; a large diamond sparkled on his hand; his clothes although of the one hue, were of a French and foppish design . . . and I wondered the more to see him in such guise, when he was but newly landed from a dirty smuggling lugger. At the same time he had a better look at me, toised me a second time sharply, and then smiled. (IX, 88-89)

The Master comes as a political and domestic enemy, a black devil who materializes cool and mysteriously well groomed out of the filth of an outlaw's barge. He is also a smiling and attractive rogue, complete with beauty mark, whose "lean, long" virility is reinforced by a small battery of masculine images. (After publication, Stevenson complained that the illustrator had not captured the Master properly at all: "Mine had a more slender body, a larger, a finer and darker countenance . . . more of the fairy prince, and more of Satan; and the black mole on his cheek [I could not tell you why] was an essential part of him.")[3] Ballantrae's identity is further enlarged and simultaneously disparaged through a comparison with the swarthy Esau, home from the hunt to claim his rights of inheritance from a mild but usurping younger brother.

The novel, which Henry James called "a pure hard crystal . . . a work of ineffable and exquisite art,"[4] opens in 1745 when word has reached the House of Durrisdeer that Prince Charlie has landed. The family consists of the head of the House, the old Lord Durrisdeer; his two sons, James, Master of Ballantrae, the wild and romantic first-born, and Henry, his colorless younger brother; and Alison Graeme, a "near kinswoman, an orphan, and the heir to a considerable fortune" who is betrothed to James. It is decided that one son should go "forth to strike a blow for King James . . . and the other stay at home to keep in favour with King George." Henry tries to persuade his older brother to remain at Durrisdeer since he is his father's heir and favorite. " 'Ay?' said the Master. 'And there spoke Envy! Would you trip up my heels—Jacob?' . . . and he swelled upon the name maliciously." The adventurous Ballantrae, of course, rides to join Prince Charlie, leaving his father, his fiancée, and his younger brother behind. In a matter of days, the rumor spreads that the Master has been killed in the field, betrayed by Henry, who neglected to send him reinforcements. The Master's death becomes a legend of heroic martyrdom and Henry's reputation is permanently tainted:

"'Ay, weel,'" says one of the neighboring rustics of Henry, "'he has his way o 't; he's to be my lord, nae less, and there's mony a cauld corp amang the Hieland heather!'" The fact is that Henry does become lord of the estate, does receive his old father's blessing, and does marry his brother's betrothed, so that when Ballantrae returns alive and well from France, he has reason to call his brother "Jacob the usurper." One night over a game of cards the Master insinuates his rightful claim to Henry's estate, wife, and the affection if not the paternity of his child: "For instance, with all those solid qualities which I delight to recognize in you, I never knew a woman who did not prefer me" (IX, 118).

The accuracy of the insult provokes Henry into striking Ballantrae across the mouth. A duel follows in which the Master is wounded. Henry, though not touched, at once falls into a nearly fatal fever (later described as a stroke), and the presumably dead body of Ballantrae disappears from the ground where it had fallen. The Master, of course, is not dead, but has been carried away by free-traders and is nursed back to perfect health.

Henry, on the contrary, never recovers the solidity of his former self, but turns into a slightly bewildered boy. "Something of the child he exhibited . . . and turned to [his wife] like a child to its mother." His terrifyingly direct confrontation with the anger of his brother has, as it were, seared out of him what slight capacity he ever had to deal with a positive threat. Mackellar's comment on the way in which Henry had "drifted from his character" is significant in view of the sorts of essays and adventure stories Stevenson had written over the past ten years:

> A great part of life consists in contemplating what we cannot cure; but Mr. Henry, if he could not dismiss solici-

> tude by an effort of the mind, must instantly and at whatever cost annihilate the cause of it; so that he played alternately the ostrich and the bull. It is to this strenuous cowardice of pain that I have to set down all the unfortunate and excessive steps of his subsequent career. (IX, 151)

It is difficult to conceive of Stevenson in 1888 writing this last sentence without being aware of its applicability to his life as an artist and moralist. In *The Master of Ballantrae,* as in nearly everything else he wrote, Stevenson is thinking of himself. And he seems, in fictional terms, to be expressing concern for the "unfortunate and excessive steps" of his own earlier "career." He heaps the petty virtues of his public personality on the inactive, sickly, and child-like Henry Durie. And he projects the "high-flying vices" of an unrealized self into the indomitable, virile, and satanic Master. After finishing ninety-two pages of the first draft, he wrote to Colvin in 1887 that "the Master is all I know of the devil. I have known hints of him in the world, but always cowards; he is as bold as a lion, but with deadly, causeless duplicity" (*Letters,* III, 43).

But in a manuscript not published until 1960, Stevenson admits quite freely that he identifies himself with his diabolical hero:

> For the Master I had no original, which is perhaps another way of confessing that the original was no other than myself. We have all a certain attitude toward our own character and part in life; we desire more or less identity between the essence and the seeming . . . and the secret of the Master is principally this, that he is indifferent to that problem. A live man, a full man, in every other part a human man, he has this one element of inhumanity.[5]

Once again, as in *New Arabian Nights,* and much of

the correspondence, Stevenson casts doubt on his own integrity. For him, it would seem, the heart of devilry is not pride or envy or wrath, but duality. What, after all, are the sins of the Master? He drinks and wenches, flirts with his brother's wife, and haunts him for money, but these are hardly the enormities to inspire a Dante or a Milton. Even on his adventures at sea and in India, where he is known to have looted with pirates and run through an occasional renegade, it is difficult against a background of the villains of Dumas, Hugo, and Scott to regard him as Lucifer personified. What elevates him to a superhuman demonic stature is not so much the nature of his crimes, which are conventional when they are not petty, but his unholy ability to flourish and thrive on them.

The image of Ballantrae arising immaculate out of the filthy smuggler's lugger sets the incongruous pattern of his black majesty. While all the drab, virtuous characters grow drabber, weaker, and homelier, the Master seems to increase in beauty and strength. When he returns to Durrisdeer after nearly twenty years' absence, Mackellar comments on the aging which was visible in every member of the family:

> The hand of time was very legible on all . . . and what affected me still more, it was the wicked man that bore his years the handsomest . . . [He] still bore himself erect, although perhaps with effort; his brow barred about the center with imperious lines, his mouth set as for command. He had all the gravity and something of the splendor of Satan in "Paradise Lost." I could not help but see the man with admiration, and was only surprised that I saw him with so little fear. (IX, 180)

Stevenson, like his puritanical narrator Mackellar, had been raised to believe that evil may often appear in a superficially attractive guise. The Calvinist mentality at its extreme regarded physical beauty and ornamentation so suspiciously that plainness and dullness became marks of virtue. In his early and impetuous break from the Church, Stevenson committed the common excess of youth and thought that to invert was to correct. Falling for a time into general agreement with the aesthetes, he believed that surface beauty in art or nature was its own virtue. He diverged almost at once, however, by constructing an optimistic morality in which health, good humor, a clear mind, and a cheerful countenance, all signify goodness. Yet in *The Master of Ballantrae* we find vigor, wit, and even a kind of good nature in the character compared with Milton's Satan and referred to by Stevenson as "all I know of the devil."

2

It becomes clear that what Stevenson knew of the devil (and of himself) had undergone considerable change in the period since *Virginibus Puerisque* and *Treasure Island.* In the boys' adventures as well as in the Gothic tales Stevenson devoted himself to disproving the devil by letting his characters have a few scares in the dark and then turning on the lights and saying, "It's only jolly John Silver, or sickly Uncle Ebenezer, or luminous paint on papier-mâché. If you stamp your foot at them, they'll go away." The situation in *The Master of Ballantrae* is quite the reverse. Henry faces his satanic brother in a duel and is left a stunted child. Mackellar attempts, without success, to push Ballantrae overboard in mid-Atlantic, and falls upon the ship's deck "overcome with terror and remorse and shame." Even Teach, the pirate captain, is reduced to a "frightened baby" by the Master's wrath:

> Teach . . . gave a barbarous howl, and swung his dirk

> to fling it, an art in which (like many seamen) he was very expert . . . "Go down to your cabin," cries Ballantrae, "and come on deck again when you are sober. Do you think we are going to hang for you, you black-faced, half-witted, drunken brute and butcher? Go down!" And he stamped his foot at him with such a sudden smartness that Teach fairly ran for it to the companion. (IX, 45)

Not since Jim Hawkins' reckless outbursts against Long John Silver has Stevenson given us a character whose invective, whose very being, renders the other inhabitants of his world ridiculous and powerless. Ballantrae's threat is effective not only against stock villains like Teach, but against the consistent innocence of his brother and the loyalty of Henry's servant, Mackellar. Stevenson has created a character who is neither pure hero nor pure villain, changeable, complex, imperfectly perceived (because he is too much like a human being to be perceived in any "total" way). And he has turned him loose in a fictional world populated by the rigid and simple constructs of Puritan allegory (Henry Durie as Long-suffering Innocence, Mackellar as Loyal Obedience) and its amoral counterpart, boy's adventure (Teach as Pirate Villain, Secundra Drass as Black Magician).

Mackellar probably comes closer than any of the other relatively simple characters to understanding Ballantrae's complexity. His descriptions of the Master become more and more involved as the plot progresses, until, during the voyage to America, his persistent attempts to redefine what Ballantrae is, though still couched in rigid terms, suggest important questions regarding the nature of human dualism:

> This outer sensibility and inner toughness set me against him; it seemed of a piece with that impudent grossness which I knew to underlie the veneer of his fine manners;

> and sometimes my gorge rose against him as though he were deformed—and sometimes I would draw away as though from something partly spectral. I had moments when I thought of him as a man of pasteboard—as though, if one should strike smartly through the buckram of his countenance, there would be found a mere vacuity within. (IX, 203-204)

Mackellar's effort to describe Ballantrae is like an inadequate attempt to catalogue a new species; it reflects the frustration of an orderly mind confronted with the unreasonable fact of a natural phenomenon. He may suspect, even hope, that the monstrous and fascinating countenance before him is a pasteboard front covering a "mere" and harmless vacuum, but the working out of the narrative hardly substantiates so tidy a vision. If anything, Henry, Mackellar, and the pirate Teach prove to be the "hollow men"—flimsy characters who collapse physically and morally in the presence of Ballantrae.

He defeats them with his doubleness. Henry he flatters in public and humiliates in private; Teach he pretends to humor and obey, and then in an instant overthrows him and loots his ship; even Mackellar is charmed and betrayed during his sea voyage with the Master. We have come upon dualism before in Stevenson—in fact, in almost every major work of fiction he produced. Probably no single story of his is better known than *Strange Case of Dr. Jekyll and Mr. Hyde.* That tale provoked sermons in the year of its publication from the pulpits of Protestant churches all over Scotland and England (including St. Paul's Cathedral, London). In 1894 Joseph Jacobs wrote that "it stands beside *The Pilgrim's Progress* and *Gulliver's Travels* as one of the three great allegories in English."[6]

It is undeniable that a good case can be made for the

story as a study of man's psyche or soul, but the emphasis in narration and tone is on gruesome effect rather than on motivation. Stevenson's tale had no serious implications at all until his wife made him rewrite it and add a "moral dimension." And even then he referred to it unpretentiously as a "Gothic gnome." Andrew Lang wrote in his "Recollections of Robert Louis Stevenson" that "the story won its great success partly by dint of the moral (whatever that may be), more by its terrible, lucid, visionary power. I remember Mr. Stevenson telling me, at this time, that he was doing some 'regular crawlers,' for this purist had a boyish habit of slang, and I *think* it was he who called Julius Caesar 'the howlingest cheese who ever lived.'"[7]

In *Jekyll and Hyde,* as in *Thrawn Janet* and *The Merry Men,* Stevenson probes the Calvinist tradition of personified evil largely for Gothic effect. Much as he came to despise the moral rigidity of his religious heritage, he remained throughout his life enchanted by its atmosphere —the damp chapels and bleak kirk-yards, the dour believers, the darkness and devilry. His picturesque "use" of the severities and superstition of Presbyterianism reminds us at first of Scott's Waverley Novels. But his attitude as a young artist toward Calvinism resembles even more closely that of some pre-Raphaelites and aesthetes toward Roman Catholicism. Walter Pater hardly cared for orthodox Christian theology as long as, figuratively, he had vestments to finger and incense to sniff.

Although Stevenson's religious aestheticism seems less decadent because Presbyterianism is not sensuous and ornate, his attitude is nonetheless strikingly like that of many of his contemporaries toward the early Church. His devils and witches, like Rossetti's drawings of angels and saints, are toys. We are charmed and amused to watch him play with them. In the best of his Gothic tales we feel some pity and a good deal of fear. But the morality, like the political ethics in *Kidnapped,* remains curiously irrelevant.

The concern with duality persists in *The Master of Ballantrae,* but in an almost entirely different way from that of *Jekyll and Hyde* with its "mad scientist" and chemical powders. In the first place, both the pure Calvinistic ideal and its reverse, the totally black outlaw, are rejected as undesirable, ineffectual human types even if they could exist on earth. Henry Durie is an obedient son, a patient and forgiving man without malice or pride. Stevenson has given him a number of Christian virtues and a large capacity for suffering. Mackellar describes him near the end of the book as

> a maimed soldier . . . A kind man, I remembered him; wise, with a decent pride, a son perhaps too dutiful, a husband only too loving, one that could suffer and be silent, one whose hand I loved to press . . . "O God . . . he did no wrong, or not till he was broke with sorrows; these are but his honourable wounds that we begin to shrink from. O cover them up, O take him away, before we hate him!" (IX, 283-284)

But in spite of his Christ-like agony, Henry cannot redeem himself. Instead it is the arch-enemy, his brother, three times risen from the grave, who seems to possess the power of resurrection and renewal. "Nothing can kill that man," groans Henry. "He is not mortal." Henry cannot save himself in this world nor in the next because his mild and defensive virtues cannot protect him from his brother's torments nor the taint of family corruption. Henry's scrupulosity, his charity, and his humility all turn out to be part of a pointless self-sacrifice, a voluntary and grotesque crucifixion without meaning. "He stood on all hands without affection or support, dear, generous, ill-fated, noble heart." Yet, despite these words, it is one of the unsentimental peculiarities of this novel that Henry's martyrdom grows increasingly barren, monotonous, and unmanly. His acceptance of affliction becomes mechanical until the sympathy of the loyal narrator (and the reader) inevitably flags.

Teach, the pirate captain, is from another world altogether, but his simplicity and single-mindedness make him as vulnerable and ineffectual in his own way as Henry is in his. He is first seen stamping about the deck of his ship "raving and crying out that his name was Satan and his ship was called Hell." But Teach, though he is capable of doing a great deal of harm, is eventually defeated by the very naiveté of his idea of what it is to be evil. "There was something about him like a wicked child or a half-witted person." Teach cannot attain truly diabolical proportions any more than Henry can give more than a pale imitation of Christ, because neither *knows* what he is doing. They are like children wearing a costume out of duty, out of habit, or out of fun, without understanding what it means. Henry's duel with Ballantrae is a diminutive and melodramatic fray in comparison with an epic encounter like the one between Paris and Menelaus, which it resembles in some superficial respects. Its cause also is an uncertain wife and an interloper who is spirited away before he can be killed, but in the novel most attempts at heroic or demonic grandeur flounder at the edge of masquerade.

Though there is inevitably an element of mock-heroics whenever an author allows his characters to attempt to assume roles too large for them, Stevenson's treatment of Teach is not primarily ironic. We find little that reminds us of Swift's satire of a miniscule Dryden encumbered by a vast Virgilian helmet. Instead, the whole process of assuming power by a symbolic association with a coherent mythic tradition (as, for example, Achilles' armor, Jason's golden fleece, King Arthur's sword Excalibur) breaks down to the point where the emblem is no less absurd than the person bearing it. To put on a "magic" cloak in an age without a common sense of the supernatural, and then to behave as though it had some sort of special power, is either childish play or outright insanity. When Teach dons his cheap disguise and goes about terrorizing the crew, he is at the same time a comic buffoon, and a grotesque and maniacal creature who, for the moment, believes in the complete invulnerability of his mask.

> Presently he comes on deck, a perfect figure of fun, his face blacked, his hair and whiskers curled, his belt stuck full of pistols; chewing bits of glass so that the blood ran down his chin, and brandishing a dirk. I do not know if he had taken these manners from the Indians of America, where he was a native; but such was his way, and would always thus announce that he was wound up to horrid deeds. The first that came near him was . . . stabbed to the heart . . . and then [he] capered about the body, raving and swearing and daring us to come on. It was the silliest exhibition; and yet dangerous too, for the cowardly fellow was plainly working himself up to another murder. (IX, 45)

Teach is not "all there," and he is quite accurately described, during his wild cavorting, as a child or a half-wit. But Henry Durie, without benefit of black-face or broken glass, is similarly described as child-like and unsound of mind after his recovery from the sickness following the duel with Ballantrae:

> Some of the heat of the fever lingered in his veins: his movements a little hurried, his speech notably more

> voluble, yet neither truly amiss. His whole mind stood open to happy impressions . . . but the smallest suggestion of trouble or sorrow he received with visible impatience and dismissed again with visible relief. It was to this temper that he owed the felicity of his later days; and yet here it was, if anywhere, that you could call the man insane. (IX, 151)

Both Henry and Teach, though at opposite poles, are partial men, stunted, underdeveloped, like children, or invalids, or madmen. Their flaw, once the singular virtue of Stevenson's boyish Romantic heroes, is lack of wholeness. The curious thing is that for the first time Stevenson has exposed his simple characters to a world more complex than they are, not only one which they cannot control, but one in which they cannot survive. Both Henry and Teach suffer total humiliation and defeat because they have defined their universe according to orderly systems of observable cause and effect which Ballantrae consistently disrupts and ultimately destroys.

Henry's system is more or less a rational Protestant one in which temperance, patience, and charity should bring about peace in this world and a just reward in the next. On the contrary, his long-suffering only increases as the years progress, until he has finally exposed his entire family to financial ruin and exile, and he himself dies of fright, a drunkard and a coward. His obedient adherence to a kind of negative and tepid version of Christian endurance has been disastrous. Instead of enlarging his perception of truth (and himself with it), it has falsified and diminished it to a degree where he is unable to cope with life at all. (It ought to be noted that Henry's problems are not exclusively with his older brother. He is not favored by his father; he proves a listless and childish husband to his wife; and he is regarded by most of his tenants and servants, save Mackellar, as a weakling and a bore.)

Stevenson by no means places all the blame on rationalism or Christianity. After he recovers from the fever, Henry's narrowness is not so much ethical or reasonable as it is defensively therapeutic and selfish. It reminds us of Stevenson's own sentimental optimism in the late seventies and early eighties. Henry "stood open to happy impressions . . . but [dismissed] the smallest suggestion of trouble or sorrow." It is a form of insanity, the narrator warns us, and Stevenson, in the working out of the tale, does nothing to contradict him. What is certain in the terms of this novel is that to restrict one's vision deliberately is unheroic, unnatural, and, at its worst extreme, self-destructive.

In this sense Teach is not so different from Henry. By permitting himself total license and fulfilling all the random urges of his animal nature, he, too, cuts out something of the man. The loss of his human identity is manifested by the painted face and his reversion to the savage. He becomes ridiculous and grotesque, a mechanical marionette dancing to a tune even more formalized, predictable, and monotonous than the one to which Henry Durie responds. Teach's doctrine is disobedience, intemperance, and abdication of reason. He is a caricature of the antithesis of Scottish Puritanism that Stevenson had treated so much more sympathetically in Long John Silver and various disreputable characters of *New Arabian Nights.* Stevenson seems, in a way, to be disparaging his own tendency to oversimplification of personality. What is most surprising is the way in which he chooses to do it: to write a novel populated by characters of varying degrees of simple-mindedness and rigidity—from a fairly dreary puritanical hero to a comic-strip pirate—and to ridicule, terrorize, and demolish them with something like a flesh-and-blood man who has the courage of his own duality.

This imbalance among the characters is finally what prevents Ballantrae from being a heroic figure or the novel from getting any further than the outskirts of epic. The split in the family, particularly since it follows Jacobite and Whig divisions and involves a fraternal rivalry which is compared with that of Jacob and Esau, sets up an expectation of national drama which is never fulfilled. A reason for this, of course, may be the historical one which would have been obvious to Stevenson in 1888. Scotland, for all the scattered instances of strife and bravery throughout her past, was destined to settle into a state of relative tranquility. Her internal enmities were not so much resolved as attenuated, exhausted, and finally made to look inconsequential beside those of the gigantic empires growing around her. Whatever epic ambitions Stevenson may have had in writing *The Master of Ballantrae* were seriously dampened by the historical actualities of Scotland's modest destiny. It is a novel of a heroic urge which has been disappointed and unfulfilled except as an incoherent and fragmentary dream of what might have been.

As the novel progresses the national and historical overtones assume less and less importance while the psychology of evil becomes the central focus of the narrative. A view of nature which previously had not been permitted by Stevenson to enter into his art or into his optimistic morality has intruded on a stage neatly set for what easily could have been a simple and straightforward romance. The externals of historical romance—the Jacobite uprising of '45, the plundering of the ships along the Scottish coast, the Master's wanderings in India—remain more or less peripheral concerns until the last seventy pages, when a long and melodramatic chase through the American woods takes narrative precedence. For most of the novel the physical struggles and open-air adventure take place *outside* the House of Durrisdeer while the reader's attention is kept at home by a narrator who is an old family servant.

David Daiches criticizes the last chapters of the novel on the basis that Stevenson has introduced "properties that belonged to a different kind of story altogether."[8] In a sense this is true, although the "properties" of popular adventure—flipping a coin to see which brother will join Prince Charlie, Chevalier Burke's account of life among the pirates, the duel by candlelight—have been fairly prominent throughout. I would suggest that, although Daiches is right in saying that *The Master of Ballantrae* reveals a "transition from the adventure story to a much more profound form of fiction," it is a mistake to assume that the events and properties associated with popular romance must give way, or are giving way in Stevenson's fiction, to different material. Stevenson may have begun to *treat* the props and incidents of open-air adventure differently, but there is no indication in the fiction written up until the day of his death that he was about to leave them alone. To make the externals of adventure serious and meaningful seems to be the uneven, but unmistakable, trend in his fiction after 1888.

If the journals of Chevalier Burke, a reckless Irishman patterned after Thackeray's Barry Lyndon, and the chase through the American woods seem weak and irrelevant, it is not so much that they introduce inappropriate elements of adventure into a psychological drama, but rather that they introduce them from the point of view of a character uninvolved with the Master except as an amusing companion in dangerous living. The excitement of the events themselves becomes more important than the characters participating in them. Temporarily, we are carried back to the world of child's play, where skill in any aspect of the game, including knocking down your best friend, supersedes questions of ethics or psychological motivation. The game is not an invention to explain the complications of the universe, but one to rule them out.

Even the chase at the end, though narrated by Mackellar, is described by a Mackellar uprooted from Durrisdeer, running through the forests with his lord. His prudent and cautious personality may be unaltered (though, if so, one can hardly imagine him coming to America in the first place), but his point of view has changed. He is no longer the voice of domestic stability and reason, viewing all phenomena in terms of their effect on his lord's household. Like so many of Stevenson's narrators, he has left home and in doing so has lost a unique vantage point; he has plunged actively into a world previously magnified and obscured by his actual as well as his temperamental distance from it. Once in the fray, Mackellar, like most of the other characters, becomes concerned with getting out of one difficulty before entering the next. And it is there that his new narrative voice, as well as the interest of the reader, discovers its limits.

3

But if *The Master of Ballantrae* contains obvious reversions to the tricks of popular adventure, it also contains a power which is generated by more than melodramatic artifice. Before he could achieve it himself, Stevenson believed that adventure could be elevated to the realm of serious art as long as the physical trials presented gave body to moral and psychological concerns, as the latter give meaning to external action:

> It is one thing to remark and dissect, with the most cutting logic, the complications of life, and of the human spirit; it is quite another to give them body and blood in the story of Ajax or Hamlet. The first is literature, but the second is something besides, for it is likewise art. (XIII, 333)

Stevenson is most an artist according to his own definition when, in *The Master of Ballantrae,* the incidents of physical action are seen in relation to the uncontrollable rivalry between the two brothers and that rivalry, in turn, is seen in the context of the irresolvable duality of the human spirit. Insofar as the subject of the novel may be taken, in the broadest and most abstract sense, to be the ominous and perpetually destructive threat chaos poses to order, the '45 uprising, the menace of coastal smugglers, the hostility of the land tenants, all *can* be pertinent and enriching to the theme of Ballantrae's disruption of the domestic security of the Durrisdeer household (through his claims on Henry's wife and money) as well as his eventual destruction of Henry's health and sanity.

While the point of view is the consistent and orderly one presented by Mackellar, the exact nature of the chaotic force remains mysterious, foreign, terrifying, by virtue of the fact that it exists darkly and portentously on the fringes of the narrator's perception. Mackellar's reports of Ballantrae's two returns to Durrisdeer (when he is seen rising out of the mist on the point of a rock and unexpectedly discovered sitting by the hearth wrapped in a great-coat) are effective evocations of a dimly visualized and ominous intrusion on the clarity and stability of a domesticated mind. As long as the Master's adventures, while he is absent from Durrisdeer, are, like his reputation among the local populace, obscured, enlarged, and "defaced with legends," he may as well be rising up out of hell as returning from France or India.

Probably the best example of Stevenson's increasing ability to inform physical action with significance beyond the immediate narrative concern for "what happens" is Mackellar's introduction to and description of the duel between the two brothers. Stripped of context and associative imagery, the incident becomes little more than a fencing bout between two opponents, possibly entertaining to watch, but hardly meaningful in any other way.

We lose the benefit, for example, of Mackellar's deliberate and detailed account of the state of nature preceding and during the duel. Although it is late February, the weather is "unseasonable, a cast back into winter: windless, bitter cold, the world all white with rime, the sky low and gray; the sea black and silent like a quarry hole." Nature is in an unnatural state of frigid paralysis which, by an unobtrusive juxtaposition, Stevenson associates with the mood of Henry Durie. We are told in the next sentence that he sits immobile by the hearth debating whether a man should "do things," whether "interference was wise."

The object of Henry's concern provides a contrast with his inaction and general lack of vigor. It is, of course, the Master, his brother, who is seen through the window by Mackellar walking with Henry's wife and daughter enjoying the day as though it were mid-spring. The Master, as usual, is seen from a distance, but what is more important is that he seems to have intruded on the rigid structure of the family as on the dead chill of the day, with a warmth and easy charm.

His presence awakens in Henry anxieties about himself which suggests, if only faintly at first, that Ballantrae may be an inverse reflection of his own worst faults, repressed, feared, even hated, but inextricably tied to him by birth and an instinctive attraction. "The weakness of my ground," Henry tells Mackellar, "*lies in myself,* that I am not one who engages love." Consciously, Henry disapproves of Ballantrae's politics, sexual and financial extravagance, disregard for family, and general irresponsibility. But he envies him all of it. Psychologically as well as literally, he is Jacob the usurper. His older brother is the living symbol of his own untried adventures and uncommitted sins—as much a rebuke as a temptation. Ballantrae is the reminder of a private part of the self Henry's public character cannot tolerate.

That the problem of the brothers' rivalry is one aspect of a natural inconsonance which may occur in the psyche of an individual as well as between seasons of the year is further stressed by Mackellar's attempt to comfort Henry. "Cheer up," he says. "It will burst of itself." The phrase may refer to a blood vessel or a bud as easily as to a showdown between brothers. Henry's latent anger is identified with an inevitable and natural process which may be destructive, creative, or both at the same time.

Stevenson does not allow the "stifling cold" or the "frozen turf" out of the reader's mind for a moment. Mackellar describes for a second time the bleak and unseasonable weather and significantly notes a brief but warm and bright intrusion, "a blink of sunshine; showing a very pretty, wintry, frosty landscape of white hills and woods." For an instant, the countryside has been transformed into something beautiful, but "with the coming of night, the haze closed in overhead; it fell dark and still and starless and exceeding cold." The scene is now set for the evening of the duel. The two brothers and Mackellar sit late into the night mechanically playing cards with no show of "love nor courtesy." In the figurative coldness of this group, the only member who reveals any warmth of spirit or body is Ballantrae. He is described disapprovingly by Mackellar as having drunk freely until he became a "trifle heated." When he can tolerate the dullness of the company no longer, he bursts into a torrent of insults, partly to provoke some kind of emotional response from his brother and partly, as he explains to Mackellar, for the diversion of toasting "you and your master at the fire like chestnuts."

If the emphasis on burning accentuates Ballantrae's passionate and satanic nature, there is a corresponding association of light imagery, which suggests Lucifer before the fall from grace and gives the Master a glint of divinity. Henry has already admitted that he is incapable of engaging love, but when he is told by Ballantrae that he possesses no "gift of pleasing," no "natural brilliancy," and that his wife prefers his brother to him, he is forced to react. But even here, Henry's reaction is as if he were dealing only with himself:

> Mr. Henry laid down his cards. He rose to his feet very softly, and seemed all the while like a person in deep thought. "You coward!" he said gently, *as if to himself*. And then, with neither hurry nor any particular violence, he struck the Master in the mouth. (IX, 119)

If Henry's behavior is deliberate and passionless, Ballantrae's response to it exalts and glorifies the cavalier: "The Master sprang to his feet like one transfigured; I had never seen the man so beautiful."

The word "transfigured" connotes no ordinary alteration, but a change in a countenance, already described as handsome, into a kind of beauty Mackellar had not seen before in the man. Inasmuch as the Transfiguration wherein the face of Jesus "did shine as the sun: and his garments became white as snow" recalls metaphorically the promise of spring described earlier by Mackellar when "a blink of sunshine . . . [showed] a frosty landscape of white hills," one wonders whether this curiously strong verb does not reflect an unconscious desire on Stevenson's part to endow Ballantrae, not with other Christ-like qualities but with a nature somehow capable of transcending that of ordinary mortals. The first words out of Ballantrae's mouth echo Captain Ahab's blasphemous threat to "strike the sun," and acknowledge the possibility of divine interference: "A blow! . . . I would not take a blow from God Almighty."

This Master, unlike the Master of the New Testament, may have been transfigured by wrath rather than by love, but the point in which he differs from and exceeds the other characters in the novel is that, for better or worse, he is in touch with some kind of deity. While the others walk mechanically about in meaningless circles—demoralized, unmanned, or mentally unhinged—Ballantrae offends them with his own metaphysical existence. The image of his soul may be a flame capable of giving off both heat and light, but then Stevenson is literal enough about his images to question whether one can exist without the other: whether the heat can be extinguished, as it is in Henry, who proves incapable of anger and lust without simultaneously losing the light of love and reason.

The light imagery continues not only in association with the Master's person, but more specifically with his sword, the token of his powerful threat to Mackellar and Henry. It is the instrument of his passion, an extension of himself. To shy away from the sexual implications of the brothers' rivalry would be a mistake in view of the fact that the immediate cause of the duel is the *inability* of one to engage love, as opposed to the other's considerable ability, not only to engage it, but to make a successful appeal to his brother's wife. It becomes clear relatively early in the novel that Henry hates his brother's virility and its brutally aggressive power to soften women and make other men look weak.

The sword is repeatedly described as "bare," "naked," and "shining." As always, the Master's overbearing manliness has archangelic as well as diabolical qualities. When Mackellar tries to intervene and stop the duel, Ballantrae uses his weapon as a kind of amulet which has unique power:

> The Master turned his blade against my bosom; I saw the light run along the steel; and I threw up my arms and fell to my knees before him on the floor . . . like a baby. (IX, 120)

When it is decided that the duel should be held outdoors, the Master commands Mackellar to bring out two candles. The servant, totally cowed by the mere exposure of Ballantrae's weapon, is rendered temporarily sightless, weak, and almost incapable of speech. The duel itself is described economically in one paragraph, and the most significant fact about it is that Ballantrae wounds himself with almost no help from Henry. Attempting foul play, he grabs his brother's blade, stumbles, falls against it, and drops to the ground. Mackellar's concluding words, in view of the Master's reputed diabolism and obstrusive masculinity, are highly appropriate: "The body [had] . . . fallen to the ground, where it writhed a moment like a trodden worm, and then lay motionless."

If the duel may be taken as Henry's attempt to cut brute nature out of his life, it is Henry rather than Ballantrae who finally suffers the consequences. It is as though he has mutilated himself. He stands looking at the body of his brother, muttering "stupidly," while Mackellar tries to give him courage: "Be yourself, sir. It is too late now: you must be yourself." The question is whether Henry can any longer "be himself," or whether the loss of his brother does not injure his identity by taking away the scale against which he measured and calculated everything he did.

Without Ballantrae, Henry may suffer no threat, but he also is left without spur, without aim, and without reference to any reality larger than the dry, humdrum, passionless existence at Durrisdeer. In psychological terms, Ballantrae's self-infliction of a wound, which renders his opponent a whimpering coward, may be regarded as a dramatic projection of Henry's destructive repression and attempted excision of his own unexpressed animal nature as personified in his brother. He runs into the house and stands shuddering by the hearth until Mackellar comes to him and comforts him with brandy, which he "forced him to swallow . . . like a child."

Upon recovering from the long illness which follows the duel, Henry is rendered permanently childish. He is described at play with his little son:

> It was pretty to see the pair returning, full of briars, and the father as flushed and sometimes as bemuddied as the child: for they were equal sharers in all sorts of boyish entertainment, digging in the beach, damming of streams, and what not; and I have seen them gaze through a fence at cattle with the same childish contemplation. (IX, 157)

It is Henry, like Mackellar and Captain Teach, who is

rendered infantile in his own attempt to combat Ballantrae; while the Master, not really dead at all, is spirited away.

As long as Ballantrae lives, his brother can find no peace in life and he cannot die. They share one existence. Though each may be the torment of the other, the Master is nonetheless a necessary link with life. As the novel progresses, he spends most of his time out of Scotland and away from Henry; yet he continues to exist in Henry's mind as a torture and a threat. Still thinking his brother has died in the duel, Henry, upon recovering from the fever, asks Mackellar where he has buried him. When the servant explains that Ballantrae is still living, Henry bursts into momentary anger: "He is bound upon my back to all eternity—to all God's eternity!"

Henry, of course, turns out to be right. When he realizes he cannot stand on his brother's grave, he refuses to acknowledge his existence and forbids his family and servants to speak of him. But as Mackellar had ominously prophesied, "It will burst of itself." And that is exactly what Henry's repressed obsession with Ballantrae does. During a visit to his lawyer, Henry conducts himself quietly and calmly until the Master's name is mentioned once too often:

> My lord's face became suddenly knotted. "I wish he was in hell," cried he, and filled himself a glass of wine, but with a hand so tottering that he spilled the half into his bosom. This was the second time, that, in the midst of the most regular and wise behaviour, his animosity had spirited out . . . It restored the certainty that we were acting for the best in view of my lord's health and reason. (IX, 184)

It becomes plain that in a sense Henry's devil is an interior one and that, try as he may to mutilate, extract, or entomb it, he succeeds only in maiming himself while the demon flourishes on the vulnerable remnants of his mind and flesh.

When Ballantrae pursues Henry and Alison in their flight to America, he is temporarily reduced to working as a tailor while they live in comfort on a large plantation. For once, Henry, though already diminished in mind and body, has the upper hand over his brother. Since it has proved impossible to banish Ballantrae from his life, Henry begins to indulge himself in his ambivalent obsession. He shows such spirit and pleasure in walking past the tailor shop that Mackellar suspects at first that he has a mistress in the neighborhood. But in following him one morning, the servant discovers that the Master is the sole object of Henry's attention and the only source of his perverted pleasure. Once again the language suggests the unnatural—this time in terms of a courtship between shy lovers:

> Here was [Henry's] mistress: it was hatred and not love that gave him healthful colours . . . I found this situation of two brethren not only odious in itself, but big with possibilities of further evil . . . There was a bench against the Master's house, where customers might sit to parley with a shopman; and here I found my lord seated, nursing his cane and looking pleasantly forth upon the bay. Not three feet from him sate the Master stitching. Neither spoke; nor (in this new situation) did my lord so much as cast a glance upon his enemy. He tasted his neighborhood, I must suppose, less indirectly in the bare proximity of person; and without doubt, drank deep of hateful pleasures. (IX, 230-231)

Not only is there an ironic and abnormal reversal of roles in this unholy affair, but there is further indication that consorting with a devil, like the previously attempted mutilation of him, occurs largely within Henry's own psyche. Ballantrae may be called the "mistress," but it is inside Henry that the seed of this obsession grows:

> "My lord, my lord," said I, "this is no manner of behaviour." "I grow fat upon it," he replied; and not merely the words, which were strange enough, but the whole character of his expression shocked me.

The ending of the book is notoriously melodramatic. After a long treasure hunt, Ballantrae is exhumed from a grave where he has lain for a week. Inappropriate and contrived as this may be in a narrative which has developed along lines of fairly conventional credibility, it does have an element of relevance to the psychological drama within the mind of Henry Durie. Detecting a sign of life in the face of his "resurrected" brother, he falls dead of a stroke, and, soon after, both brothers are buried together in the same grave. Treated less literally than Stevenson treats it (he tries to convince the reader that the body could have been kept alive by plugging up the ears and nostrils) and described with less clearly visualized exactitude, the scene might have been an effective symbolic culmination of the brothers' enmity. As it is, the sensational clichés of popular adventure prevail in the last pages, but not without considerable harassment from a more serious world.

"I have great trouble finishing *The Master of Ballantrae,*" wrote André Gide in 1913. "Odd book in which everything is excellent, but heterogeneous to such a degree that it seems the sample card of everything in which Stevenson excels."[9] Gide's remark points up the curious fact that the best parts of the novel often appear to be at cross purposes with one another. The concern for the tragic destiny of an ancient Scottish family, supplemented by the sweeping range of exploits in India, piracy on the high seas, and flight to colonial America, sustains the adventurous and epic qualities. Yet the direction is not that of classical epic. It is *from* the national and historical *to* the individual and perennial, rather than the other way around. The behavior of individual characters does in some obvious ways suggest national traits and historical divisions within Scotland. But Stevenson grows increasingly interested in Scottish tradition and heroic gesture for what they reveal of the human mind in the encounters through which it enlarges itself or contracts and dies.

Ballantrae is the embodiment of an impossible romantic dream of old Scotland—the dashing, indomitable Jacobite—a fighter, a hard drinker, an "unco man for the lasses." But he is much more. He is the most unwelcome of intruders into the realm of boyish romance: a sexually potent male and a harbinger of death. Henry Durie is Jim Hawkins and David Balfour turned middle-aged and set in stone. (More than a few of Stevenson's heroes grow older with their author.) Henry is the chaste, loyal, thrifty Scotsman his predecessors were, without their youthful defenses. What is charming in a boy of twelve or sixteen becomes madness in a man of forty. The challenge Ballantrae presents to his brother is the elemental and relentless one of process—growth and its concomitant, decay. Henry's attempt to deny to his consciousness the pleasures and responsibilities of the fully developed male is, in the end, a rejection of old age and death.

Stevenson's whole career as an artist, but this novel especially, is a melodramatic reminder of a dilemma more delicately and sensuously expressed in Keats's "Ode on a Grecian Urn." Eternal youth may be wished for, but Stevenson, like Keats, came to recognize the barren comfort of such an immortality. *The Master of Ballantrae* is not a "cold pastoral" but it is true to its subtitle—a cold adventure, "a winter's tale." Through fear, denial, and pretense, Henry distorts the mixed phenomena of natural existence into an unqualified menace. His adventure begins as an attempted escape from that menace, his life: its center is humiliation; and death is the inevitable, almost happy, ending.

4

There would be little sense in claiming that *The Master of Ballantrae* and *Weir of Hermiston* are, in any strict sense, epics. We have already found that Stevenson's satires were not pure satires, nor his fables ordinary fables. But there is more than Procrustean convenience in suggesting these classifications. There is value, for one thing, in seeing the ways in which an author deviates from formal convention. There is also value in noticing and trying to explain predominant tendencies toward satire, allegory, and epic in works which admittedly contain a good deal else. It is less important to prove whether *Weir of Hermiston* is or is not a true epic (I should say it is not) than to see how certain epic strains in the novel reflect a development in Stevenson's attitude toward fiction.

He had always appreciated the magnitude of epic literature. He wrote often in his early letters and essays of the indelible impression left upon him by Homer and Virgil, and of the grandeur of vision of Milton's *Paradise Lost.* But later in life, especially during and after the writing of *The Master of Ballantrae,* he speaks more specifically of his own desire to compose epic narratives. The references, as so often when Stevenson deals with matters which concern him deeply, are evasive, consciously whimsical, and half-apologetic. He jokes about his lack of creative power for attempting anything so ambitious and complains about having been born into a "small age." But the ambition of his last years is increasingly for largeness—to write a book with more weight and seriousness than he had before "with an epic value of scenes, so that the figures remain in the mind's eye forever."

In the summer of 1893 he confides to Henry James that he wants to write a book which will transcend his own past performances as well as the conventional fiction of the period:

> How to get over, how to escape from, the besotting *particularity* of fiction. "Roland approaches the house; it had green doors and window blinds; and there was a scraper on the upper step." To hell with Roland and the scraper! (*Letters,* IV, 232)

However tentative and self-conscious Stevenson's ambitions may be, his increasing references to a frustrated wish to write at least one great book with epic qualities indicates a change in his attitude toward his own adventurous fiction. Having once produced romances with a formal simplicity almost independent of the moral and psychological confusion of life, he seeks in the nineties to embody some kind of truth about the human condition, to capture a glimpse of the mind and soul in the external actions of the body; not only to root his legend in time and place, but to associate it, by means of continuous allusion, with comparable episodes in recorded history and mythological tradition.

In 1891 he wrote to his New York publishers of a plan to write a history of the internal warfare in Samoa:

> Here is, for the first time, a tale of Greeks—Homeric Greeks—mingled with moderns, and all true; Odysseus alongside of Rajah Brooke, proportion gardée; and all true. Here is for the first time since the Greeks (that I

> remember) the history of a handful of men, where all know each other in the eyes, and live in a few acres, narrated at length, and with the seriousness of history.
> (*Letters,* III, 375)

The result of this plan, *A Footnote to History,* or *Eight Years of Trouble in Samoa,* is an unpolished and undistinguished work, but it is Stevenson's attitude toward it, and the effect of that attitude on the writing of *Weir of Hermiston,* which are of interest. The primary excitement for Stevenson in trying to write a nineteenth-century epic in reduced scale is that it is true, "all true," in a sense he would have rejected for fiction ten years earlier. That subject matter may have sufficient substance to be treated "with the seriousness of history" has clearly become a positive advantage in Stevenson's eyes. In *Weir of Hermiston,* as a result, a basically fictitious situation is set in a definite historical time in Scottish history from which it absorbs mood and credibility without involving the characters in actual historical events of importance. The novel borrows regional traditions and the inevitability of history to give seriousness and a sense of fatality to fiction, while his earlier historical romances, like *Kidnapped,* borrow historical fact to give color and authenticity to relatively uncomplicated adventures.

The second point emphasized in the letter comparing Samoans with Homeric Greeks is that epic should convey, along with the seriousness of history (if not always its literal accuracy), a feeling for the human personality in touch and perhaps even in sympathy with his enemies. Stevenson's villains have always been interesting, often more so than his heroes, but the emphasis in *A Footnote to History* seems to be on something more than "outlaw" glamor. The opponents in the Samoan strife to which Stevenson refers do not fit into neat categories of noble warriors versus wicked but attractive villains. Part of the tragic dignity of the conflict lies in the fact that the men involved know their enemies well enough to entertain strong personal feelings of hate, respect, and even love for them. Unlike the large mechanical wars of the nineteenth century, it is a conflict which elevates and enhances personality rather than obliterating it.[10]

During this period of growing interest in epic literature Stevenson wrote to Henry James that he had drafted three chapters of a new novel, *The Justice-Clerk* (later changed to *Weir of Hermiston*), and in the same letter, praises his life in Samoa:

> And anxious friends beg me to stay at home and study human nature in Brompton drawing-rooms! *Farceurs!* And anyway you know that such is not my talent. I could never be induced to take the faintest interest in Brompton *qua* Brompton or a drawing-room *qua* a drawing-room. I am an Epick writer with a k to it, but without the necessary genius. (*Letters,* IV, 157)

Adventure fiction, from Stevenson's point of view in 1892, was a kind of epic *manqué*. *Weir of Hermiston* was not to be a radical departure from his earlier romances, but an extension of them, a deepening and humanizing of an art form which had been originally cultivated to "give joy." As in *The Master of Ballantrae,* the intense physical activity normally associated with adventure fiction sets a mood for the novel, but does not assume a central position in the narrative. Throughout *The Master of Ballantrae* the wild exploits (uprisings, piracy, mutiny, frantic chases) take place away from Durrisdeer and are presented to the reader by means of digressions or, more importantly, through their effect upon the lives of those who cannot participate in them.

In *Weir of Hermiston* the high adventure is removed

not in place but in time. The most obvious single example of this is the digression of the old housekeeper, Kirstie, who, "like one inspired," tells how in "1804, at the age of sixty, [her father] met an end that might be called heroic." It is a weird and lusty tale of ambush, robbery, and murder, and of the bloody revenge taken by the old man's four sons on his assassins. "Some centuries earlier," Stevenson comments at the conclusion of the legend, "the last of the minstrels might have fashioned the last of the ballads out of that Homeric chase and fight; but the spirit was dead" (XX, 72).

The spirit is apparently not quite dead, or Stevenson would not have bothered to have Kirstie tell the story at such length. In fact, the basic theme of the novel is that the crude energies of the heroic past continually inform and affect contemporary life. As an undercurrent of the plot, it carries with it a profound truth about individual psychology as well as a concept of history which is unexpectedly modern in emphasis. An explanation which would please any Jungian is offered for how the most gentle of the avenging sons was able to perform the gory deed in his father's behalf:

> Some Barbarossa, some old Adam of our ancestors, sleeps in all of us till the fit circumstance shall call it into action; and for as sober as he now seemed, Hob had given once for all the measure of the devil that haunted him. (XX, 73)

Haunted is the right word. *Weir of Hermiston* is a psychological drama of the nineteenth century, haunted by the epic grandeur and savagery of the past. Not only are the individual characters occasionally moved and even possessed by uncontrollable passions which seem to rise up out of an unremembered ancestry, but the whole rigid structure of society is continually buffeted and reshaped by the existence of members whose roughness and magnitude resist accepted moral categories. Stevenson deals with time past in this novel, not like Scott or Reade or Kingsley, not regarding it distantly and nostalgically as a completed moment, separate and distinct from time present. He liked to think, even as a student, that a city as small and conservative as Edinburgh contained within its boundaries the evidence of centuries, just as every human being is the cumulative product of generations:

> Our conscious years are but a moment in the history of the elements that build us . . . And though today I am only a man of letters, either tradition errs or I was present when there landed at St. Andrews a French barber-surgeon . . . I have shaken a spear in the Debatable Land and shouted the slogan of the Elliots . . . Parts of me have seen life, and met adventures, and sometimes met them well . . . The threads that make me up can be traced by fancy into the bosoms of thousands and millions of ascendants: Picts who rallied round Macbeth . . . fleers from before the legions of Agricola . . . star-gazers on Chaldean plateaus. (XIII, 247-248)

Stevenson's revery resembles the *Widsith,* an Anglo-Saxon poetic catalogue of the seventh century, which is a boast of participation in heroic deeds throughout the ages and a lament that those times are past. The tone of *Weir of Hermiston* is very much the same. The heroes of that novel attain a stature unlike that of any other of Stevenson's characters, with the exception of Ballantrae, through their symbolic as well as genetic association with great figures of recorded history and mythology. The destiny of the protagonists is pathetic rather than epic, however, because they exist in a world of passive and devious adversaries who agree neither on the terms of the struggle nor on the definition of defeat.

The four major characters of the novel are Adam Weir, the Lord Justice-Clerk; his wife Jean; their son Archie; and Kirstie, the housekeeper at the family estate. Stevenson died after having completed only one hundred fifty-one pages, but he was far enough along in the plot for the dramatic situation to have developed considerably. The advocate is described as a brilliant but merciless judge with a reputation for sending criminals and radicals to their execution without a sign of pity or a moment's hesitation. His wife Jean is a "pious, anxious, tender, tearful, and incompetent" woman who unwittingly raises her son to hate his father by teaching him endless lessons of Christian meekness and mercy. When Mrs. Weir dies, Archie grows to young manhood in his father's home in Edinburgh and becomes daily less sympathetic toward the judge.

One day, while still a student at the University, Archie attends one of Hermiston's trials, hears him pronounce the death sentence, witnesses with horror the public hanging a few days later, and denounces his father's act loudly among his acquaintances as a "God-defying murder." When Weir gets word of his son's disloyal behavior he banishes him to the country estate at Hermiston, where the remorseful boy goes obediently, grateful to bury himself away from further public shame. The relationship between father and son (particularly the language Stevenson uses to describe it) resembles that in *The Ebb Tide* between Robert Herrick and the God-like Attwater:

> Lord Hermiston was coarse and cruel; and yet the son was aware of a bloomless nobility, an ungracious abnegation of the man's self in the man's office. At every word, this sense of the greatness of Lord Hermiston's spirit struck more home; and along with it that of his own impotence, who had struck—and perhaps basely struck—

> at his own father, and not reached so far as to have even nettled him. "I place myself in your hands without reserve," [Archie] said. (XX, 43-44)

At Hermiston, Archie falls under the care of old Kirstie Elliot, who fills his head with heroic legends of clan warfare and splendid deeds of familial loyalty. As Archie is beginning to fall in love with Kirstie's niece and discover some happiness in his exile, he is visited by Frank Innes, a university acquaintance, who maliciously sets about destroying his reputation in the region. The story breaks off as Archie tries to explain to his beloved that he must meet her less frequently for appearance's sake. We know from letters and hints early in the novel that Archie was to shoot Frank for getting the girl with child, and possibly to come into his own father's court (though Stevenson questioned the legality of it) for trial.

There is some doubt whether, even in this masterful and mature work, Stevenson would have been able to avoid a melodramatic ending. The evidence provided by his stepdaughter to Sidney Colvin—including an unlikely break from prison and flight to America—is that he would not.[11] But if his large tragic vision was to falter as Conrad's did at the end of *Nostromo,* its weak finale could not have destroyed the artistry that preceded. The likelihood of a mechanical conclusion suggests that Stevenson, once again, as in *The Master of Ballantrae,* was about to involve himself in an artistic problem and a moral dilemma for which he could see no satisfactory conclusion.

The subject of the novel is history—not a record of dates and events, but the general evolution and repetition of human conduct; the problem is to find in the intersection between public event and private experience some moral pattern. The conflict is not between carefully abstracted ideologies or even between models of virtue and vice according to the premises of a single ideology, but rather between generations at different stages of development. It is father dominating the son and the son trying to usurp his father's place; it is, in universal terms, the collision of present and past, which necessarily involves partial destruction of both in order to bring about the creation of the future.

The two characters in the book who represent an "older" generation are Hermiston and the housekeeper Kirstie. Mrs. Weir is still a young woman when she marries Adam, who is already past forty, and she seems to belong more to the generation of her son than to that of her husband. It is no coincidence, moreover, that the names of Weir and Kirstie are repeatedly associated with heroic figures from the pre-Christian traditions of Greece, Rome, Israel, and semibarbaric Scotland, while Mrs. Weir and Archie derive their symbolic identity almost exclusively from the New Testament.

Adam Weir himself is the most impressive character in the novel and one of the great characterizations in the Stevenson canon. He is called Rhadamanthus because of his inflexibility as a judge, "an aboriginal antique," an "adamantine Adam," and a "usurping devil . . . horned and hoofed." We are told in the first sentence of the book that "the Lord Justice-Clerk was a stranger in that part of the country," and reminded ever after that he seems to derive his preternatural vigor from some other time or place. Even when Archie seems most to hate his father, he grants that "he struck me as something very big," and wonders whether his filial defiance is against "God or Satan." A kind old judge, who is a friend both to father and son, tells Archie one day that his father "has all the Roman virtues: Cato and Brutus were such; I think a son's heart might well be proud of such an ancestry of one." But the boy's mother regards her husband without benefit of the classics. She compares him with her own great-great-grandfather who "had drawn the sword against the Lord's anointed."

> Nor could she blind herself to this, that had they lived in these old days, Hermiston himself would have been numbered alongside of Bloody MacKenzie and the politic Lauderdale and Rothes, in the band of God's immediate enemies. (XX, 8)

When Archie confesses to Hermiston that he has looked through some of his trial proceedings, Weir associates it with the sin of Noah's sons who spied their father's nakedness. Hermiston may be a hero or a villain, depending on the point of view of those around him, but of one matter there seems to be no doubt in his own or any of the other characters' minds—that he is "something very big."

Kirstie is also a character larger than life, who draws her strength and grandeur from ancient heroines and *femmes fatales*. She is described as having been "once a moorland Helen, and still comely as a blood horse and healthy as the hill wind." She is regarded by Hermiston as a "skirling Jezebel"; and when her mistress dies, she breaks into a high note of "barbarous mourning, such as still lingers modified among Scots heather." Above all, she is a kind of northern goddess, blonde and buxom, but born into a century that has little use and no reverence for her:

> Kirstie was now over fifty, and might have sat to a sculptor. Long of limb and still light of foot, deep-breasted, robust-loined, her golden hair not yet mingled with any trace of silver, the years had but caressed and embellished

> her. By the lines of a rich and vigorous maternity, she seemed destined to be the bride of heroes and the mother of their children; and behold, by the iniquity of fate, she had passed through her youth alone, and drew near to the confines of age, a childless woman . . . She carried her thwarted ardours into housework, she washed floors with her empty heart. (XX, 60-61)

Mrs. Weir, too, is referred to as a goddess, but she is a deity of a different religion. Old Kirstie, in fact, pampers the young bride, makes "a goddess and an only child of the effete and tearful lady." "It seems strange to say of this colourless and ineffectual woman, but she was a true enthusiast, and might have made the sunshine and the glory of a cloister." When Mrs. Weir dies, one of the great scenes of the novel is of Hermiston standing over her bed looking down at the dead body like a barbarian hero who has come unexpectedly on a fragile shrine built by feminine hands to an idea he does not understand: "the very image of the insignificant."

Little Archie is raised by his nun-like mother whose "philosophy of life was summed up in one expression—tenderness," and whose favorite text is, interestingly enough for a Lord Justice-Clerk's wife, "Judge not that ye be not judged." The boy is repeatedly referred to as his mother's "lamb," and compared to the child Jesus among the temple doctors when, at the age of seven, he questions Mrs. Weir about his father's "sinful" profession.

There is small wonder that as Archie grows into his teens his father thinks him "just his mother over again—daurna say boo to a goose!" The point upon which the novel turns is that Archie is also Hermiston's son and resembles the judge most when he is defying him. When the boy publicly denounces Weir's severe handling of a petty criminal, Stevenson comments that his father, "if he must have disclaimed the sentiment, might have owned the stentorian voice with which it was uttered." Later the same evening, while presiding at his university debating society meeting, Archie again behaves with uncharacteristic spirit: "He little thought, as he did so, how he resembled his father."

Archie's resemblance to his father, like Kirstie's legend of heroic revenge, is an instance of a sudden and temporary outburst of passion. The mixture of bloods and the effect of his upbringing prevent the boy from sustaining the extraordinary powers of the will for more than a moment. Those characters, like Weir and Kirstie, who carry their strength and magnitude about with them continually, are isolated from the society into which they have been born, like oversized creatures of another species. Their tragedy is that they must spend the enormous intensity of their emotion on minds and hearts so much weaker and more sensitive than their own that it goes unheeded or, what is worse, annihilates its object. Archie's major objection to his father's treatment of Duncan Jopp in court is that he used the strength of his own character and position to deride and terrify an insignificant, wretched criminal, until "the loathsomeness of Duncan Jopp enveloped and infected his judge."

Weir also relentlessly destroys his own fragile and insipid wife, not through any deliberate plan, but merely by being what he is: "Being so trenchantly opposed to all she knew, loved or understood, he may well have seemed to her the extreme, if scarcely the ideal, of his sex." In the first place, his virility wilts and diminishes her rather than engendering in her a complementary feminine reaction. Secondly, the fact that he is a judge and "persecutor" does not fit into her simple notion of Christian mercy. While Archie is still a boy, his mother gradually loses her senses; she is described as bewildered and frightened; "she seemed to loose and seize again her touch with life." On her last day, she turns suddenly to Kirstie and speaks of her husband as though he were something too big and too strange, which had intruded into her mind and body and unwittingly strained and broken them:

> "Kirstie!" she began, and paused; and then with conviction, "Mr. Weir isna speeritually minded, but he has been a good man to me."
>
> . . . When Kirstie looked up at the speaker's face, she was aware of a change. "Godsake, what's the maitter wi' ye, mem?"
>
> . . . "I do not ken . . . but he is not speeritually minded, my dear." Kirstie helped and forced her into my lord's own chair.
>
> "Keep me, what's this?" she gasped. "Kirstie, what's this? I'm frich'ened." They were her last words. (XX, 16)

"Helped and *forced* into my lord's own chair," Mrs. Weir expires, actually and metaphorically trying to fill a position which confuses and terrifies her. The pathos of Mrs. Weir's life is comparable to that of Henry Durie's defenselessness against his older brother. Both Henry and Mrs. Weir are morally, intellectually, and physically incapable of coping with an intrusion into their lives which carries with it a scent of bestiality. A demonstration of moral frailty, in both cases, precedes and in a way brings about the mental and physical breakdown. The neat moral pattern Mrs. Weir finds in history does not provide her with a basis for comprehending the rugged and complex nature of her own husband:

> Her view of history was wholly artless, a design in snow and ink; upon the one side, tender innocents with psalms upon their lips; upon the other, the persecutors,

> booted, bloody-minded, flushed with wine; a suffering Christ, a raging Beelzebub. (XX, 8)

Weir seems inexplicably to combine attributes from both extremes of the polarity. On the one hand he is a respected member of society, a good provider for his family, a symbol of law and order; on the other, he has a wild temper, seems incapable of demonstrating affection, and takes pleasure in persecuting the most wretched of criminals. Puzzled to the point of derangement by the inconsistencies of her husband's character and her inability to justify them to Archie according to her own notions of morality, she goes into a decline and dies. Before she succumbs, Mrs. Weir can only pronounce, with a kind of uncomprehending resignation, the paradox which has disrupted her moral security and unhinged her mind: "Mr. Weir isna speeritually minded, but he has been a good man to me."

It is one of the virtues of this novel fragment (as Stevenson considered it to be one of the virtues of the narratives of old epic struggles) that the reader's sympathy is not consistently engaged by one character at the expense of another. Weir may indeed be the "devil" which haunts and eventually destroys his wife, but, as in *The Beach of Falesá* and *The Master of Ballantrae,* the "devil's work" is made easier by the limitations of his victims' perceptions. Evil, Stevenson had implied in his earlier novels, was primarily a matter of misinformation. In *The Master of Ballantrae* and *Weir of Hermiston* he has not discarded this position, but added to it by presenting evil as a constant element of the human condition which assumes a variety of forms depending upon the peculiarities of the individual. That there is an irrational and purely destructive force in all men which abhors soundness of mind and body and serenity of spirit seems no longer to be doubted by Stevenson. The additional truth which he begins to uncover in *Weir of Hermiston,* and which serves as a partial indictment of his own former attitude, is that since each man participates in creating the shape, if not the essence, of his own devil, he is condemned to suffer its torments in isolation.

Stevenson gradually took to be true of individuals what he had learned about whole societies: that from the outside a foreign concept of evil may appear exaggerated, trivial, even ridiculous, and at the same time be real for those who hold it. Stevenson did not travel to the South Seas to trade the "horned and hoofed" Beelzebub of the Highlands for a Samoan fetish. He was ready to scoff at both. But disbelieving in an anthropomorphized Satan, like dynamiting the painted masks at Falesá, proved of little use in preventing pride, envy, brutality, anger, and malice from tormenting him, both from the outside and from within. He came to believe that it was characteristic of the psyche to project the cause of destructiveness into human or symbolic beings external to itself; which means not that man invents evil, but that he defines it, gives shape to what threatens him. Stevenson has moved from a position which stressed the subjectivity of evil to one which grants it an objective existence that is made manifest in a variety of subjective ways.

Weir himself is beset by devils who frustrate, undermine, and betray him by souring the potential nobility and magnitude of his passions with their unwillingness or inability to respond. Archie recognizes that "the loathsomeness of Duncan Jopp enveloped and infected the image of his judge." But what takes him much longer to see is that the tearful incompetence of the wife and the effeminate superiority of the son envelop and infect Adam Weir as well. If the nature of Mrs. Weir's anguish is "overstrain," objectified by the physical imbalance between her robust husband and herself, Hermiston's tragedy is unfulfillment—emotional, moral, and physical. Lacking an enemy of equal dimension, lacking a lusty mistress and a manly successor, he is condemned to waste his rage on petty criminals and to conceal his passion from a wife and son who misunderstand and fear him.

In this book filled with characters and episodes that parallel and illuminate one another, Kirstie's dilemma repeats in a feminine key that of her master. As he was fit to lead clans in ancient warfare, she was fit to be the mistress of a great warrior and the mother of brave sons. But her fertility and strength are left untapped in an age which prefers refinement and respectability. When Archie is sent in exile to Hermiston, old Kirstie is his only companion for months. Though many years his senior and his inferior in social rank, she lavishes upon him the unspent affection of two decades, which amounts in intensity to a sexual passion:

> Her feeling partook of the loyalty of a clanswoman, the hero-worship of a maiden aunt, and the idolatry due to a god . . . Her passion, for it was nothing less, entirely filled her. It was a rich physical pleasure to make his bed or light his lamp when he was absent, to pull off his wet boots or wait on him at dinner when he returned. A young man who should have so doted on the idea, moral and physical, of any woman, might be properly described as being in love. (XX, 62)

But Kirstie's role as a lover, like Hermiston's as a heroic chieftain, is impossible. She must feed her unacknowledged passion on distant glimpses of the beloved or servile acts performed for her youthful master, just as Hermiston must play Rhadamanthus to a docket of petty criminals and Noah to a weakling son. Stevenson's somewhat Carlylean point is that strong human passions, when joined or opposed with something like equal energy and transformed into the concrete (a mortal enemy defeated, a dynasty founded), can appear productive, noble, and even heroic. But when they are spent upon themselves without response from or relevance to society, when they increase and grow inward without the dignity of public acknowledgment or the protective claim of utility, they appear strangely fruitless and ignoble. For an artist who had spent nearly a lifetime avoiding explosive accumulations of passion in his fiction, Stevenson surprises us by presenting in Kirstie a moving and pathetic portrait of a middle-aged woman infatuated with a young man.

Kirstie's attachment to Archie is obviously complicated and modified by conventional maternal sentiments of admiration and respect. But along with this is a fundamental and unsatisfied physical appetite which Stevenson makes no attempt to conceal:

> This perpetual hunger and thirst of his presence kept her all day on the alert. When he went forth at morning, she would stand and follow him with admiring looks. As it grew late and drew to the time of his return, she would steal forth to a corner of the policy wall and be seen standing there sometimes by the hour together, gazing with shaded eyes, waiting the exquisite and barren pleasure of his view a mile off on the mountains. (XX, 63)

Kirstie's behavior is described as a desperate attempt to put off the prospect of solitude, old age, and death. Her fondness for Archie, with all its potential absurdity and sadness, carries with it the nobility of genuine feeling and a willful protest against desiccation. When Archie falls in love with her niece (also named Christina) he spends less time at home, thus depriving the older woman of the pleasure of seeing and talking with him. She suffers torments of jealousy and loneliness:

> To her it was as if the whole world had fallen silent; to him, but an unremarkable change of amusements. And she raged to know it. The effervescency of her passionate and irritable nature rose within her at times to bursting point. (XX, 135)

Kirstie sees herself in an imaginary role which in the "real" world of youth and age has no validity. The pathos of the situation is that her imagined guise does not alter the circumstances. She cannot assume a mask and act upon it the way Jim Hawkins and his comrades could when they named themselves admiral and crew of the *Hispaniola* and sailed for Treasure Island. Nor can she don a false hair-piece and engage in a temporary "fling" like the mad-cap characters of *New Arabian Nights.* She bears more of a resemblance to figures in Stevenson's later fiction: like Catriona, who in the midst of daydreaming that she is a "man-child" remembers she cannot use a sword; or Robert Herrick in *The Ebb Tide,* who has changed his name and fled to Tahiti, but cannot throw off the reality of his own weakness.

The shattering of Kirstie's dream comes swiftly and suddenly when she realizes that Archie is in love with her pale, dark-haired niece:

> She had seen, in imagination, Archie wedded to some tall, powerful, and rosy heroine of the golden locks, made in her own image, for whom she would have strewed the bride-bed with delight; and now she could have wept to see the ambition falsified. (XX, 136)

But the habit of many months does not permit Kirstie to yield her dream easily. As circumstances make it appear more hopeless than ever, her fantasy intensifies and reveals itself with a force no longer ameliorated by the respectable "loyalty of a clanswoman" or "hero-worship of a maiden aunt."

> She lay tossing in bed . . . besieged with feverish thoughts . . . Now she saw, through the girl's eyes, the youth on his knees to her, heard his persuasive instances with a deadly weakness, and received his over-mastering caresses. Anon, with a revulsion, her temper raged to see such utmost favours of fortune and love squandered on a brat of a girl, one of her own house, using her own name. (XX, 136-137)

When Kirstie hears her young master's foot on the stair she decides to make one final attempt at acting out her desired and imagined role. She prepares to visit Archie's room to advise him against seeing her niece again. Her avowed reason is to safeguard the girl's virtue, since Archie's higher social rank will probably prevent him from marrying her.

The scene depicts a love made impossible by time and morality, communicated imaginatively across the gap of a generation, but incapable of fulfillment. Archie is confronted by Kirstie as Robert Herrick had been by the majestic wooden figurehead beckoning to him on the beach of Attwater's New Island. Both feminine symbols are compared to goddesses out of a rich and glorious past, which the nineteenth-century protagonist can mournfully acknowledge but not embrace. It may also, and not altogether coincidentally, capture the mood of the Victorian romantic novelist, enchanted, haunted, all but obsessed, by the persistent image of epic adventure which, except in brief moments of exceptional vision, appears to him worn and barren.

But both the woman and the faded ideal of an art can,

if only in momentary flashes, become magnificent and alive again by sheer exertion of the will and concentration of imaginative power. When Kirstie rises from her bed, she is confused and unsteady, both the noble female, "hating the wrong, loyal to her own sex," and the *femme fatale,* "cherishing next her soft heart . . . hopes she would have died sooner than have acknowledged." As she prepares to go to Archie's room she seems to cast off the "middle-aged housekeeper" and take on the appealing and compassionate woman:

> She tore off her nightcap, and her hair fell about her shoulders in profusion. Undying coquetry awoke. By the faint light of her nocturnal rush, she stood before the looking glass, carried her shapely arms above her head, and gathered up the treasure of her tresses. (XX, 138)

Having performed the preparatory ritual, she is ready to enter her young master's bedroom as a woman. As soon as she crosses his threshold, she is temporarily transformed into an apparation of beauty and youth. Like the Master of Ballantrae, who had never looked so beautiful as when his brother struck him across the face, she is transfigured, made momentarily divine by the intensity of her passion, as he had been by his.

> Something—it might be in the comparative disorder of her dress, it might be the emotion that now welled in her bosom—had touched her with a wand of transformation, and she seemed young with the youth of goddesses. (XX, 139)

The passions of Ballantrae and Kirstie are hardly generous; his is supreme anger and hers borders on lust, but the two are magnified, almost deified by them. Yet it seems all but useless for the ancient gods to reveal themselves to the inhibited mortals of the Victorian world.

Archie, like his mother and the mild Henry Durie, is bewildered and intimidated; he is unable to comprehend the vision of intense passion which confronts him. Kirstie, again like the transfigured Ballantrae, is figuratively ablaze with heat and light. But as she reaches out toward the object of her passion he can only respond with a sympathetic but inadequate gesture:

> Kirstie, her eyes shining with unshed tears, stretched out her hand towards him appealingly; the bright and dull gold of her hair flashed and smouldered in the coils behind her comely head, like the rays of an eternal youth; the pure colour had risen in her face; and Archie was abashed alike by her beauty and her story. He came towards her slowly from the window, took up her hand and kissed it. (XX, 141)

It is not difficult to see in this novel the recurrent pattern of potential love transformed by repression or frustration into a destructive passion. The theme is introduced by the perpetual anger of the mismated Adam Weir, the mental decline of his wife, the infatuation of the barren Kirstie. It apparently was to come to a climax in the murderous wrath of the overly fastidious Archie. It would be an exaggeration to read the late Stevenson as a precursor of D. H. Lawrence, even though in some ways the two share similar objections to the hypocrisies of Victorian morality. But it would be a greater mistake and a continuation of the old disservice which criticism has done to Stevenson to disregard the way he began to employ severe emotional and sexual inhibition ("sad, senseless self-denial") as one token of the several ways in which man dries up the creative sources of life or diverts them into pernicious channels.

Stevenson seems at times even more of a Calvinist and a pessimist than Lawrence. He is more of a Calvinist because, long after he had given up the Presbyterian orthodoxies of his parents, he recognized an extra-theological truth in the doctrine of the Fall. He spent most of his life searching the globe and his own mind for a "pure, dispassionate adventure," but beyond the world of boys' dreams, he never found a "pure, dispassionate" human being to carry it out. He is more pessimistic than Lawrence about the possibility of healthy relations among people because he believed that to cut out the evil or destructive energy in man requires a maiming of the soul and body which renders him impotent as soon as it renders him harmless.

Weir of Hermiston, in its acknowledgment of the human tragedy represents the final shattering by Stevenson of his own rigid romantic convention which had been designed to keep the "dazzle and confusion of reality" out of his fiction. His early attempts to subordinate character to incident simply do not extend to *The Master of Ballantrae* or *Weir of Hermiston.* But personality is not the only element Stevenson has allowed to enter with vigor into his art. Accompanying it with full force is a good deal of the monstrousness, illogic, and poignancy of life; we find morality, for a change, instead of moralizing; and into a mold still somewhat cumbersome and brittle with boyish inexperience pours a torrent of adult passion.

5

The question that has to be asked, then, is whether such a book belongs in a discussion of the fiction of adventure. *Weir of Hermiston,* in the usual sense, certainly is not a pure adventure story. But Stevenson had started what Conrad was to fulfill with genius in a career that began with the publication of *Almayer's Folly* in 1895, the year after Stevenson's death. In *The Master of*

Ballantrae and *Weir of Hermiston,* Stevenson began to probe the ironic and symbolic possibilities of the conventional properties of adventure: the mysterious hints of destiny, the digressive monologues of characters recalling the past, journeys of exile or discovery into desolate regions, and unexpected outbursts of anger, fear, and desire in an otherwise monotonous repetition of lifeless habit and politely modulated despair.

In *Weir of Hermiston* the well-edited simplicity of the distant past both mocks and enhances the muddled, shapeless, and complex experience of the present, in much the way Hermiston and Kirstie seem to do as they stand large and sharply etched above the self-defeating uncertainties of Mrs. Weir and Archie. But the "editing," we soon discover, is done by moderns like Archie and his mother. Neither Adam nor Kirstie (nor the Scottish past which they evoke) is as monolithic as the new generation at first supposes. The oversimplified vision of the past, whether religious or romantic, whether a design, like Mrs. Weir's, "in snow and ink," or like Archie's, "of velvet and bright iron," is repeatedly weakened and repudiated by the ignoble ambiguities of the present moment.

When Archie first hears his father sentence a pathetic criminal to be hanged, his mind escapes into a romantic vision of history as he rushes horrified out of the court into the street:

> He saw Holyrood in a dream, remembrance of its romance awoke in him and faded; he had a vision of the old radiant stories, of Queen Mary and Prince Charlie, of the hooded stag, of the splendor and crime, the velvet and bright iron of the past; and dismissed them with a cry of pain. He lay and moaned in the Hunter's Bog, and the heavens were dark above him and the grass of the field an offense. "This is my father," he said. (XX, 30)

The unadorned assertion of filiation ("the flesh upon my bone is his") appalls Archie as an obstacle between himself and the honorable Scottish past with which he would like to be identified. But Archie's concept of history, like the young Stevenson's theory of fiction, is full of incident and almost void of humanity. History, for Archie, is dehumanized event. Until he can conceive of the Scottish past in terms more sophisticated and *natural* than that which is conjured up by "velvet and bright iron," he can make peace neither with his father nor with himself.

Stevenson launched his young hero this time on a journey he may or may not have been prepared to have him complete. That, we can never know. Like most Stevenson heroes, Archie is young and inexperienced, forced early in the narrative to leave the home of his father and strike out on a new life for which his childhood was only meager preparation. He does not go to sea, nor to the continent, nor to a tropical island, but to the ancient and isolated homestead of his dead mother's family, and his encounter there is with himself. We have repeatedly seen in Stevenson's fiction the first part of a familiar ritual: the son's rejection (sometimes involving symbolic murder) of the father. But in *Weir of Hermiston* the protagonist, for the first time, pursues the psychological consequences of that defiant act. He returns to the home of his dead mother, comes temporarily under the sway of a matriarchal housekeeper, and eventually falls in love with her niece, who coincidentally has the same name. Both Kirsties present aspects of the desired female parent. When the young Christina meets Archie by the Weaver's Stone where he used to walk as a child with Mrs. Weir, the mother and mistress become indistinguishable in his mind:

> By one of the unconscious arts of tenderness the two women were enshrined together in his memory. Tears, in that hour of sensibility, came into his eyes indifferently at the thought of either, and the girl, from being something merely bright and shapely, was caught up into the zone of things serious as life and death and his dead mother. (XX, 111)

Archie lives for many months the life of a recluse. His retreat from the world, like Henry Durie's, is psychological as well as physical. He was "parsimonious of pain to himself, or of the chance of pain, even to the avoidance of any opportunity of pleasure." The common tragedy of Robert Herrick, Henry Durie, and potentially of Archie Weir, is that they mistake, as the young Stevenson once did, the primary source of their personal misery as something external to themselves: physical illness, Victorian society, a malicious older brother, a merciless father. But each one discovers that trying to force the mind to abjure the painful is as useless as trying to escape it by fleeing to America, Tahiti, or a Highland retreat.

The journey becomes a symbol of an unsuccessful attempt to withdraw from human suffering by retreating into the self. The torment continues and intensifies in emotional isolation, and, in the case of Herrick and Durie, so weakens the supple power of the will that it cracks under the strain of human encounter. The deliberate cultivation of a closed vision, which had once been the source of innocent charm for Stevenson's boyish heroes, has become a dangerous form of self-deception, nurtured on cowardice and conducive to insanity. The lives of both Herrick and Durie end in moral catastrophe.

Archie Weir's encounter with himself in the isolation of the Highlands shows signs of being an adventure from which he may return alive and sane, but permanently transformed. After a protected childhood in which he learned neat formulas regarding "love," "mercy," "justice," and "evil," and was taught a history of Scotland which presented "upon the one side, tender innocents with psalms upon their lips; upon the other, the persecutors, booted, bloody-minded, flushed with wine," he is sent into manhood virtually uneducated. In the seclusion of Hermiston, Stevenson confronts Archie with three characters who are flesh-and-blood embodiments of the abstractions he had heard about as a child. Like figures in a dream or a modern morality play, Kirstie, Frank Innes, and Christina pass before Archie's eyes with the aspects of Caledonia, Pure Evil, and Romantic Love.

Of Kirstie and her incarnation of a rugged national tradition which has passed its prime without proper fulfillment, I have already spoken. Through her, Archie encounters an image of Scottish history which is still noble, but marred with pettiness, disappointment, and failure. In his dim awareness of the ambiguity and difficulty of his relationship with her, he begins to perceive, with some maturity, the less romantic aspects of his family heritage. Aside from being a partial embodiment of the old clan tradition, Kirstie is more explicitly a mentor who teaches Archie an attitude toward the past which is the reverse of his former escapist fantasies. She shows him, among other things, how to look back in time and find models of himself.

Kirstie's tale of her gentle brothers' violent revenge against their father's murderers does have an analogue in Archie's life when an ancient instinct prompts him (in a part of the book never written) to avenge the ruined Christina by killing Frank Innes.

Archie's university colleague makes his major appearance in a chapter entitled "Enter Mephistopheles." He has decided to pay Archie a long visit in the country in order to avoid debtors' prison in Edinburgh. "Frank was the very picture of good looks, good humour, and manly youth. He had bright eyes with a sparkle and dance to them, curly hair, a charming smile, brilliant teeth . . . the look of a gentleman." Practiced readers of Stevenson are not surprised to find in this "Apollo" among "rustic Barbarians" one serious, damning and irredeemable fault. He is envious.

As much out of boredom as anything else, Innes sets about destroying Archie's reputation by hinting that in his seclusion he has developed dark and low habits and is hiding "perhaps a vicious mystery." From the beginning, his behavior can only bring injury to Archie without appreciably improving his own position. His crime fits Dr. Johnson's definition of envy as "mere unmixed and genuine evil; it pursues a hateful end by despicable means, and desires not so much its own happiness as another's misery."[12]

As a purveyor of "mere unmixed and genuine evil," Innes indeed enters as Mephistopheles or, more accurately, as a *diabolus ex machina,* who has no function in the plot but to destroy peace and bring out the worst in Archie, whom he was eventually to provoke to homicide. But even before the murder, Innes has provided Archie with an unwanted mirror of himself, or at least that aspect of himself from which he had tried to escape when he left Edinburgh: the glib, supple-witted, self-pampered law student with nothing but contempt for those with rougher and perhaps larger minds than his own.

Archie's crime against his father is, after all, in the some category as Innes's crime against Archie: defamation of character. Like Innes and Kirstie, who cover rather disturbing motives with rationalizations of benevolence,

Archie had convinced himself of a humanitarian objection to capital punishment when it is clear, long before the trial of Duncan Jopp, that he nurses less intellectualized feelings of resentment toward his powerful and virile father. The very purity and simplicity of Innes's crime against Archie provides the young Weir with a naked image of his own soul and the sin of envy committed against his father. Once again, as in *The Master of Ballantrae,* Stevenson has confronted a character with a double in whose countenance he sees not a grotesque mask induced by chemical powders, but an undisguised glimpse of the darkness that lies within.

But all is not black along the route of Archie's retreat into the back lands of his country and his soul. If he finds in his race and in himself an instinct for annihilation, he discovers almost simultaneously a tender and creative urge to grow and to live, which becomes all the more sacred in view of the odds nature places against it. On the Sunday morning when he first sees Christina in church, Archie's body and spirit have already begun to awaken with the earth:

> There was no doubt that the spring had come at last . . . The grey, Quakerish dale was still only awakened in places and patches from the sobriety of its wintry colouring . . . His heart perhaps beat in time to some vast indwelling rhythm of the universe. (XX, 86)

Stevenson is preparing the reader for the natural innocence of Archie's immediate sexual attraction to Christina. If, as in the case of the avenging son of Kirstie's legend, "some Barbarossa, some old ancestor," awakened a wildness within, there is a heritage and instinct of tenderness in man which is equally elemental and strong. Even inside the church the sounds and fragrances of spring

> rose like exhalations from some deeper, aboriginal memory, that was not his, but belonged to the flesh on his bones. His body remembered; and it seemed to him that his body was in no way gross, but ethereal and perishable like a strain of music; and he felt for it an exquisite tenderness as for a child, an innocent, full of beautiful instincts and destined to an early death. (XX, 87)

Half-playfully and half-seriously, Stevenson insists upon the animal naturalness of Archie's first flirtation with Christina by describing it in terms of the hunter pursuing his quarry:

> He looked at her again and yet again, and their looks crossed. The lip was lifted from her little teeth. He saw the red blood work vividly under her tawny skin. Her eye, which was great as a stag's, struck and held his gaze.

And later on:

> Like a creature tracked, run down, surrounded, she sought in a dozen ways to give herself countenance. (XX, 91-92)

Archie's attraction to Christina is as instinctive, pure, and irrational in its way as Innes's envy and his own resentment of his father are in theirs. His journey to Hermiston has been, then, not only a removal from the city into one of the most primitive areas of Scotland, but a symbolic passage backward through time to a point where human lives are irrevocably bound to the earth and human motives are unobscured by the rationalizations and hypocrisies of civilized society. Still, this book is not a work of social protest, even in the indirect sense of *The Ebb Tide* and *The Beach of Falesá*. Edinburgh is known primarily through Archie's cluttered, busy, often confused consciousness, while Hermiston, in the fullest sense, is a retreat where a man may very well be forced to look into himself out of a simple lack of familiar scenery.

It would be an unnecessary exaggeration to label Stevenson's topographical detail as a metaphorical description of Archie's psyche, though we need only recall the picturesque "background" landscape of *Kidnapped* to see the increased psychological pertinence of the description of Archie's path to exile:

> The road to Hermiston runs for the great part of the way up the valley of a stream, a favorite with anglers and with midges, full of falls and pools, and shaded by willows and natural woods of birch. Here and there, but at great distances, a byway branches off, and a gaunt farmhouse may be descried above in a fold of the hill; but the more part of the time, the road would be quite empty of passage and the hills of habitation. Hermiston parish is one of the least populous in Scotland. (XX, 56)

The journey into an isolated valley provides an appropriate prelude to Archie's psychological trials through the remainder of the book. We may continue to expect physical adventure, but we do not expect Highland robbers or hi-jacking pirates to leap at random out of the bush. The focus of the narrative is on the vulnerability of Archie's mind more than on the invulnerability of his body. What physical encounters he does become involved in (as the lover of Christina, as the rival of Innes) are important primarily because of what they tell us about him as a whole man.

Archie, whose bringing-up reversed the Wordsworthian sequence from animal innocence to a maturity deadened by the ways of the civilized world, travels backward in search of the natural self. Trained early and rigidly by a pious mother in the ways of the Puritan ethic, he is all but born into the "shades of the prison-house," already at the age of seven a "little Rabbi," nursed on Rutherford's "Letters" and Scougal's "Grace Abounding." When, at twenty, he feels himself awakening with the spring, he regards his body with a feeling of "tenderness as for a child." He is encountering his own flesh, it would seem, for the first time. And the demands it will make are about to provide him with an altogether new picture of himself and eventually of the young Christina.

The story breaks off at a tantalizing point. (Stevenson died suddenly in the late afternoon of the day on which he had dictated the last lines.) Archie has told Christina that he must stop seeing her, and she has flung away from him in a passion. He races after her and takes her in his arms, but is nearly overwhelmed by the intensity of her emotion:

> [He felt] pity, and at the same time a bewildered fear of this explosive engine in his arms, whose works he did not understand, and yet had been tampering with. There arose from before him the curtains of boyhood, and he saw for the first time the ambiguous face of woman as she is. In vain he looked back over the interview; he saw not where he had offended. It seemed unprovoked, a willful convulsion of brute nature . . . (XX, 151)

Archie promises to be a character, unlike Henry Durie, Robert Herrick, and his own mother, who can look into the *ambiguous* face of nature and remain alive and whole. Earlier in the book when he shouts, "Everything's alive. Thank God, everything's alive!" it is already becoming clear that he is finding out what that means. It is not an empty shout of enthusiasm over a spring day, but a discovery that life continues by means of death; that his own flesh, like that of all organic nature around him, has been nourished by the dying, yielded room by the dead, and will in its turn give way to new life. It is not an entirely comforting thought for any man, least of all for a literal-minded Scot like Stevenson without Donne's religious faith or the extraordinary imagination of Keats. He left Edinburgh and the "sour piety" of Scotch Calvinism partly to escape the "damp smell of the graveyard [which] finds its way into the houses where workmen sit at meat." Yet years later, writing in his tropical Samoan retreat, he creates a character who, in the midst of exhilaration over the rebirth of nature, is

> struck with a sense of incompleteness in the day, the season, and the beauty that surrounded him—the chill there was in the warmth, the gross black clods about the opening primroses, the damp earthy smell that was everywhere intermingled with the scents.[13]

Archie feels the "chill" of death even at the peak of his physical and imaginative vigor, and it is to be able to live with this, to accept the limitations of his body without losing respect for himself, that promises to be his final heroic achievement. It is the melancholy fate of Robert Herrick and Henry Durie (and of Henry Jekyll insofar as his story can be said to have a serious meaning) that neither can survive the knowledge of what seems to be his own peculiar deformity.

The universal "defect" of individual life is that it dies. According to Judeo-Christian theology, death is the wage of sin, the permanent curse laid upon man for his first disobedience of the divine will. In itself, then, it is not only an ending and a mystery, but a continual reminder of guilt, a physical image of human corruption. Although in his early youth Stevenson repudiated the religious explanation of man's "sense of incompleteness," he painfully and gradually came to acknowledge its psychological, if not its supernatural, validity. He implies repeatedly in his last years that sin and guilt are corollaries of death; that man is perennially humiliated, oppressed, and maddened by the awareness that he must die. It is a knowledge that belittles him in his own eyes and one for which he holds himself in some way responsible. Death seems to be nature's reproach of man for having been born with an idea of perfection and permanence into a world and a body unable to fulfill it.

But excessive concern with human imperfection, as Stevenson found it in the Scottish Church, eventually led to a morbid obsession with *the* human imperfection—mortality. His flight from a sin-centered ethic was therefore, as much as anything else, a flight from fatality. But the belief of his later years (reflected in "Pulvis et Umbra," *The Master of Ballantrae, The Ebb Tide,* and *Weir of Hermiston*) was that guilt and awareness of death remain, even after orthodox theology has been dismissed, as elements inherent in human experience. To avoid the "painful sides" in one's view of nature, Stevenson demonstrates in his later works, is to mutilate the world as it is and, what is worse, to render one's self defenseless against the most common trials of existence.

In his early career he saw his task as artist and moralist not to hold a mirror up to nature, but to construct a verbal surface around experience and then to suck the life out of its center. The most successful results of this process—*Treasure Island,* some of *New Arabian Nights,* and several of the early essays—are exquisite and captivating shells, beautifully contrived, a pleasure to behold, but brittle, insubstantial, and irrelevant. Irrelevance can, of course, be part of the charm of an adventure, but the irrelevant moralizing of which Stevenson shows himself capable in *Prince Otto* and "A Christmas Sermon" (in which he suggests as a noble epitaph, "Here lies one who meant well") is not very charming. There is some question whether the Vailima Prayers, written toward the end of his life, are a result of uxorial pressure, as Henley suggests, or an indication of a voluntary return to conventional piety. Whatever the case may be, it is important, in following Stevenson's development as a novelist, to notice that as he grew older he introduced fewer easy moral epigrams into his fiction.

Stevenson had once hoped that he could "give joy" by avoiding pain, fear of death, and brute nature (which usually means sexuality) in his art. But an awareness of the little success he had in his own life in trying to ignore the defects of an imperfect body, the morality of his parents, and the morbidity of his national religion gradually infiltrated his creative imagination. In "The House of Eld," one of the most moving and significant of his moral fables[14] he answers a question about the nature of man, which he had raised as early as 1878 in "Will o' the Mill." A young boy lives in a community all of whose members wear shackles on their right legs. In an effort to eradicate this superstitious habit, he slays ghosts which resemble his catechist uncle and his parents because he is told by traveling foreigners that they are not the bodies of his "true" relatives but the masks of a sorcerer who holds the villagers under a spell. On his way home from killing the "harmful" spirits in the woods, he discovers from passersby that the former custom has indeed changed, but it has given way to a new one; now everyone wears a shackle on his left leg. To make matters worse, he finds upon returning to the house of his parents that he has murdered them in fact as well as in spirit.

Old is the tree and the fruit good,
Very old and thick the wood.
Woodman, is your courage stout?
Beware! The root is wrapped about

> Your mother's heart, your father's bones;
> And like the mandrake comes with groans. (XX, 470)

It is appropriate that Stevenson should use the image of the tree to conclude a fable which warns against destroying the good fruits of life while attempting to extract the roots of evil. Since the Fall, the two have grown together and formed the tree of the knowledge of good and evil. And however pious the intent, to stunt that tree, this natural life, is to avoid hell at the expense of heaven. "It is one thing to enter the kingdom of heaven maim," Stevenson writes in 1888; "another to maim yourself and stay without." As in so many other cases, he uses a Christian vocabulary and scriptural symbol to describe a human vision, the theological validity of which he does not presume to judge. He seems always to have maintained faith in a divine Creator, but in 1886, in a letter to Gosse, he scoffed at "this fairy tale of an eternal tea-party," where a man goes after his death believing "that his friends will meet him, all ironed out and emasculate, and still be lovable" (*Letters,* II, 314).

By the time he wrote *The Master of Ballantrae* and *Weir of Hermiston,* Stevenson had clearly tired of "emasculate" visions, whether of heaven or earth. His various heroes—from Jim Hawkins, through Will o' the Mill, David Balfour, Robert Herrick, James Durie, and Archie Weir—are all images and products of one imagination at various stages of rebellion. It is significant that the Fall of Man at the foot of the tree of knowledge should be associated with a child's fantasy of murdering his parents, because at the center of all adventure is the necessity of the youth breaking with authority, either by chance, because his parents have died, fallen into poverty, or gotten lost, or deliberately and willfully in conscious disobedience.

The difference between boyish adventure (the kind Stevenson wrote in his early years) and serious adventure (in the style of his late novels and the best works of Melville and Conrad) is that in the former the act of dissociation or disobedience permits the escapade without permanent consequences. It is a new rendering of the story of Adam and Eve taking the apple, but not "for keeps." They can taste the fruit, but somehow put it back whole, and nobody (including themselves) is any the wiser. It is the wonderful, pathetic, and perennial dream of being born into a world without death, in which we each see ourselves free to commit the sins of our parents, but *this time* without getting caught. It is in fact a very real world into which all men are born and dwell for five, ten, or fifteen years. Stevenson is perhaps unique among English novelists for having fashioned this universe so well that in adulthood we read his early books like faintly remembered travelogues of a country we can no longer reach.

At all levels of sophistication, adventure turns on disobedience—on the breaking of a law: For Robinson Crusoe, Tom Jones, Frank Osbaldistone, and Archie Weir it was the law of the father (or male guardian); for Captain Singleton, Midshipman Easy, and Long John Silver, it was the law of the navy; for Huckleberry Finn, Gerard Eliassoen, Natty Bumppo, and David Balfour it was the law of social custom; and for any or all of them it might be the law of their own conscience which Lord Jim momentarily abandons at the instant he leaps from the *Patna*. What distinguishes adventure from other types of fiction dealing with disobedience is that the act is generally a violent and physical one (often intensified by sudden death, natural catastrophe, public scandal, or war), which requires the disobedient hero to work out the physical and moral consequences of his "crime" at a distance from the authority which has been repudiated.

The realization that that authority, whether it assumes the name of God, father, super-ego, or romantic ideal, is inescapable—as much a part of the self as the irrational urge to defy it—brings the adventure into the realm of universal human experience regardless of bizarre locale and unlikely quality of incident. The heroes of nonserious adventure (for example, Leo Vincey, Captain Singleton, Amyas Leigh, Jim Hawkins) can temporarily "get away" from the laws of society to which other men are subject, and this in turn exempts them from many of the common laws of nature. They discover in their life outside conventional society unexpected, almost superhuman, powers of survival, limitless reserves of ingenuity and courage, which natural catastrophe and enormously unfavorable odds have no capacity to destroy.

The heroes of Stevenson's late novels, especially Henry Durie (who flees to America), Robert Herrick (who seeks anonymity in the South Seas), and Archie Weir (exiled to Hermiston), discover, on the contrary, that flight from conventional society is no exit from the universe of which their own being is both part and image. If anything, they see themselves more clearly in relative isolation than they had in the cluttered, civilized world. The flamboyant gesture toward release may very well expand the range of vision sufficiently to provide an unexpected view of the natural limitations of the self.

The challenge to the hero of this kind of adventure is whether or not he can bear to live with the knowledge of his own imperfection. If so, as Stevenson seems to have intended in the case of Archie Weir, he will emerge stronger and more humane than he had dreamed upon first striking out in his youthful act of rebellion. If not, as in the instances of Robert Herrick and Henry Durie, the recognition of interior weakness can annihilate the will and, in Durie's case, destroy the body. It is interesting to conjecture about the direction *Weir of Hermiston* would have taken had Stevenson lived to finish it. Supposedly, according to his plan, Archie and Christina were to have fled to America, married, and lived happily ever after. But one wonders whether the pessimistic mood of *The Master of Ballantrae* and *The Ebb Tide* would have taken over and caused Stevenson to allow Archie's sins to pursue and destroy him.

It is perhaps fruitless to theorize over the ultimate extent of optimism or pessimism in Stevenson's later works. He admitted often that as a writer of fiction he preferred beginnings and never thought himself very good at endings. As we have often seen, whether it was a journey or a novel he was usually willing to begin again, regardless of the consequences of the previous attempt. This has led some people to think of him as an incorrigible optimist or a fool. But, for Stevenson, to begin a book or an expedition was to protest against things as they were, not by means of direct criticism (and rarely by invective), but by a simple rejection of *rigor mortis.* If protest is a necessary sign of life—"man's first disobedience," the cry of a newborn baby, Shelley's "scream in the shape of a theory"—then let it out.

In spite of moods of resignation, reflected in letters and stories like "Will o' the Mill," Stevenson's major tendency was always toward remonstrance. What changes and broadens is not this tendency but the object of his protest. First, in the rebelliousness of his youth, it is against his parents and their Scottish Puritanism, then against Victorian society and contemporary art, and finally against a universe in which innocence is always spoiled and even "clear-eyed" boys grow old and die.

As early as 1874 he writes with distaste of people whose "eyes [are] sealed up with indifference . . . going automatically to offices and saying they are happy or unhappy out of a sense of duty . . . Is it not like a bad dream? Why don't they stamp their feet upon the ground and awake?" (*Letters,* I, 183)

Ten years later he prays in one of his best-known poems that the Lord will stir him to life with pain or sin rather than let him exist in spiritual torpor. He calls God the "Celestial Surgeon," a title which evokes the medieval and Latinate stress on the virtues of compunction and reminds us of Eliot's "wounded surgeon" in *East Coker.*

> Lord, Thy most pointed pleasure take
> And stab my spirit broad awake;
> Or, Lord, if too obdurate I,
> Choose Thou, before that spirit die,
> A piercing pain, a killing sin,
> And to my dead heart run them in![15]

In the same year he confided in a letter to Trevor Hadden an analogous anxiety about art:

> The great lack of art just now is spice of life and interest; and I prefer galvanism to acquiescence in the grave. All do not; 'tis an affair of tastes; and mine are young. Those who like death have their innings to-day with art that is like mahogany and horsehair furniture, solid, true, serious and dead as Caesar. (*Letters,* II, 214)

In 1894, two days before his death, Stevenson commented on a poem of Gosse's which included the lines:

> I live to watch, and meditate,
> And dream,—and be deceived.[16]

Stevenson replies:

> Not I, I must confess. It is all very well to talk of renunciation, and of course it has to be done. But, for my

> part, give me a roaring toothache! . . . You are going on sedately travelling through your ages . . . And here am I, quite out of my true course, and with nothing in my foolish elderly head but love stories . . . I believe the main distinction is that you have a family growing up around you, and I am a childless, rather bitter, very clear-eyed, blighted youth. I have, in fact, lost the path that makes it easy and natural for you to descend the hill. I am going at it straight. And where I have to go down it is a precipice.
> (*Letters,* IV, 379)

The adventure which Stevenson launches again and again in his fiction has changed considerably since *Treasure Island.* He began, like some of his own most memorable characters, hoping to plunge deeply enough into a literary dream to leave the world behind. When he discovered that the images in his dreams were only inverted, distorted, or oddly colored fragments of nature, he tended for a while, like the storytellers in *New Arabian Nights,* to think of them as shams, and of himself as a trickster. *The Master of Ballantrae* and *Weir of Hermiston* begin to show the impressive consequences of the transition in Stevenson's fiction from sleight-of-hand to artistry, from adventure as an entertaining counterfeit to adventure as a symbolic chart of the formidable risks in which life involves all men.

SELECTED BIBLIOGRAPHY
NOTES   INDEX

SELECTED BIBLIOGRAPHY

The standard Stevenson bibliographies are: W. F. Prideaux, *A Bibliography of the Works of Robert Louis Stevenson* (New York, 1903; revised by F. V. Livingston, 1917), and J. H. Slater, *Robert Louis Stevenson: A Bibliography of His Complete Works* (London, 1914). For information on more recently published material on Stevenson, the reader is referred to the *Cambridge Bibliography of English Literature* (New York and Cambridge, 1941), III, 520-525, to T. G. Ehrsam and R. H. Deily, *Bibliographies of Twelve Victorian Authors* (New York, 1936), and to George L. McKay, *A Stevenson Library: Catalogue of a Collection of Writings by and about Robert Louis Stevenson formed by Edward J. Beinecke* (New Haven, 1951), 5 vols. An excellent and recent list of the "crucial published material on Stevenson" may be found in J. C. Furnas, *Voyage to Windward* (New York, 1951).

The following list is by no means comprehensive but contains major titles which may be of use to those who wish to pursue their study of Stevenson. It includes representative biographies and critiques of Stevenson published during the past seventy years and related works of critical theory and literary history which have been of particular help in the preparation of this book.

Aldington, Richard. *Portrait of a Rebel: The Life and Work of Robert Louis Stevenson.* London, 1957.

Baildon, Henry B. *Robert Louis Stevenson: A Life Study in Criticism.* London, 1901.

Balfour, Graham. *The Life of Robert Louis Stevenson.* 2 vols. New York, 1901.

Barrie, J. M. *An Edinburgh Eleven.* The Kirriemuir Edition. 10 vols. London, 1922.

Benson, E. F. *As We Were: A Victorian Peep Show.* London, 1930.

Brown, Alice. *Robert Louis Stevenson: A Study.* Boston, 1895.

Buckley, Jerome Hamilton. *William Ernest Henley: A Study in the Counter-Decadence of the Nineties.* Princeton, 1945.

——— *The Victorian Temper.* Harvard, 1951.

Caldwell, Elsie Noble. *Last Witness for Robert Louis Stevenson.* University of Oklahoma Press, 1960.

Carré, Jean Marie. *The Frail Warrior.* Translated by Eleanor Hard. New York, 1930.

Chapman, John Jay. *Emerson and Other Essays.* New York, 1898.

Charteris, Evan Edward. *The Life and Letters of Sir Edmund Gosse.* London, 1931.

Chesterton, G. K. *Robert Louis Stevenson.* New York, 1928.

Chrétien, L. E. *La Vocation de Robert Louis Stevenson.* Paris, 1930.

Cohen, Morton. *Rider Haggard, His Life and Works.* London, 1960.
Cooper, Lettice. *Robert Louis Stevenson.* London, 1947.
Cornford, L. Cope. *Robert Louis Stevenson.* Cambridge, 1899.
Daiches, David. *Robert Louis Stevenson.* Norfolk, 1947.
——— *Stevenson and the Art of Fiction.* New York, 1951.
Dalglish, Doris N. *Presbyterian Pirate.* London, 1937.
Dark, Sidney. *Robert Louis Stevenson.* London, 1931.
Elwin, Malcolm. *The Strange Case of Robert Louis Stevenson.* London, 1950.
Fiedler, Leslie. *No! In Thunder.* Boston, 1960.
Fisher, Anne B. *No More a Stranger.* Stanford, 1946.
Furnas, J. C. *Voyage to Windward: The Life of Robert Louis Stevenson.* New York, 1951.
Gosse, Edmund. *Biographical Notes on the Writings of Robert Louis Stevenson.* London, 1908.
——— *Critical Kit-Kats.* New York, 1903.
Green, Roger Lancelyn. *Andrew Lang: A Critical Biography.* Leicester, 1946.
Guthrie, Charles J. *Robert Louis Stevenson: Some Personal Recollections.* Edinburgh, 1920.
Hamilton, Clayton. *On the Trail of Stevenson.* New York, 1915.
Hellman, George S. *The True Stevenson, A Study in Clarification.* Boston, 1925.
Henley, William Ernest. *Essays.* London, 1921.
Isler, Anne Roller. *Happier For His Presence.* Stanford, 1949.
Jacobs, Joseph. *Literary Studies.* London, 1895.
Japp, Alexander H. *Robert Louis Stevenson: A Record, An Estimate, and A Memorial.* New York, 1905.
Johnstone, Arthur G. *Recollections of Robert Louis Stevenson in the Pacific.* London, 1905.
Kelman, John. *The Faith of Robert Louis Stevenson.* Edinburgh, 1903.
Lang, Andrew. *Adventures Among Books.* London, 1905.
——— *Letters to Dead Authors.* London, 1886.
——— *A Short History of Scotland.* New York, 1912.
Masson, Rosaline. *The Life of Robert Louis Stevenson.* Edinburgh, 1923.
——— (ed.) *I Can Remember Robert Louis Stevenson.* Edinburgh, 1922.
McGaw, Sister Martha Mary, C.S.J. *Stevenson in Hawaii.* Honolulu, 1950.
Phelps, William Lyon. *Essays on Modern Novelists.* New York, 1910.
Quiller-Couch, A. T. *Adventures in Criticism.* London, 1896.
Raleigh, Walter. *Robert Louis Stevenson.* London, 1895.

Rice, Richard Ashley. *Robert Louis Stevenson: How to Know Him.* Indianapolis, 1916.

Rickett, Arthur. *The Vagabond in Literature.* London, 1906.

Saintsbury, George. *A History of Nineteenth Century Literature.* New York, 1899.

Schwob, Marcel. *R.L.S.* Portland, 1920.

Simpson, E. Blantyre. *Robert Louis Stevenson's Edinburgh Days.* London, 1898.

Smith, Janet Adam. *R. L. Stevenson.* London, 1937.

——— (ed.) *Henry James and Robert Louis Stevenson: A Record of Friendship and Criticism.* London, 1948.

Steuart, John A. *Robert Louis Stevenson: A Critical Biography.* 2 vols. Boston, 1924.

Stevensoniana. Edited by J. A. Hammerton. Edinburgh, 1903.

Strong, Isobel and Lloyd Osbourne. *Memories of Vailima.* New York, 1902.

Swinnerton, Frank. *R. L. Stevenson: A Critical Study.* London, 1914.

Sykes, F. H. *Notes for Lectures.* N.P., privately printed, n.d.

Symons, Arthur. *Studies in Prose and Verse.* London, 1904.

Tillyard, E. M. W. *The Epic Strain in the English Novel.* London, 1958.

Warner, Oliver. *Captain Marryat: A Rediscovery.* London, 1953.

Young, G. M. *Victorian England.* London, 1936.

NOTES

INTRODUCTION: A LITERARY REPUTATION

1. George Saintsbury, *A History of Nineteenth Century Literature (1780-1895)* (London, 1896), pp. 339-340.
2. *The Letters of Gerard Manley Hopkins to Robert Bridges,* ed. Claude Colleer Abbott (Oxford, 1935), p. 238.
3. A. T. Quiller-Couch, "Robert Louis Stevenson," *Adventures in Criticism* (London, 1896), p. 184. (This article is reprinted from *The Speaker,* December 22, 1894.)
4. *Henry James and Robert Louis Stevenson,* ed. Janet Adam Smith (London, 1948), p. 249.
5. The complete poem is entitled "Apparition" and is number XXV in the series *In Hospital* (1873-1875):

> Thin-legged, thin-chested, slight unspeakably,
> Neat-footed and weak-fingered: in his face—
> Lean, large-boned, curved of beak, and
> touched with race,
> Bold-lipped, rich-tinted, mutable as the sea,
> The brown eyes radiant with vivacity—
> There shines a brilliant and romantic grace,
> A spirit intense and rare, with trace on trace
> Of passion and impudence and energy.
> Valiant in velvet, light in ragged luck,
> Most vain, most generous, sternly critical,
> Buffoon and poet, lover and sensualist:
> A deal of Ariel, just a streak of Puck,
> Much Antony, of Hamlet most of all,
> And something of the Shorter-Catechist.

(From *The Works of W. E. Henley,* London, 1908, I, 40.)

6. Joseph Jacobs, *Literary Studies* (London, 1895), pp. 175, 180-181. (This article is reprinted from the *Athenaeum,* December 22, 1894.)
7. *Stevensoniana,* ed. J. A. Hammerton (London, 1903), p. 242.
8. Lionel Johnson, "*The Wrecker* by Robert Louis Stevenson," *The Academy,* 42: 103-104 (August 6, 1892).
9. Arthur Symons, *Studies in Prose and Verse* (London, 1904), p. 81.
10. Walter Raleigh, *Robert Louis Stevenson* (London, 1895), p. 64.
11. Alice Brown, *Robert Louis Stevenson, A Study* (Boston, 1895), pp. 45-46.
12. Edmund Gosse, *Critical Kit-Kats* (New York, 1903), p. 302.

13. Andrew Lang, "Recollections of Robert Louis Stevenson," *Adventures Among Books* (London, 1905), p. 42.
14. John A. Steuart, *Robert Louis Stevenson, A Critical Biography,* 2 vols. (Boston, 1924), II, 307, 309.
15. Thomas Beer, *The Mauve Decade: American Life at the End of the Nineteenth Century* (Garden City, 1926), pp. 177-178.
16. Gower Woodseer, in Meredith's *The Amazing Marriage,* was partly inspired by Stevenson. And, although the incident related in James's *The Author of Beltraffio* was based on an anecdote told about John Addington Symonds, several of the author's physical and temperamental traits were borrowed from Stevenson. John Steinbeck put Stevenson in a story called "How Edith McGillicuddy Met R.L.S.," first published in *Harper's Magazine* in August 1941.
17. James M. Barrie, "Robert Louis Stevenson," *An Edinburgh Eleven* (London, 1924), p. 113.
18. *Letters of Henry Adams,* (1858-1891), ed. Worthington Chauncey Ford (Boston, 1930), pp. 452-453.
19. Gérard Jean-Aubry, *The Sea Dreamer: A Definitive Biography of Joseph Conrad* (New York, 1957), pp. 190-192.
20. *Hopkins to Bridges,* p. 228.

CHAPTER I: THE AESTHETICS OF ADVENTURE

1. Janet Adam Smith, *Henry James and Robert Louis Stevenson, A Record of Friendship and Criticism* (London, 1948), p. 277.
2. *Ibid.,* pp. 130-132.
3. G. K. Chesterton, *Robert Louis Stevenson* (New York, 1928), pp. 190-191.
4. George Saintsbury, *A History of Nineteenth Century Literature* (London, 1896), p. 337.
5. Émile Zola, *The Experimental Novel and Other Essays,* trans. Belle M. Sherman (New York, 1893), p. 43. The essays in this volume originally appeared in Russian and French reviews between 1875 and 1880. They were collected and published in a single volume for the first time in France in 1880, and it is in this form that they were probably available to Stevenson. For a further discussion of the chronology and influence of Zola's critical works, see Fernand Doucet, *L'Esthétique d'Émile Zola et son application à la critique* (The Hague, 1923), pp. 231-243.
6. *Adventures Among Books,* pp. 279-280. For a more complete exposition of Lang's part in "the battle between the crocodile of Realism and the catawampus of Romance," see his "Realism and Romance," *The Contemporary Review,* November 1887; "Romance and the Reverse," *St. James's Gazette,* November 1888; and Roger

Lancelyn Green's *Andrew Lang, A Critical Biography* (Leicester, 1946), pp. 109-123.

7. Zola, *The Experimental Novel,* pp. 25-26.

8. *Ibid.,* pp. 54, 209.

9. *The Correspondence of Gerard Manley Hopkins and Richard Watson Dixon,* ed. Claude Colleer Abbott (Oxford, 1935), p. 114.

10. "A Note on Realism," *The Works of Robert Louis Stevenson,* 25 vols. (London, 1912), XVI, 236.

11. As quoted in Gérard Jean-Aubry, *The Sea Dreamer: A Definitive Biography of Joseph Conrad* (New York, 1957), p. 273.

12. "A Note on Realism," Swanston Edition, XVI, 239-240.

13. "The Art of Fiction," *Henry James and Robert Louis Stevenson,* ed. Smith, p. 75.

14. Samuel Taylor Coleridge, "On Poesy or Art," *Literary Remains,* ed. H. N. Coleridge, 4 vols. (London, 1836), I, 220.

15. William Hazlitt, "On Poetry in General," *The Complete Works of William Hazlitt,* ed. P. P. Howe, 21 vols. (London, 1934), V, 1-18.

16. *Hopkins and Dixon,* p. 114.

17. In a great number of the books written about Stevenson during the twenty-year period following his death, it was generally assumed that, on the basis of his interest in childhood and nature, he was clearly and indisputably a Romantic. A characteristic example of this opinion may be found in L. Cope Cornford's *Robert Louis Stevenson* (Edinburgh, 1899), chap. vi.

18. Coleridge, "Shakespeare's Judgment Equal to His Genius," *Literary Remains,* II, 66-67.

19. Lang, *Adventures Among Books,* p. 213.

CHAPTER II: ADVENTURE AS BOY'S DAYDREAM

1. From Lord Guthrie's *Robert Louis Stevenson,* as quoted in *I Can Remember Robert Louis Stevenson,* ed. Rosaline Masson (Edinburgh, 1922), p. 72.

2. Chesterton, *Robert Louis Stevenson,* p. 199.

3. J. C. Furnas, *Voyage to Windward, The Life of Robert Louis Stevenson* (New York, 1951), pp. 389-390.

4. George S. Hellman, *The True Stevenson, A Study in Clarification* (Boston, 1925), p. 27.

5. Leslie Fiedler, *No! In Thunder* (Boston, 1960), p. 81.

6. Doris N. Dalglish, *Presbyterian Pirate, A Portrait of Stevenson* (London, 1937), p. 69.

7. David Daiches, *Stevenson and the Art of Fiction* (New York, 1951), p. 10.

8. John Conway discusses the athletic contest as a kind of "allegory," "the type of all talent," in "Standards of Excellence," *Daedalus,* 90: 683-684 (Fall 1961). Though he is speaking specifically of athletics in American society, his point is relevant to Stevenson insofar as he describes the game as cutting across and avoiding moral and cultural complications by presenting "in its purest and most abstract form a skill and its simple realization . . . which can be appreciated by everybody, irrespective of education or background or individual gifts."

9. David Daiches, *Robert Louis Stevenson* (Norfolk, Connecticut, 1947), p. 72.

10. *James and Stevenson,* p. 239.

11. The author makes grateful acknowledgment to the Harry Elkins Widener Collection at Widener Library, Harvard University, for permission to quote from the intermediate manuscript of *Catriona.*

12. Daiches, *Robert Louis Stevenson,* p. 86.

13. Robert Browning, "Saul," *The Works of Robert Browning,* 10 vols. (London, 1912), III, p. 196, 1. 295.

14. *James and Stevenson,* p. 131.

15. Joseph Conrad, *A Personal Record* (Garden City, 1927), pp. 36-37.

CHAPTER III: ADVENTURE AS COMIC SATIRE

1. William Archer, "In Memoriam: R.L.S.," *New Review,* January 1895, as quoted in *Stevensoniana,* p. 175.

2. Last stanza of "Et Tu in Arcadia Vixisti," Swanston Edition (London, 1912), XIV, 82.

3. As told by Sherriff Maconochie in *I Can Remember Robert Louis Stevenson,* p. 80.

4. Although at one time Stevenson's wife was thought to have written most of *The Dynamiter,* it is now generally acknowledged that, though several of the ideas were hers, he reworked and rewrote nearly everything she suggested. In any case, there has never been serious doubt that the framework and recurrent thematic patterns are Stevenson's, in that they follow a mode he had established, well before his marriage, in *New Arabian Nights.* For a further discussion of the authorship of *The Dynamiter,* see Malcolm Elwin, *The Strange Case of Robert Louis Stevenson* (London, 1950), pp. 186, 197.

5. Daiches, *Stevenson,* p. 5.

6. Andrew Lang, *Letters to Dead Authors* (London, 1886), pp. 123-124.

CHAPTER IV: ADVENTURE AS FABLE OF FARAWAY PLACES

1. "And as he stands there with beating heart and kindling eye, the cool breeze whistling through his long fair curls, he is a symbol, though he knows it not, of brave young England longing to wing its way out of its island prison, to discover and to traffic, to colonise and to civilise, until no wind can sweep the earth which does not bear the echoes of an English voice." Charles Kingsley, *Westward Ho!, The Novels and Poems of Charles Kingsley,* ed. Maurice Kingsley (New York, 1899), I, 15-16.

2. H. Rider Haggard, *She, A History of Adventure* (London, 1887), p. 207.

3. Samuel Johnson, "Gray," *The Lives of the English Poets, The Works of Samuel Johnson,* LL.D., ed. Arthur Murphy, 12 vols. (London, 1806), XI, 374.

4. "Songs of Travel, xxxv," Swanston Edition (London, 1912), XIV, 243.

5. *Ibid.,* "xxxvi," p. 244.

6. Dylan Thomas's adaptation of the story for the screen has been published by Stein and Day (New York, 1963).

7. Albert J. Guerard, in *Conrad the Novelist* (Harvard, 1958), has noted the external resemblance between this section of *The Beach of Falesá* and the devil's compound in Conrad's *Heart of Darkness.* He points out that to determine whether or not Conrad read Stevenson's novella (and it is likely that he did) is not so important as recognizing the difference in the handling of similar material. Mr. Guerard speaks of "the inert jungle of Stevenson's South Pacific" in contrast with "the charged symbolic jungle of Conrad's Congo." And he concludes that "*The Beach of Falesá* is a good manly yarn totally bereft of psychological intuition" (p. 43). Mr. Guerard's basic point is indisputable, but I would not state it as emphatically as he does. Stevenson's "manly yarn" does show some signs of interior strain, which is caused by psychological intuition in conflict with popular convention. The convention prevails, but with a difficulty we did not find in *Treasure Island* or *Kidnapped,* for example.

8. *The Journals of André Gide,* trans. Justin O'Brien, 4 vols. (New York, 1947), I, 147.

9. "A sailor, a shepherd, a schoolmaster—to a less degree, a soldier—and (I don't know why, upon my soul, except as a schoolmaster's unofficial assistant, and a kind of acrobat in tights) an artist, almost exhaust the category (of the few possible and dignified ways of life)" *Letters,* IV, 357.

10. *In the South Seas,* XIX, 106-107. It is interesting to compare this passage with that in *Heart of Darkness* in which Conrad describes a French man-of-war "shelling the bush . . . In the empty immensity of earth, sky, and water, there she was, incomprehensible, firing into a continent . . . There was a touch of insanity in the proceeding . . . and it was not dissipated by somebody on board assuring me earnestly there was a camp of natives—he called them enemies!—hidden out of sight somewhere." Joseph Conrad, *Heart of Darkness* (Garden City, 1927), pp. 61-62. The image is a memorable one, and it takes on symbolic connotations in Conrad, which it obviously does not in Stevenson's travel journal. Nonetheless, it is characteristic and revealing that Stevenson's attitude should fall somewhere between that of the "self-righteous old ship-captains" and Conrad's troubled narrator.

11. "A Visit to Robert Louis Stevenson," by S. R. Lysaght, as quoted in *I Can Remember Robert Louis Stevenson,* p. 264.

12. "The Woodman," Swanston Edition (London, 1912), XIV, 252-253.

CHAPTER V. ADVENTURE AS MODERN EPIC

1. *The Phantom Ship* by Captain Frederick Marryat was published in three volumes in 1839. It is a fictional reconstruction of the legend of the *Flying Dutchman,* and is Marryat's second historical novel.

2. "The Genesis of 'The Master of Ballantrae,' " Swanston Edition, XVI, 341.

3. Elsie Noble Caldwell, *Last Witness for Robert Louis Stevenson* (University of Oklahoma Press, 1960), p. 118.

4. Smith, *James and Stevenson,* p. 185.

5. Caldwell, *Last Witness for Robert Louis Stevenson,* p. 118.

6. Joseph Jacobs, *Literary Studies* (London, 1895), p. 179.

7. Andrew Lang, *Adventures Among Books* (London, 1905), p. 46.

8. Daiches, *Stevenson,* p. 79.

9. *The Journals of André Gide,* I, 343.

10. Stevenson would seem to agree with Charles Reade's sentiment expressed in *The Cloister and the Hearth:* "Gunpowder has spoiled war. War was always detrimental to the solid interests of mankind. But in old times it was good for something: it painted well, sang divinely, furnished Iliads. But invisible butchery, under a pall of smoke a furlong thick, who is any the better for that?" Charles Reade, *The Cloister and the Hearth, A Tale of the Middle Ages* (London, 1862), p. 219.

11. This evidence was contested by S. R. Lysaght in December 1919 in a letter to *The Times* reprinted in part in *I Can Remember Robert Louis Stevenson,* p. 263: "In one . . . point [the plan he told me of] differed from the notes furnished by Mrs. Strong . . . The strongest scene in the book—[that] he had ever conceived or would ever write—was one in which the younger Kirstie came to her lover when he was in prison and confessed to him that she was with child by the man he had murdered. His eyes flashed with emotion as he spoke about it, and I cannot think that he had abandoned this climax."

12. "The Rambler," Number 183, *The Works of Samuel Johnson, LL.D.*, VI, 253.

13. *Weir of Hermiston,* XX, 87. The mood of this passage brings to mind a letter Keats wrote to his brother Thomas from Carlisle, Scotland, on July 1, 1818. As Archie Weir had stood near the churchyard and been struck "with a sense of incompleteness in the day," so also had Keats, at the tomb of Burns, felt "the chill there was in the warmth." He included this sonnet in the letter:

> The Town, the churchyard, and the setting sun,
> The clouds, the trees, the rounded hills all seem
> Though beautiful, cold—strange—as in a dream,
> I dreamed long ago, now new begun.
> The short lived, paly summer is but won
> From winter's ague, for one hour's gleam;
> Though sapphire warm, their stars do never beam,
> All is cold Beauty; pain is never done.
> For who has mind to relish Minos-wise,
> The real of Beauty, free from that dead hue
> Sickly imagination and sick pride
> [Cast] wan upon it! Burns! with honor due
> I have oft honored thee. Great shadow, hide
> Thy face, I sin against thy native skies.

(From *The Letters of John Keats,* ed. Hyder Edward Rollins, Harvard University Press, 1958; I, 308-309.)

14. For a discussion of the dating of Stevenson's moral fables, see J. D. Furnas, *Voyage to Windward,* pp. 412, 540. On the basis of internal evidence I would agree with Furnas's conclusion that "most of them were written or else radically rewritten in Louis's last nine or ten years."

15. "The Celestial Surgeon," Swanston Edition (London, 1912), XIV, 86-87.

16. This quotation is from a poem entitled "Clasping the Cloud":

INDEX

* * * * * * *